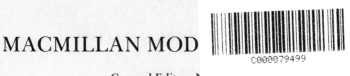

MACMILLAN MOD

General Editor: N

MACMILLAN MODERN NOVELISTS

Published titles

ALBERT CAMUS   Philip Thody
FYODOR DOSTOEVSKY   Peter Conradi
WILLIAM FAULKNER   David Dowling
GUSTAVE FLAUBERT   David Roe
E. M. FORSTER   Norman Page
ANDRE GIDE   David Walker
WILLIAM GOLDING   James Gindin
GRAHAM GREENE   Neil McEwan
CHRISTOPHER ISHERWOOD   Stephen Wade
HENRY JAMES   Alan Bellringer
JAMES JOYCE   Richard Brown
D. H. LAWRENCE   G. M. Hyde
ROSAMOND LEHMANN   Judy Simons
DORIS LESSING   Ruth Whittaker
MALCOLM LOWRY   Tony Bareham
THOMAS MANN   Martin Travers
GEORGE ORWELL   Valerie Meyers
ANTHONY POWELL   Neil McEwan
MARCEL PROUST   Philip Thody
BARBARA PYM   Michael Cotsell
JEAN-PAUL SARTRE   Philip Thody
SIX WOMEN NOVELISTS   Merryn Williams
MURIEL SPARK   Norman Page
JOHN UPDIKE   Judie Newman
EVELYN WAUGH   Jacqueline McDonnell
H. G. WELLS   Michael Draper
VIRGINIA WOOLF   Edward Bishop

Forthcoming titles

MARGARET ATWOOD   Coral Ann Howells
SAUL BELLOW   Peter Hyland
IVY COMPTON-BURNETT   Janet Godden
JOSEPH CONRAD   Owen Knowles
GEORGE ELIOT   Alan Bellringer
F. SCOTT FITZGERALD   John Whitley
JOHN FOWLES   James Acheson
ERNEST HEMINGWAY   Peter Messent
FRANZ KAFKA   Ronald Speirs and Beatrice Sandberg
NORMAN MAILER   Michael Glenday
V. S. NAIPAUL   Bruce King
PAUL SCOTT   G. K. Das
PATRICK WHITE   Mark Williams

MACMILLAN MODERN NOVELISTS

JEAN-PAUL SARTRE

Philip Thody

First published 1992 by
MACMILLAN EDUCATION LTD
Houndmills, Basingstoke, Hampshire RG21 2XS
and London
Companies and representatives
throughout the world

ISBN 0–333–53754–8 hardcover
ISBN 0–333–53755–6 paperback

A catalogue record for this book is available
from the British Library.

Printed in Hong Kong

Series Standing Order

If you would like to receive future titles in this series as they are
published, you can make use of our standing order facility. To place a
standing order please contact your bookseller or, in case of difficulty,
write to us at the address below with your name and address and the
name of the series. Please state with which title you wish to begin your
standing order. (If you live outside the United Kingdom we may not
have the rights for your area, in which case we will forward your order
to the publisher concerned.)

Customer Services Department, Macmillan Distribution Ltd
Houndmills, Basingstoke, Hampshire, RG21 2XS, England.

Contents

Acknowledgements   vi
General Editor's Preface   vii

1   The Life and Times of Jean-Paul Sartre   1
2   *La Nausée*   13
    Philosophy and obsessions   13
    Satire and politics   39
    Literature and autobiography   50
    Freedom and responsibility   61
3   *Le Mur*   67
    Advice   67
    Madness   93
    Discrepancies   106
4   *Les Chemins de la liberté*   109
    Characters, ethics and plot   109
    Identity, choice and politics   122
    Technique, ideas and a sense of ending   142

Notes   160
Select Bibliography   175
Selective Index   176

Acknowledgements

If Andrew Rothwell and David Shaw had not been ready to share their knowledge of computer technology, not a single word of this book would have been written.

The author and publishers wish to thank Random Century Group, Mrs Laura Huxley and HarperCollins Publishers Inc. for permission to use 'The Fifth Philosopher's Song' in *Collected Poetry of Aldous Huxley*, Chatto and Windus, copyright © by Aldous Huxley.
  Every effort has been made to trace all copyright holders, but if any have been inadvertently overlooked the publishers will be pleased to make the necessary arrangement at the first opportunity.

To Fred and Ileana Bridgham

General Editor's Preface

The death of the novel has often been announced, and part of the secret of its obstinate vitality must be its capacity for growth, adaptation, self-renewal and self-transformation: like some vigorous organism in a speeded-up Darwinian ecosystem, it adapts itself quickly to a changing world. War and revolution, economic crisis and social change, radically new ideologies such as Marxism and Freudianism, have made this century unprecedented in human history in the speed and extent of change, but the novel has shown an extraordinary capacity to find new forms and techniques and to accommodate new ideas and conceptions of human nature and human experience, and even to take up new positions on the nature of fiction itself.

In the generations immediately preceding and following 1914, the novel underwent a radical redefinition of its nature and possibilities. The present series of monographs is devoted to the novelists who created the modern novel and to those who, in their turn, either continued and extended, or reacted against and rejected, the traditions established during that period of intense exploration and experiment. It includes a number of those who lived and wrote in the nineteenth century but whose innovative contribution to the art of fiction makes it impossible to ignore them in any account of the origins of the modern novel; it also includes the so-called 'modernists' and those who in the mid- and late twentieth century have emerged as outstanding practitioners of this genre. The scope is, inevitably, international; not only, in the migratory and exile-haunted world of our century, do writers refuse to heed national frontiers – 'English' literature lays claim to Conrad the Pole, Henry James the American, and Joyce the Irishman – but geniuses such as Flaubert, Dostoievski and Kafka have had an influence on the fiction of many nations.

Each volume in the series is intended to provide an introduction to the fiction of the writer concerned, both for those approaching him or her for the first time and for those who are already familiar with some parts of the achievement in question and now wish to place it in the context of the total *oeuvre*. Although essential information relating to the writer's life and times is given, usually in an opening chapter, the approach is primarily critical and the emphasis is not upon 'background' or generalisations but upon close examination of important texts. Where an author is notably prolific, major texts have been made to convey, more summarily, a sense of the nature and quality of the author's work as a whole. Those who want to read further will find suggestions in the select bibliography included in each volume. Many novelists are, of course, not only novelists but also poets, essayists, biographers, dramatists, travel writers and so forth; many have practised shorter forms of fiction; and many have written letters or kept diaries that constitute a significant part of their literary output. A brief study cannot hope to deal with all these in detail, but where the shorter fiction and the non-fictional writings, public and private, have an important relationship to the novels, some space has been devoted to them.

NORMAN PAGE

1

The Life and Times of Jean-Paul Sartre

1844, 12 June: Birth of Charles Schweitzer at Pfaffenhofen, Alsace, one of three sons of a schoolmaster, Philippe-Chrétien, who according to *Les Mots* had so many children that he had to become a grocer. Charles's brother Louis became the father of Albert Schweitzer of Lambaréné, who was thus Anne-Marie Sartre's cousin.

1874, 6 August: Birth at Thiviers, in the Dordogne, of Jean-Baptiste Sartre, son of a country doctor. According to *Les Mots*, Jean-Baptiste's father was so furious with his wife when he discovered, after the marriage, that she had brought him no dowry, that he never spoke to her again.

1882, 22 July: Birth of Anne-Marie Schweitzer, the fourth child of Charles Schweitzer and Louise née Guillemin, daughter of a Catholic lawyer.

1904, 3 May: Marriage of Jean-Baptiste Sartre, by that time a naval officer, and Anne-Marie Schweitzer.

1905, 21 June: Birth in Paris of Jean-Paul-Charles-Aymard Sartre.

1906, 17 September: Death of Jean-Baptiste Sartre, of a fever contracted in Indochina. Anne-Marie, having neither a job nor any money, goes back to live with her parents, first of all at Meudon, then at the rue Le Goff in Paris. Sartre is simultaneously pampered and neglected. His grandfather is so devoted to him that he will not expose him to the normal risks of going to school. At the same time, a leucoma is

1

allowed to grow over his right eye. Nothing is done to counteract its effects, so that Sartre is left with only one good eye.

1914–1918: First World War. Sartre writes a story in which a French soldier takes the Kaiser prisoner, challenges him to a duel, and defeats him. He is an unhappy, lonely child, who does not go to school until he is ten and a quarter.

1917, 26 April: Anne-Marie Sartre marries Joseph Mancy, an engineer, who becomes director of the shipyards at La Rochelle. Mancy tries to educate Sartre to follow his own profession, thus adding to an already heavily charged emotional atmosphere. Mancy was not, in fact, a particularly successful member of the middle class which Sartre grew up to dislike with such violence. In 1922, the La Rochelle shipyards went bankrupt. So, too, in 1924, did a factory managed by Joseph Mancy at Saint-Etienne. Sartre gets on badly with his schoolmates, steals money from his parents to try and buy their friendship, is caught and punished. His academic results improve, and he becomes quite a competent Greek scholar.

1917, October: Russian revolution brings Bolsheviks to power.

1920, October: Sartre moves to the Lycée Henri IV in Paris, where he meets up again with his friend Paul Nizan and is much happier.

1924–1928: After coming seventh in the very competitive examination to enter the Ecole Normale Supérieure, Sartre spends four very happy years there, compensating for his failure to pass the *agrégation* on his first attempt in 1928 by coming first in his second, in 1929. He signs a petition against compulsory military service, and takes part in a number of student demonstrations. In 1929, he meets Simone de Beauvoir, who comes second in the *Agrégation de Philosophie* the year that Sartre comes first.

1929, November: Begins eighteen months compulsory military service, where he is a private in the meteorological section, with Raymond Aron as the sergeant who instructs him.

1931, March: Appointed professeur de philosophie (= sixth-form master with special responsibility for philosophy) at the Lycée Le Havre.

1933–1934: Year at the Institut français de Berlin, where like most French students there (but not Aron, who was Jewish) is unimpressed with Hitler and convinced that the Nazi movement will soon collapse; even after Hitler has come to power on 30 January 1933.

1934: Resumes teaching at Le Havre, where he enjoys informal contact with pupils but dislikes the rigid atmosphere of the *lycée*.

1936, 7 March: Hitler sends troops into the Rhineland, thus breaking the article in the Versailles treaty which made it a demilitarised area. He encounters no resistance and proceeds to construct the Siegfried Line to defend the region against any attack by the French. Sartre remains apolitical, being principally concerned with his book 'Melancholia', the first version of what was to become *La Nausée*. It is eventually accepted for publication by the leading publishing house of Gallimard, the director Gaston Gallimard himself choosing the title.

Appointed to a teaching post in Laon, a town which he dislikes but which has the advantage of being closer to Paris than Le Havre.

1937: Publication of the short story 'Le Mur' in the July number of *La Nouvelle Revue Française*.

1938, 15 March: *Anschluss* (merging) of Germany and Austria, forbidden by the Treaty of Versailles.
April: Publication of *La Nausée*. Appearance in review form of three more of the stories that will make up *Le Mur*.
28 September: signature of the Munich agreement whereby Great Britain and France allow Hitler to take over the

Sudetenland mountains, inhabited by German-speaking citizens of Czechoslovakia. The crisis caused by Hitler's demands forms the subject matter of *Le Sursis*, the second volume in *Les chemins de la liberté*.

1939, February: Publication of *Le Mur* in book form.

March: German troops occupy the rest of Czechoslovakia. Great Britain and France renew their guarantee to Poland. On 1 September, German troops invade Poland. Great Britain and France declare war. Sartre is called up, and serves in Alsace, convinced that the war will be a short one but equally conscious that it has cut his life in two.

April: When on leave, receives the Prix du roman populiste for *Le Mur*.

10 May: German troops invade Holland and Belgium; and on 13 May, France. Sartre is taken completely by surprise by the rapidity of the German victory, and on 21 June is taken prisoner at Padoux without firing a shot. He is later transferred to a prisoner-of-war camp at Treves, where he quite enjoys the experience of communal life and makes many friends. These include a priest called Marius Perrin, who later publishes a book about Sartre as he knew him (*Avec Sartre au stalag X11*, Delarge, 1980). At Christmas 1940, Sartre performs the role of King Balthazar in the production of his own play, *Bariona*, set in Roman-occupied Palestine, and in which the main character organises a rearguard action which enables Joseph and Mary to escape with the infant Christ before Herod's soliders arrive.

1941, March: Recovers the manuscript of *L'Age de raison* from a German officer who had tried to confiscate it, and succeeds in having himself released on the grounds that he is a civilian captured by accident. The fact that he has only one eye lends credence to his story, the Germans not having suffered from anything like *la dénatalité française*, the fall in the birth rate which required the French to recruit anybody and everybody into the armed services. Returns to Paris, to the teaching post at the Lycée Pasteur to which he had been appointed in 1937. Writes *L'Etre et le néant* very quickly, the ideas being already clear in his head. He does most of his writing at the café de Flore, where Simone de Beauvoir describes how they both used to arrive early enough in the morning to take and occupy a seat near the stove for the rest of the day.

Sartre lives in various hotels, refusing on principle to own anything, but gets on better with his stepfather because of Joseph Mancy's disapproval of the policy of collaboration recommended by Marshal Pétain after his meeting with Hitler at Montoire on 24 October 1940.

1943, 2 June: First performance of *Les Mouches*, at the Théâtre de la Cité. Meets Camus at the first night, having already published his *Explication de 'L'Etranger'* in February.

June: Publication of *L'Etre et le néant*. Takes time off from writing *Le Sursis*, having completed *L'Age de raison* in 1942, to write *Huis Clos*. The original idea for a play with three characters unable to escape from their situation was the technical one of providing three actors with a work in which none of them would be off stage when the best lines were spoken, and in which each would have roughly the same amount to say. Although the theme of the play – 'Hell is other people' – is said to have come later, it does closely resemble some of the ideas set out in *L'Etre et le néant*.

Sartre never claimed to have played an active part in the resistance movement, but did write articles for the clandestine press.

1944, 22 May: First performance of *Huis Clos*, Sartre's most successful play in box office terms.

6 June: Allied armies invade France. 23–25 August, liberation of Paris. Beginning of vogue of what hostile critics describe as 'Résistentialisme': the coming together of Sartre's philosophy of freedom with the left-wing hopes of the resistance movement, whose slogan was 'De la Résistance à la Révolution'.

1945, January: Visits New York as special envoy of the newspaper *Combat*. Death of Joseph Mancy. In 1946, Sartre goes to live with his mother at 42, rue Bonaparte, staying there until 1962, when his campaign against the policy of *L'Algérie Française* leads to a series of bomb attacks against the apartment building.

September: Publication of *L'Age de raison* and *Le Sursis*; and of *Huis Clos* in book form.

October: First number of *Les Temps Modernes*. On 24 October, the lecture 'L'Existentialisme est un humanisme' causes a sensation, and Sartre is at the height of his fame.

1946: Publication of Sartre's preface to Baudelaire's *Ecrits Intimes*, later to appear in book form as *Baudelaire*. Its last sentence – 'Le choix libre qu'un homme fait de soi-même coincïde absolument avec ce qu'on appelle sa destinée' (the free choice that a man makes of himself coincides absolutely with what is called his destiny) – sums up Sartre's basic philosophy of liberty.

8 November: First performance of *La Putain respectueuse* (The Respectable Prostitute) at the Théâtre Antoine. Within a year, the term *une respectueuse* becomes accepted slang for a prostitute.

1947: Visits United States with Simone de Beauvoir. Publication of his *Théâtre*, of the *Baudelaire* in book form, and of the plea for committed literature, 'Qu'est-ce que la littérature?' in review form in *Les Temps Modernes*.

1948, March: In collaboration with David Rousset and others, launches the *Rassemblement Démocratique Révolutionnaire*, and attempts to find a viable left-wing movement without the Communists and in spite of their hostility to him. The RDR is not a success, and Sartre leaves it in October 1949.

6 April: First performance of *Les Mains Sales*, welcomed by conservatives as an exciting denunciation of Communist ruthlessness and opportunism, denounced by the Communists as a Cold War manoeuvre financed by the CIA.

May: Supports the creation of the State of Israel.

1949: Publication of *La Mort dans l'âme* and of Simone de Beauvoir's *Le Deuxième Sexe*.

30 October: The whole of Sartre's work placed on the index.

1950, January: Denunciation in *Les Temps Modernes* of the slave labour camps in the Soviet Union.

25 June: Troops from Communist North Korea invade

South Korea. Sartre soon takes the view that the North was provoked and that the person really responsible for the war was General MacArthur (*Les Temps Modernes*, December 1950).

1951, 7 June: First performance of *Le Diable et le Bon Dieu*, with Pierre Brasseur in the title role, a play which seems to prefigure the support which Sartre was to give to the French Communist Party a year later.

1952: Publication of *Saint Genet, comédien et martyr*.
28 May: The French Communist Party organises a major demonstration against the arrival in Paris of General Ridgeway, accused of using germ warfare in Korea. The demonstrations are not very successful, but the secretary of the Communist Party, Jacques Duclos, is arrested for plotting to overthrow the state, an important item of evidence against him being two pigeons in the boot of his car. The government claims that these were to be used to send the news of the street fighting back to Moscow; Madame Duclos says she is going to cook them with fresh peas. Sartre has just finished reading Henri Guillemin's *Le Coup du 2 décembre*, an analysis of the way Napoleon III had violated the Constitution of the Second Republic in 1851 in order to make himself first of all President for ten years and then Emperor.
Sartre is convinced that the French government of 1952 is planning a similar move to replace a democratic republic by an authoritarian dictatorship directed against the working class, and writes the articles entitled *Les Communistes et la Paix*. These appear in *Les Temps Modernes* in May and June 1952, and argue that the working class in France can achieve its identity as a class only through the Communist Party.
August: Publication in *Les Temps Modernes* of an exchange of letters between Sartre and Albert Camus, marking a final break in their friendship. In October 1951, Camus's *L'homme révolté* had contained a number of criticisms of Marxism with which Sartre and the *Temps Modernes* team did not agree.
19 November: Forbids the performance of *Les Mains Sales* in Vienna on the ground that it will be used as Cold War propaganda against the Soviet Union.

1953, October: Publishes *L'Affaire Henri Martin*, a series of articles defending a young French sailor for protesting against the attempt by the French to hold on to Indochina by force.

1954, May–June: Visits Soviet Union. Falls ill and is taken to hospital. On his return, publishes in *Libération* a series of articles in which he states that Soviet citizens have complete freedom to criticise the government and that material conditions in the Soviet Union are improving every day.

1955, January: Together with Francis Jeanson, declares his support and that of *Les Temps Modernes* for the Algerian *Front de Libération Nationale*, whose campaign for Algerian independence had begun on 1 November 1954.
6 June: First performance of *Nekrassov*, a play satirising the anti-communism of the French right-wing press.
November: Adapts Arthur Miller's *The Crucible* for the cinema under the title *Les Sorcières de Salem*.

1956, February: *Les Temps Modernes* express support for French soldiers refusing to serve in Algeria.
October–November: Sartre condemns the Franco-British attack on Egypt but devotes more space to denouncing the Soviet Union for putting down the Hungarian rebellion by force of arms. Breaks with the French Communist Party, which supported the Russian intervention in Hungary.

1957, September–October: Publishes in *Les Temps Modernes* two long articles entitled 'Questions de Méthode' in which he argues that a valid philosophy is one which reflects the way a rising class interprets the world and makes sense of its experience; and that since, in 1957, the new rising class is the proletariat, the only valid philosophy for to-day is Marxism.

1958: With a contempt for his own physical comfort which Ronald Hayman's biography presents as a permanent characteristic, fills himself full of a drug called corydrane in order to write *La Critique de la raison dialectique*.
6 March: Publishes his preface to Henri Alleg's *La Question*, 'Une Victoire', in *L'Express*, which is then seized by the police.
17 April: Joins with Camus, Malraux and Martin du Gard in

demanding that the government condemn the use of torture by the French army in Algeria.

13 May: Representatives of the European population in Algiers, supported by the French army, establish a *comité de salut public* in order to stop the government in Paris from beginning negotiations with the Algerian *Front de Libération Nationale*. Sartre protests against the use made of this incident to bring de Gaulle to power, and remains implacable in his opposition to him.

1959, 24 September: First performance of *Les Séquestrés d'Altona*, a political allegory in which the behaviour of the French in Algeria is assimilated to that of the Germans in Russia during the Second World War.

1960, May: Publication of *La Critique de la raison dialectique*, an attempt to bring together existentialism and Marxism. Sartre's argument that the existence of scarcity – as in W. H. Auden's 'Hunger allows no choice/To the citizen or the police'; though without the addition of the line: 'We must love one another or die' – makes conflict inevitable links the tone of the book to that of *L'Etre et le néant*.

March: Visits Cuba and reports enthusiastically on Fidel Castro's revolution.

May: Nikita Khrushchev, in Paris for a summit meeting over Berlin which never takes place, holds a reception at the Soviet Embassy which Sartre and Simone de Beauvoir attend. I have not been able to find anywhere in Sartre's published work any reference to the fact that this conference was to be held because the Russians had threatened to blockade West Berlin; or to the construction of the Berlin Wall on 13 August 1961; or to the explosion by the Soviet Union of a hundred megaton bomb as part of the series of nuclear experiments held in September 1961.

1961–2: Continues his campaign against the policy of *L'Algérie Française*, while refusing to support any of de Gaulle's moves to end the conflict. Has to move from his apartment in the rue Bonaparte because of attempts to blow him up by right-wing extremists. In April 1962, receives a letter of encouragement and support from Albert Schweitzer, to which he replies with affection and gratitude.

June 1962: Visits Russia.

Makes no public comment on the granting of Algerian independence on 1 July 1962.

1963: Visits Russia and Czechoslovakia.

October–November: Publication of *Les Mots* in *Les Temps Modernes*. In book form, the autobiographical fragment will be dedicated to Madame Z., a pseudonym for Sartre's Russian translator and interpreter, Lena Zonima.

1964, 26 October: Sartre is awarded the Nobel Prize for literature, but refuses it.

1965, 18 March: Adopts Arlette El Kaïm.

10 March: First performance of *Les Troyennes*, Sartre's adaptation of Euripides' *The Trojan Women* at the *Théâtre National Populaire*.

Refuses to go on a lecturing tour in the United States in order to protest against American policy in Vietnam. Visits Russia, where he speaks on 13 July in favour of a motion demanding the withdrawal of American troops from Vietnam.

December: Supports François Mitterrand in his bid to defeat de Gaulle in the election to the Presidency. Sartre's first and only direct intervention in conventional French politics.

1967, July: Agrees to take part in Bertrand Russell's International Tribunal on American War Crimes in Vietnam. This absorbs much of Sartre's time in the following year.

Supports Israel's claim to free navigation in the gulf of Akaba. Franz Fanon's widow refuses to allow Sartre's 1961 preface to *Les Damnés de la terre* to be published in future editions of her husband's book.

1968, May: Supports the student protest movement on the grounds that it is a genuine attempt to achieve political liberty.

August: Condemns the intervention of Soviet troops to crush the Prague Spring.

1970, April–May: Defends the continued publication of the revolutionary newspaper *La Cause du Peuple*, banned because of its
support for violence.
October: Stands on a barrel outside the Renault car factories
in order to address the workers.

1971, May: Publication of the first two volumes of the biography of
Flaubert, *L'Idiot de la Famille*, containing over a million
words. Sartre argues that Flaubert's childhood was oversha-
dowed by the fact that his mother wanted a girl, and by the
impossibility of his ever catching up with his brilliant elder
brother, Achille. This led him to choose, like Sartre himself,
to live in the imaginary world of literature.

1972: Publication of volume III of *L'Idiot de la Famille*. Sartre is
actively involved in a number of protests against working
conditions in the Renault car factory, and supports the
24-hour kidnapping of one of the managers.

1973, January: Describing parliamentary elections in a bourgeois
democracy as 'un piège à cons' (booby trap) urges mass
abstention in the forthcoming legislative elections.
February: Gives an interview in *Der Spiegel* in which, while
disapproving of what they did, he takes up the defence of the
Bader–Meinhoff 'Red Army faction'.
22 February: Publication of the first issue of *Libération*, a
left-wing daily newspaper of which Sartre is the titular
editor, his increasing blindness preventing him from playing
a more active role.

1974: Publication of *On a raison de se révolter*, a short book of
interviews by Sartre and others on the need for revolutionary violence.
November: Breaks off all contact with UNESCO after that
organisation had yielded to pressure from the Arab states to
exclude Israel.
Visits the German revolutionary leader Andreas Baader in
prison. Says that he disapproves of the kind of violence
practised by the Baader–Meinhof group, but criticises the
conditions under which Baader is imprisoned.

1977: Marks the official visit of Leonid Brejnev to Paris by taking part in a public meeting of dissident Russian intellectuals.

1979: Takes part in a number of demonstrations in favour of the 'boat people' escaping from Communist Vietnam.

1980: Supports boycott of Moscow Olympic Games in protest against Russian invasion of Afghanistan.
15 April: Death of Sartre. On 19 April, his body is taken to the Cimetière Montparnasse, escorted by a crowd of some 50,000 people. The President of the Republic, Valéry Giscard d'Estaing, pays tribute to him as 'une grande lueur d'intelligence'.

A fuller account of the major events in Sartre's life can be found in the *Pléiade* edition of his novels and short stories, from which much of the above information is taken.

2

La Nausée

Philosophy and Obsessions

Jean-Paul Sartre's first novel, *La Nausée*, was published in Paris in April 1938. It was an immediate success and was seriously considered for the most prestigious of French literary prizes, the Prix Goncourt. In 1950, when Sartre was at the height of his fame, it was selected by a literary jury as one of the best French novels of the half century. It was then that it appeared in its first French paperback edition, the *Collection Pourpre*, before becoming a Gallimard *Livre de Poche* in 1956. It was reprinted twice within a year of its first hardback publication, and by 1988 had sold over 2 million copies. In an interview in 1964, just after he had become the first and so far the only writer to turn down the Nobel Prize for Literature, Sartre said that *La Nausée* was the best book he had written from a literary point of view, and most critics agree with him in seeing it as his best work of fiction.

Although it broke new ground in a number of ways, and is considered one of the most successful attempts to use the novel to express philosophical ideas, *La Nausée* can still be read as fiction of a fairly traditional kind. It does, for example, tell a story, describing how an amateur historian, Antoine Roquentin, makes a discovery about the nature of existence. It explains what this discovery is, gives a long account of how Roquentin reacts to it, and ends by sketching out the solution which he intends to give to the problems which it has created for him. In 1971, when talking to a group of journalists making a film about his life, Sartre said that *La Nausée* was a kind of detective story. In the beginning, Roquentin does not understand why he is so physically uncomfortable. About half way through the book, he finds the answer. 'Le coupable', Sartre said in 1971, 'c'est la contingence'[1] (The criminal is contingency). What makes Roquentin so unhappy is the realisation that the universe

13

has come into being through a series of accidents and exists for no purpose.

The answer which the Sartre of 1938 suggested to the problems created by what the text of *La Nausée* also called the 'essential absurdity' of the world was to make Roquentin write a book. This would have all the qualities which the natural world lacked. It would not be 'contingent', in the sense that Roquentin uses the word in *La Nausée*: unpredictable, unjustifiable, existing for no purpose, overflowing with the absurdity of life to the point of making him feel physically sick. It would, in contrast, contain its own internal necessity within itself. It would be moulded and harmonious, carrying its own definition of what it is in its perfectly proportioned and mathematically self-evident form. Sartre never wrote such a book, and did not pursue this attempt to make art provide the solution to Roquentin's problems. It was his decision to give pride of place to the idea that the world has no meaning which made Sartre into one of those authors, more numerous in France, Russia and Germany than in the United Kingdom or the United States, who are genuinely worried by the fact that there is no God. It was not the attempt to find an answer in art.

Sartre was the most versatile of writers, and used plays, essays, interviews and lectures as well as novels and short stories to put his ideas across. In October 1945, in a well-attended public lecture in Paris, he explained what he meant by the word 'Existentialism', the philosophy which he did more than any other writer to make into a household word. While recognising that there were thinkers who, like the nineteenth-century Danish theologian Søren Kierkegaard, were Christian existentialists, he defined his own version of this philosophy as

> un effort pour tirer toutes les conséquences d'une position athée cohérente.[2] (an attempt to draw every possible conclusion from a position of total atheism.)

For the Christian, he explained, the world has the best of all reasons for existing: God made it. Everything that exists does so because God decided that it would exist, and took the decision to give it precisely the form it has. For the Christian, as for the Voltairean deist, the world is no more absurd than a clock. The clock exists because the clock-maker made it to tell other human beings what the time is. The world exists to proclaim the glory of God and to provide man with the opportunity of learning to love

and worship Him. He gave the people living in His world a number
of clear rules to tell them how to behave, and informed them about
the difference between right and wrong. But once God disappears,
there ceases in Sartre's view to be any reason for anything,
especially the rules separating right from wrong, to exist at all. One
of the reasons for Sartre's importance as a writer, and for the
interest his ideas still have for the modern reader, lies in a phrase
which he himself wrote in 1950 about an earlier French author
whom he greatly admired, André Gide: that in his work and life,
Gide had lived out 'l'agonie et la mort de Dieu'[3] (the final death
agony of God).

For a variety of reasons, *La Nausée* has not been as popular in
English-speaking countries as some of Sartre's other works, especially his plays. It was first translated, perhaps rather misleadingly,
as *The Diary of Antoine Roquentin*, but even its later appearance in
the Penguin Modern Classics in 1965 under the title of *Nausea* was
not particularly successful. This is not because of the translation.
The version by Robert Baldick in the Penguin Classics exactly
renders the blend of ironic observation and black poetry with
which Roquentin tells his story. This obviously comes over better in
Sartre's vigorous, racy, highly idiomatic French, but the book loses
much less in translation than Camus' *L'Etranger*, which has always
been very successful with English readers. The main reason, apart
from frivolous ones such as the impatience traditionally felt by
English readers with unhappy intellectuals and the difficulty for
anyone who listened to the BBC in the 1930s of forgetting that the
comedian Arthur Askey had a girl friend called Nausea Bagwash,
is the fact that the basic idea inspiring the book has been around
for rather a long time.

It is true that it has been more visible in scientific writing and in
poetry than in fiction. In 1785, for example, James Hutton wrote in
his *Theory of the Earth* that the world had 'no vestige of a beginning,
no prospect of an end', and the poetry of the Victorians is rich in
evocations of the anticipation which Tennyson gave to one of the
main themes in Darwin's *The Origin of Species* when he asked, in the
poem *In Memoriam*, in 1851:

> Are God and Nature then at strife,
> That Nature lends such evil dreams?
> So careful of the type she seems,
> So careless of the single life

only to realise that even this was an optimistic way of looking at the
world and continue

> 'So careful of the type?' but no.
> From scarped cliff and quarried stone
> She cries, 'A thousand types are gone:
> I care for nothing all shall go'.

If God is all powerful and all good, as Christian doctrine has
always taught, and if there consequently is a divine providence
lying behind everything, then why have so many species arisen and
died out for no apparent reason? Why has there been all the
suffering inseparable from the existence of biological life? What
purpose has it served, since the only possible reason for physical
suffering is to enable human beings to become morally better, and
human beings did not appear until less than half a million years
ago? Why did so many other creatures have to suffer and die
before man finally made his appearance? Unlike Tennyson, Sartre
never writes the equivalent of

> I stretch lame hands of faith, and grope,
> And gather dust and chaff, and call
> To what I feel is Lord of all,
> And faintly trust the larger hope.

He does not faintly trust anything. In 1964, in one of the best of his
interviews, he showed how fully he endorsed the gloomiest inter-
pretation of the Darwinian hypothesis when he said:

L'univers reste noir. Nous sommes des animaux sinistrés.[4] (The
universe is still shrouded in darkness. We are animals struck with
disaster.)

One of the most consistent themes in Sartre's thinking is that
there is no God and that history has no meaning. But the idea of
the death of God, proclaimed by Nietszche in *Thus Spoke Zarathustra*
in 1883, was already there for English readers in Matthew Arnold's
Dover Beach in 1880.

> The sea of faith
> Was once, too, at the full, and round earth's shore

Lay like the folds of a bright girdle furled;
But now I only hear
Its melancholy, long, withdrawing roar,
Retreating to the breath
Of the night wind down the vast edges drear
And naked shingles of the world.

Sartre does not quote Matthew Arnold, any more than he quotes *In Memoriam*. Until the publication in 1983, three years after his death, of his *Lettres au Castor et à quelques autres* (*Letters to Simone de Beauvoir and others*), there was little evidence in his published work of his interest in English literature, and of his admiration for Shakespeare.[5] The foreign authors whom he wrote about in his published work in his lifetime were Americans, especially the novelist Dos Passos whose narrative technique he imitated in his novel about the 1938 Munich crisis, *Le Sursis* (*The Reprieve*), and the German philosopher Husserl, whose ideas greatly influenced his views on the imagination. Neither did Sartre show much enthusiasm at any point in his career either for the natural or for the biological sciences. Simone de Beauvoir reports him as being as dismissive in the 1930s of scientific modes of thought as he was of conventional ethics.

'Science,' he was wont to say, 'c'est peau de balle. Morale, c'est trou de balle.'[6] (Science is the outer surface of the ball. Morality its inner emptiness.)

The basic problem in *La Nausée* is nevertheless familiar to anyone who has thought about Darwin's theory of the evolution of species, especially if they have also come across more recent developments in palaeontology.

Thus it is not merely an accident of language that the book which the American biologist and palaeontologist Stephen Jay Gould published in 1990, *The Burgess Shale*, should use the word 'contingency' almost as much as Sartre does. What emerges from the fossils laid down 570 million years ago in the mud of Northern Canada is that the evolutionary process which eventually gave birth to man might never have happened at all. A drop of a few degrees in temperature at a particular moment in the palaeolithic age could have eliminated all forms of biological life, thus rendering impossible the genetic variations which eventually gave birth to man. The

evidence offered by the Burgess Shale supports the view of the
Christian theologians who say that we are, as a species, quite
unique. But so is every other species, and this is not because the
Lord God made us all. It is because the accident which produced us
was a one-off, accidental, unrepeatable event. When somebody said
to Mae West: 'My Goodness, what diamonds', she replied: 'Goodness had nothing to do with it'. The title of another of Stephen Jay
Gould's books is *Wonderful World*. But God had nothing to do with
that either.

Once God the creator is removed, any idea of the different
species as we know them, including our own, having come into
existence by anything but an accident totally disappears. A few
highly individualistic thinkers like George Bernard Shaw might
persist in believing in some kind of dynamic evolution manifesting
itself as a Life Force and pursuing ends which point to the
existence of some kind of motivation in the universe. But even if
this motivation did exist, it would not have the necessity stemming
from a divine providence ordered and engineered by God the
Father, and which Arthur Campbell Ainger summed up when he
wrote in his most famous hymn that:

God is working his purpose out, as year succeeds to year
God is working his purpose out, and the time is drawing near
Nearer and nearer draws the time, the time that shall surely be
When the earth shall be filled with the glory of God as the waters
    cover the sea.

One of the best ways of appreciating the intellectual reasons
lying behind Roquentin's anguish is to think about how the world
seems to a convinced Christian or a devout Muslim: totally free of
absurdity, entirely non-contingent, full of meaning because willed
into existence by an all-powerful creator in order to serve a definite
purpose. *La Nausée* is the exact opposite of this, and in the
European as well as the Islamic intellectual tradition shows what
can happen when human beings stop trying to make sense of their
experience through God. Nothing could be further from Sartre's
way of seeing the world than the vision which the Psalmist
expressed when he sang that: 'The Heavens declare the glory of
God and the firmament showeth his handiwork'.

This does not mean that Sartre is in any way nostalgic for an age
of faith or that he is consciously sorry that people have stopped

believing in God. The one mention of Christ in his published work
presents Him as a political agitator executed by the Romans.[7]
Neither did Sartre deliberately set out to write a novel which
expressed the consequences of the realisation which came over
Darwin, as he examined the evidence and compared the various
species one with another, that there was no way in which this could
all have been produced by a deliberate act of divine creation.
Darwin is said to have replied to the question as to whether his
researches had taught him anything about God the Creator with
the remark: 'Yes. He has an extraordinary fondness for spiders'.
Sartre did not make jokes of this kind. If he mentions insects, it is
with the same horrified fascination with which he evokes what he
sees as the nightmarish world of shellfish.

Although *La Nausée* can be approached intellectually in terms of
the Darwinian theory of evolution, Sartre did not conceive his
novel in these terms, and it would have been a very dull one if he
had done. It would certainly not have had the flashes of humour
which make it one of the best accounts of a French provincial town
in the period between the two world wars, and it would not have
been a book which presents the ordinary reader as well as the
literary critic with so fascinating a set of literary and intellectual
problems. One of the most important of these is that of trying to
decide whether the nausea which overwhelms Roquentin whenever
he thinks about himself or about the physical world is a cleverly
chosen device to express Sartre's ideas on contingency, or whether
it expresses a state of mind in both the fictional Roquentin and the
real Sartre which is best described as pathological.

Roquentin's feelings of nausea begin to take on a definitive form
when he picks up a pebble on the beach with the intention of
skimming it across the water. But the pebble suddenly ceases to be
merely something he can play with in an innocent game of ducks
and drakes. Roquentin feels, in his hands, 'une espèce d'écoeurement douceâtre', a kind of 'sickly-sweet nausea' which prevents him
from treating the pebble as a tool. He finds himself increasingly in
a world in which objects become separated from their names, in
which everything he sees, whether artefacts such as the benches in
a café, natural objects like the chestnut tree in the park, or
biological entities like other human beings, takes on the same
terrifying, burgeoning over-fullness. The climax comes when he
looks at the chestnut tree, on which the wind has just settled 'like an
overblown fly', and realises the truth about himself and about

everything that exists. This is that everybody is 'de trop', unnecessary, excessive, plethoric, empty of meaning but overflowing with absurdity, accidental in the sense that it ought never to have been there in the first place.

The only escape from this nauseating superabundance is into a world of pure form, of the hard, metallic necessity of mathematical formulae and passages of music. As Roquentin explains, there is nothing absurd about a circle. It carries its own definition within itself, is defined by what makes it into a circle: the rotation of a straight line about a fixed point. It does not matter whether the straight line is a piece of tautly held string, the edge of a ruler or a piece of chalk. Indeed, since a circle is essentially a concept, it is better if it is not thought of as a physical object at all. There are no straight lines in nature. Circles, squares, oblongs and triangles are creations of the human mind, not objects which actually exist. This is why, in Roquentin's world, people who compose or perform music represent so perfect an ideal. By creating something which exists only in the pure world of abstractions, the Jew who Roquentin says has composed the song and the Negress who sings it have 'washed themselves free from the sin of existing' (se sont lavés du péché d'exister).[8]

The action of *La Nausée* takes place sometime in the late 1920s or early 1930s in the French provincial seaport of Bouville (Mudtown), modelled partly on La Rochelle, a town in which Sartre had spent his unhappy adolescence, and partly on Le Havre, where he later had a spell as a teacher. Roquentin is a bachelor, lives in a hotel, and spends quite a lot of his spare time in a café called Le Rendez-vous des Cheminots (The Railwaymen's Rest). There, in a juke box, is a record of Sophie Tucker singing 'Some of these Days', and one of the few ways in which Roquentin can find temporary respite from his nausea is by listening to this song. It, too, he reflects, is like a mathematical formula in that it is beyond the world of existence. If you broke the record and tore up the music, the song would still be there. It is not like a tree or a human being, the product of the coming together of a number of accidental physical circumstances. It is beyond existence, in the sense that nothing that happens in the world of real objects can possibly touch it.

In 1963, twenty-five years after the publication of *La Nausée*, Sartre wrote in his autiobiography *Les Mots* (Words) that his father had versé les quelques gouttes de sperme qui font le prix ordinaire d'un enfant[9] (shed the few drops of sperm needed to make a child).

It is a memorable phrase, encapsulating the truth of which all adults become aware when they think about the moment at which they were conceived. The postponement of their parents' love-making until the following morning might have meant that they had quite a different physical constitution. They might not, for example, have the rather clumsy build which they and their brother have obviously inherited from their paternal grandfather's side of the family. Instead, they might have the physical dexterity which their sister derives from the genes on their mother's side. But while we are all the fruit of unrepeatable couplings and accidental genetic variations which are still – fortunately – beyond human control, musical phrases are not like that. They are the product of conscious choice, the result of the observance of rules to produce a deliberately chosen effect. They cannot be destroyed, as a human mind can be destroyed, by the accident of a microbe getting out of control. They cannot be reduced to idiocy and incontinence by a few cells proliferating in a place where love and self-interest say they should not, and forming a tumour on the brain.

Roquentin is no composer, and *La Nausée* does not end with his decision to try to write a tune as memorable as 'Some of These Days', or as Scott Joplin's 'The Entertainer'. It does, however, end with his decision to write a book. This will, Roquentin hopes, have some of the qualities which he finds in musical airs and mathematical formulae, and which cannot be found in the flabbiness and sickening over-fullness of the material world. It will be, as he says 'belle et dure comme de l'acier'[10] (beautiful and hard as steel). It will also 'make people feel ashamed of their existence' (fera honte aux gens de leur existence). This is a phrase which gives a second meaning to the book which Roquentin intends to write: it will have a private, aesthetic value, thus providing an answer to Roquentin's worries about contingency; but it will also have a public, moralising function, in that it will make anybody who reads it feel that Roquentin has seen the world as it really is.

There is no particular problem about the first of these two meanings. The idea of art as having a form that life lacks, of a poem lasting longer than anyone alive when the poet writes it, is one of the oldest ideals in literary history. Flaubert wanted to write a book:

> sur rien, un livre sans attache extérieure, qui se tiendrait de lui-même par la force interne de son style[11] (about nothing, with no links with the outside world, which would stand upright by the inner strength of its style).

Mallarmé also claimed that 'tout, au monde, existe pour aboutir à un livre'[12] (everything in the world exists to culminate in a book) and Roquentin is in a well-established tradition in arguing that art alone can have the significant form lacking in ordinary experience. It is when the implications of the idea that Roquentin's book will 'make people feel ashamed of their existence' start to sink in that the argument of *La Nausée* presents problems.

To concentrate, as Sartre does, on the sensation of feeling sick is a very good way of explaining what contingency means. Unless we are unfortunate enough to suffer from sea-sickness or food-poisoning, we feel sick because we have eaten or drunk too much. Since the theory which Sartre is developing in *La Nausée* implies that there is no good and sufficient reason for anything to exist at all, a description of the experience of feeling sick is a very good way of expressing why Roquentin is so unhappy: he feels that there is just too much of everything. We sympathise with him, recognise him as a very unusual person, and admire the skill with which Sartre brings him to life. Roquentin is one of the most amusing and perceptive observers in the history of the French novel. He is not only a very unusual and sensitive man. He is also very funny with it. But it is difficult to see him as a kind of philosophical hero whose thoughts and feelings are those which we would all have if we thought honestly about ourselves. Most people do not feel sick, and do not see any reason why they should.

When Sartre's philosophical works first became known in England, soon after the end of the Second World War, A.J. Ayer pointed out that *La Nausée* expressed what the logical positivists would call 'a pointless lament'.[13] A world that satisfied Roquentin's criteria of innate necessity and mathematical inevitability would, Ayer pointed out, be a very odd one. It would be one in which matters of fact would be logically necessary, and by definition this can never be the case. If they were, Bouncing Boy would win the 3 o'clock at Cheltenham with the same absolute predictability that three sevens make twenty-one, and this would do more than put

the bookmakers out of business. It would create a world so
different from the one we know that there would be no living in it.
Nobody would disagree with Sartre's view that the world exists for
no purpose. What seems odd is that he should create a hero who is
so upset by this that he wants to write a book which will make
people 'ashamed of their existence'.

Ayer's criticism of Sartre was more than a clash of personalities.
It was the expression of a whole difference of philosophical temper
and cultural attitudes. Most literate Englishmen of Ayer's generation had become so accustomed to regarding the death of God with
the same equanimity with which they accepted the death of
Gladstone that Roquentin seemed to be making rather an unnecessary fuss. It had been understandable for the Victorians to be
worried about the death of God. They had, after all, quite often
grown up believing in Him, and it is understandable to be upset
about the loss of an old and valued friend. Thomas Henry Huxley
was affectionately known as 'Darwin's bulldog', and won hands
down when he debated the case for the evolution of species against
the continued belief of Bishop Wilberforce, or 'Soapy Sam', in the
literal truth of the account of the creation of the world in the first
book of Genesis. But there is more than a twinge of anxiety in
Thomas Huxley's comment to Darwin, in a letter written on 20
February 1871, about the possibility that a person might fall victim
to insanity 'because his nth ancestor had lived between tide
marks'.[14]

Thomas Henry's grandson Aldous had also published, in 1920, a
poem unwittingly anticipating the implications of Sartre's later
remark about his father 'shedding the few drops of sperm needed
to make a man'. In *The Fifth Philosopher's Song*, he wrote of how
extraordinary it was that out of the 'million million spermatozoa' in
the ejaculation which had set into motion the process leading to his
birth, only one of them – himself – should have survived.

In the novel *Antic Hay*, in 1923, Huxley had shown himself even
more worried about living in a universe in which a little piece of the
body of the person you most loved suddenly 'began to obey the
second law of thermodynamics', so that they developed cancer and
died. The world which he described in his early novels was one in
which

the tragedies of the spirit are mere struttings and posturings on
the margin of life, and the spirit itself only an accidental

exuberance, the product of spare vital energy, like the feathers on the head of a hoopoe or the innumerable population of useless and foredoomed spermatozoa.[15]

But Huxley's reaction was an unusual one, and the predominant reaction in English intellectual circles was not to go on quite so much about being the accidental product of a blind evolutionary process governed by a mixture of genetic chance and selective necessity. To the cold eye of English common sense, it seems rather odd for anyone to react as Roquentin does to the discovery of the accidental nature of biological existence and to write, as he does, that

tout existant naît sans raison, se prolonge par faiblesse et meurt par rencontre[16] (everything that exists is born without reason, carries on living by weakness and dies by chance).

After all, there are plenty of people who have had precisely the opposite reaction. Like the G. K. Chesterton of *Orthodoxy*, they have rejoiced in the extraordinary accident which has produced them and nobody else. The horror which Roquentin feels is very convincing and quite understandable. But it is hard to see why it is a more logical or honest reaction than that of the person who says that there is something rather wonderful about an evolutionary process which has produced a digestive system capable of dealing just as well with bacon and eggs as with bananas; especially when this process also occasionally gives birth to a Michelangelo or a Mozart as well.

To readers such as these, who feel relatively at home in the world, *La Nausée* would be a much better novel if Roquentin were presented as an odd rather than an exemplary figure, someone whose sickness was not something we all ought to feel but simply a kind of metaphor, a rhetorical device for expressing one possible reaction to the death of God. There are occasional hints that *La Nausée* might be read in this way. A note at the beginning of the novel presents it as made up of notebooks discovered among Roquentin's papers, with the implication either that he is dead or that he has gone mad. The text itself also occasionally suggests that Roquentin is a man driven slightly insane by his discovery of contingency. However wittily and perceptively he describes other people, he is a pathological case, a man made more vulnerable than a normal person would be to a world whose absurdity does not prevent the common run of humanity from living in it without too much difficulty. In this reading of the novel, Sartre would be using Roquentin as Flaubert uses Emma Bovary, as an example of what happens if you allow yourself to be carried away by a particular idea. After all, as Wittgenstein pointed out in his *Philosophical Investigations*, the confusions which it is the task of philosophy to dispel arise when 'language is like an engine idling, not when it is doing work'.

If we want to stop slipping and start to walk then we must, as Wittgenstein says, 'get back to the rough ground',[17] and it is a piece of advice which Roquentin seems to echo when he comments on how his Tante Bigeois used to tell him about the dangers of gazing at yourself for too long in the looking-glass. When *La Nausée* first appeared in English, under the title of *The Diary of Antoine Roquentin*, *The Times Literary Supplement* described Roquentin as a 'favourite type with French novelists', a 'superior man' whose Byronic gloom went hand in hand with an 'overwhelmingly egotistical, thwarted personality', and the mistaken belief that he had 'seen through everything life has to offer'.[18] The inclusion of Tante Bigeois' remark means that it is Sartre himself who is suggesting the aggressively commonsensical comment that Roquentin would not be so unhappy if he had some proper work to do.

It is tempting to interpret *La Nausée* as a first-person narrative in which one of the main targets for the satire is the narrator himself. Similarly, it is possible to argue that commentators on Sartre's work have done him a disservice by concentrating on the 'horrible ecstasy' which comes over Roquentin as he gazes at the chestnut tree in the park. This is far from being the best or most interesting passage in the book. The scenes in the Café des Cheminots, where Roquentin watches the men playing cards and listens to their conversation, are much better. So, too, is the description of the people waiting in the cinema queue, eagerly waiting for the time they could sink into its magic world, only to find that, as usual, the film would be no good, they would be sitting next to an old man with a stinking pipe, their old pain would start up again, or their boy friend would be having one of his moods.[19]

Similarly, when Roquentin notes the delight which he used to take at seeing an old shop, with its 'cynical, obstinate look' which rappelait avec insolence les droits de la vermine et de la crasse, à deux pas de l'église la plus coûteuse de France[20] (insolently recalling the rights of vermin and filth a stone's throw from the most expensive church in France),

he is much better at gaining the reader's sympathy than when he describes how he feels himself existing and writes of the slow, nauseating feeling of existence that comes over him every time he swallows.[21]

Were it possible to take *La Nausée* in isolation, accepting the convention that it is merely the papers of a man who has now disappeared, there would be no problem. It is quite acceptable for a fictional character to write that:

> Où que je la mette, elle continuera d'exister et je continuerai de sentir qu'elle existe; je ne peux pas la supprimer, ni supprimer le reste de mon corps, la chaleur humide qui salit ma chemise, ni toute cette graisse chaude qui tourne paresseusement, comme si on la remuait à la cuiller, ni toutes les sensations qui se promènent là-dedans, qui vont et viennent, remontent de mon flanc à mon aisselle ou bien qui végètent doucement, du matin jusqu'au soir, dans leur coin habituel.[22] (Wherever I put my hand, it will continue to exist and I shall continue to feel that it exists; I cannot get rid of it, or get rid of the rest of my body, of the damp heat that dirties my shirt, nor free myself from this warm fat which turns lazily as if stirred by a spoon, from these sensations which walk about inside me, which come and go, move from my side to my armpit, or which softly vegetate, from morning to evening, in their accustomed corner.)

Such a man would be, like the Augustus Carp who presents his autobiography as that of 'A Really Good Man', or the more agreeable Mr Pooter in *The Diary of a Nobody*, somebody who invites criticism by the very way he describes his experience. He would be a sick man whose illness comes through in the very way he talks about his symptoms. However, once the inevitable happens and *La Nausée* is placed in the context of Sartre's other works, it soon becomes clear that he would have been very unhappy to see his book interpreted in this way. Indeed, Sartre is so far from wanting Roquentin's experience to be seen as pathological that he refers to his sickness as though it were the only possible way in which an honest person can react to existence.

In 1943, for example, he wrote a play called *Les Mouches* (*The Flies*), an adaptation of the Greek legend of the murder of Agamemnon by his wife Clytemnestra and her lover Aigisthos. In it, he presented Agamemnon's son Orestes as the man who quite rightly avenges his father's murder by killing not only the usurper Aigisthos but his own mother as well. At the time, it was easy to see Orestes as a political hero. He liberates France by killing the German invader Aigisthos, and he wreaks vengeance on the treacherous collaborators personified by the unfaithful Clytemnestra as well. Perhaps it was because Orestes was also a philosophical hero that the Germans did not notice its political implications and ban the play. *Les Mouches* does have quite a lot of philosophising in it, especially when Orestes proclaims as he disappears into the sunset, after freeing his fellow citizens from Aigisthos' tyranny by killing him, that 'la vie humaine commence de l'autre côté du désespoir' (human life begins on the other side of despair). Orestes might well, in this respect, be the man to write at least part of Roquentin's book for him, for when Jupiter accuses him of being about to tell the inhabitants of Argos about

leur obscène et fade existence, qui leur est donnée pour rien[23] (their obscene and tasteless existence, which is given to them for no purpose)

he agrees completely. Yes, he says, this is precisely what he is going to do, and there is a very clear link between his desire to make people see what life is really like and Roquentin's aim to write a book which will make people feel ashamed of their existence. It is the images as well as the ideas in Sartre's early work which make it clear that Roquentin's experience of the world is intended to be seen not as pathological but as privileged. Sartre's first major philosophical interest was in the workings of the imagination. After writing a short, academic-style book called *L'Imagination* in 1936, which gives relatively little idea of what he himself thought, he published in 1940 a long book entitled *L'Imaginaire*, which he sets out his own views. In the closing chapter, he described what happens when you stop listening to Beethoven's Seventh Symphony. You leave an ordered, satisfactory but imaginary world, and come back to what Sartre calls

l'écoeurement nauséeux qui caractérise la conscience réalisante[24]
(that nauseating sickness which characterises our consciousness
of reality).

The argument is very similar to the one in *La Nausée*, with the
Seventh Symphony playing the same illustrative role as 'Some of
These Days'. But there is no obvious need for Sartre to use the
same images in a work of philosophical analysis that he exploits in a
novel. Readers of philosophical works as difficult as *L'Imaginaire* do
not need these particular aids to understanding. If Sartre includes
them, it must be for one of two reasons: either these images
constitute for him a kind of King Charles's Head, the equivalent of
the obsession with the unfortunate monarch's execution which the
Mr Dick of *David Copperfield* could not prevent finding its way into
whatever he wrote; or it is because he really believes, emotionally as
well as intellectually, that everybody who looks honestly at their
existence not only ought to have the same thoughts as Roquentin
but also inevitably experiences the same sensations.

Sartre's first and most important philosophical work, the 750-
page *L'Etre et le néant* (*Being and Nothingness*), was published in
1943. Like *La Nausée*, it takes for granted the non-existence of God.
Nowhere in Sartre's work is there anything like the moral argument against the existence of a Christian God presented in Camus'
La Peste (The Plague). Sartre is not interested in the impossibility of
reconciling the existence of an all-powerful and all-merciful God
with the fact of a child dying of a painful natural disease, any more
than he is concerned about the inconsistencies in the biblical texts
which, in the nineteenth century, made Ernest Renan give up the
priesthood rather than believe in something so manifestly false as
the literal truth of the Old and New Testaments.[25] The only
account which he gives of his religious development is in *Les Mots*,
where he attributes his early loss of faith to the fact his grandfather, who was a Protestant, constantly made fun of his grandmother's Catholic beliefs, and vice versa. He simply assumes that
his readers will know enough about the various intellectual reasons
for not believing in God, rather as he assumes that they will not
need the reasons for disliking the bourgeoisie spelt out to them in
detail.

In this, as in other respects, his work offers a valuable if not
always conscious commentary on the realities of intellectual life in
mid-twentieth-century France. *L'Etre et le néant* is also very like the

other books in which Sartre 'draws the consequences from a
consistently atheistic position' in containing phrases which suggest
that Roquentin's 'horrible ecstasy' is not to be seen as an illness but
as an experience which reflects the way things are. Thus Sartre
writes that

> Une nausée discrète et insurmontable révèle perpétuellement
> mon corps à ma conscience[26] (A dull and inescapable feeling of
> sickness perpetually reveals my body to my mind),

and he later attributes exactly the same experience to other people.
The sentence

> Cette facticité, c'est précisément celle qu'il (= autrui) *existe* dans
> et par son pour-soi; c'est celle qu'il vit perpétuellement par la
> nausée comme saisie non-positionnelle d'une contingence qu'il
> est, comme pure appréhension de soi[27]

can be fully translated as

> This facticity is exactly what the other person *exists* in and
> through the for-itself; it is the facticity which it experiences
> through nausea as a non-positional apprehension of contingency
> that he is.

What it means in ordinary English is that everybody really feels as
sick as Roquentin, though without always realising it. A few pages
earlier in *L'Etre et le néant*, just after he has evoked the nausea which
'discreetly reveals his body to his mind', Sartre goes out of his way
to dismiss the idea that Roquentin's nausea is merely a metaphor.
'C'est au contraire', he writes

> sur son fondement (= de la nausée) que se produisent toutes les
> nausées concrètes et empiriques (nausées devant la viande pour-
> rie, le sang frais, les excréments, etc.) qui nous conduisent au
> vomissement.[28]

Once again, a translation gives something like:

> On the contrary, it is this nausea which provides a basis for all the
> occasions when we are actually sick (as in the presence of rotten
> meat, fresh blood, excrement, etc.),

and the actual meaning of the sentence suggests a kind of variant of Plato's view that the colour red exists because of a divine archetype, lying beyond space and time, by virtue of which all the objects which we recognise as red are really red and not a disguised green. For the Sartre of *L'Etre et le néant*, we feel sick on specific occasions only by virtue of a permanent nausea which underlies our whole experience of reality. For him, if one is to believe the texts which he wrote in the 1930s and 1940s, nausea is almost as transcendental as the notion of goodness in Plato.

Neither is it only when Sartre is writing about philosophy that he uses language which suggests that Roquentin is a character whose experience is important and significant because it reflects the way we all experience the world, even if we are not always conscious of it at the time. In the first volume of his *Situations*, a collection of essays published in 1947, and in which he talks about novelists such as Giraudoux, Mauriac, Camus, Dos Passos and Faulkner, Sartre describes the world in very Roquentin-like terms when he refers to it as

> cette pâte molle parcourue d'ondulations qui ont leur cause et leur fin hors d'elles-mêmes[29] (this soft paste shot through with waves that have their cause and ending outside themselves).

It is the frequent and almost obsessional repetition of this kind of imagery which makes it very difficult to accept the view that the images in *La Nausée* are merely a rhetorical device which Sartre uses to make his ideas more understandable. It is true that he said in an interview in 1971 that he personally had never had 'une nausée' of the type attributed to Roquentin, and equally true that his posthumously published letters to Simone de Beauvoir do not show any nausea from which he might have suffered ever diminishing his appetite. In July 1938, he particularly enjoyed

> une belle côte de boeuf aux haricots verts et une tarte en lisant un roman policier (a splendid side of beef with French beans while reading a detective story)

and he later wrote to thank her for sending him a packet containing tins of sausages, tuna fish and foie gras while he was serving in the army in the first months of the Second World War. He was also, he wrote in the same letter, looking forward to eating 'une truffe sous la cendre' (truffles baked in hot ash) when he came home on leave, and the various biographies published of him since his death suggest an appreciation of food which at times came near to gluttony. But if Sartre the private individual always, as his friend and biographer Francis Jeanson wrote, 'fait bon ménage avec son corps' (got on well with his own body),[30] the image which he gave of himself in his published work was very different. There, whether he is writing about fictitious characters such as Roquentin, or illustrating philosophical or literary ideas from his own experience, he comes back again and again to the same images of sickness and discomfort, of the plethoric unpleasantness of nature, which he assumes that other people share with him.

This remained the case throughout his literary career. In the 1963 autobiographical fragment *Les Mots*, he talked about the 'écoeurante fadeur'[31] which overcome him every time he thought about his 'disponibilité', the fact that he had been born for no obvious reason. When, eventually, he is allowed to go to school and to play with other children, the adjectives which he uses to describe his delight are exactly those with which Roquentin evokes his emergence from contingency into the necessary harmony of the work of art. He too, as he emerges from the stifling atmosphere of home, where everyone plays a part, feels himself.

'sec, dur et gai', and, like Roquentin, 'lavé du péché d'exister'[32] (dry, hard and cheerful . . . freed from the sin of existing).

Even when writing for an audience of only one, in his early letters to Simone de Beauvoir, Sartre speaks of nature in exactly the same terms as Roquentin, describing an invasion of cockchafers as 'con et répugnant' (stupid and repugnant), and finding the little town of Gien full of

la nature, une nature aqueuse, verte et molle, pleine de ces plantes vertes qui donnent l'impresssion qu'il en sortirait du lait si on pressait dessus[33] (nature, a wet, soft and watery nature, full of those green plants which look as though milk would come out if you squeezed them).

Sartre is one of the few writers actually to say that he was an existentialist – Camus, for example, always vigorously denied it – and he is certainly in the tradition of the nineteenth-century

Danish philosopher and theologian Søren Kierkegaard in seeing
more value in the experience of the isolated, unhappy and alien-
ated individual than in the well-integrated member of middle-class
society. There is a good case for seeing the seventeenth-century
mathematician and theologian Blaise Pascal as the first existentialist, and the basic argument in his *Pensées* was that it was important
for human beings to realise how unhappy they were since this
made them more aware of how much they needed God. One of the
best known prayers in the Anglican Communion Service reminds
us that 'if we say we have no sin, we deceive ourselves and the truth
is not in us'. It needs only a slight shift of angle to see the remark in
L'Etre et le néant about everyone feeling as sick as Roquentin does,
though without realising it, as a recasting of this idea in a form
suitable to an atheistic awareness of what *La Nausée* also calls 'le
péché d'exister'[34] (the sin of existing).

In the immediate post-war period in France, when the clash of
the rival totalitarianisms of Fascism and Communism threatened to
destroy Western civilisation almost completely, Sartre's insistence
on the inevitability of human unhappiness took on a new and
highly topical air. Indeed, his philosophy so fitted the doom-laden
atmosphere of the time that when he wrote about what it was like to
be alive during the German occupation of France, he gave the
impression of glorying in the way that history was rubbing people's
noses in the more unpleasant truths of the human condition.

> L'exil, la captivité, la mort surtout que l'on masque habilement
> dans les époques heureuses, nous en faisions les objets perma-
> nents de nos soucis, nous apprenions que ce ne sont pas des
> accidents évitables, ni même des menaces constantes mais ex-
> térieures: il fallait y voir notre *lot*, notre destin, la source de notre
> réalité d'homme.[35] (Exile, captivity and death above all which are
> skilfully hidden from us in happy times, became matters of
> permanent daily concern. We learnt that they are not avoidable
> accidents and not even constant but external threats. We had to
> see them as our fate, our destiny, the very roots of our human
> reality.)

There is nevertheless a difference between the sensation of
permanent sickness by which all Sartre's characters come to realise
that they exist and the cruelty and violence which swept over
Europe between Hitler's coming to power in Germany in 1933 and

the end of the Second World War in 1945. Even if he lived in a society as stable as Switzerland, the Mathieu Delarue of the next novel which Sartre published after *La Nausée*, *L'Age de raison* (*The Age of Reason*) in 1945 would still feel 'that old taste of blood and rusty iron' which he thinks of as his taste, and would still say to himself,

> Exister, c'est ça: se boire sans cesse[36] (that is what to exist means, to drink oneself without being thirsty).

Even if he had written his poems in the security of an Oxford college, the Charles Baudelaire of Sartre's 1946 essay would still be as Sartre described him, 'filled with his own being, filled to overflowing' with a self which is

> une humeur fade et vitreuse, privée de consistance, de résist-ance, qu'il ne peut ni juger ni observer, sans ombres ni lumières, une conscience babillarde qui se dit elle-même en longs chuchotements sans qu'on en puisse jamais presser le débit[37] (nothing but a tasteless, glassy mood, without consistency or resistance, without light or shade – a garrulous consciousness which declared it was itself in a long murmur that could never be hastened).

Even in a society in which there were not any Jews for them to hate, the people satirised in Sartre's 1946 essay 'Réflexions sur la question juive' would still, on his analysis, find somebody to be angry with in order to run away from the 'inconsistance profonde' which causes them such fear whenever they try to examine their own personality. The unhappiness which Sartre sees as symptoma-tic of the human condition can be made more intense by political disasters or historical accidents. These, as Sartre is very ready to admit, can make people more aware of what they are really like, in the same way that shining a bright light on a statue can bring out its shapes and angles more clearly. But the statue itself, the 'slow self-tasting' which characterises Baudelaire's awareness of himself will still be there, and Baudelaire will still be like Roquentin in that he

> a dégusté jusqu'à la nausée cette conscience sans rime ni raison, qui doit inventer les lois auxquelles elle veut obéir[38] (has tasted

until he feels sick this meaningless consciousness which must invent the laws which it wants to obey).

The Sartre of *La Nausée*, of *L'Etre et le néant*, of the essay on Baudelaire and the 'Reflexions sur la question juive' is a philosophical writer in the sense of claiming to put forward a view of human experience which is true at all times and all places, and for all sorts and conditions of men. This was also what Graham Greene did when he gave one of his novels the title of *Brighton Rock*. Wherever you break a piece of Brighton rock, you see the same words: 'Brighton Rock'; and wherever you look at human experience, you will find, in Graham Greene's view, the same permanent realities of sin, damnation and – if you are very lucky – redemption. For Sartre, wherever you look at human experience, you will find the same uncertainty about your own identity, as well as the same profound revulsion and disgust. Similarly, in Pascal's view, you will find the same boredom, uncertainty and anguish (ennui, inconstance, inquiétude) characterising the human conditon wherever you are.

It is easy to agree with the phrase in *Baudelaire* about the human mind 'having to invent the laws which it wants to obey'. Once you accept that there is no God, then there is no ultimate justification to be good rather than bad. You may decide to try to be good on the grounds that you want to live in a society that has rules, and think it is a good idea to give an example, or because you have found by experience that you make people happier, and therefore more inclined to treat you well, if you try to love your neighbour as yourself. But your decision to be good presupposes that you have already decided that you want society to exist, and there is no way in which you can justify your choice to the anarchist who says that it would be better if it didn't. In *The Problem of Knowledge*, A. J. Ayer accepts that there is no final reply to the objections of the person he calls the 'total sceptic', and that there is no way of finally refuting his claim that no knowledge is totally reliable. The existentialism of *Baudelaire* and *L'Etre et le néant* also recognises that there is no final way of refuting the moral sceptic. In the final analysis, it is we and we alone who make up the values by which we live. But we can recognise the validity of Sartre's arguments about what conclusions should or should not be drawn from the non-existence of God without agreeing that Roquentin's nausea is a feeling that we all ought to have if we think honestly about the world and about our place in it.

Like a number of avant-garde works of art and philosophical
novels, *La Nausée* makes the reader feel so pleased with himself at
having been clever enough to understand what it means that he
quite forgets that he is supposed to be deeply disturbed by it as
well. Sartre gives a particularly dangerous hostage to fortune by
making it too easy for the reader who does not normally feel sick,
and who indeed feels physically at ease with himself for most of the
time, to dismiss Roquentin in the same terms that Voltaire criticised
Pascal in the *Lettres philosophiques*. Voltaire argued that Pascal
should not, because he personally is unhappy, expect other people
to feel the same as he does; and the Sartre of *La Nausée* is
vulnerable to exactly the same objection. There is naturally a
difference, in that Pascal was using his unhappiness to try to
persuade people to accept a set of religious beliefs which were
almost certainly wrong, whereas Sartre is arguing in favour of a
philosophy which is probably right. But anyone who maintains that
a particular philosophy is true because it corresponds to the way he
feels is vulnerable to the objections that it isn't right for me because
it doesn't correspond to the way I feel.

This is one of the major problems of the philosophical novel, or
indeed of philosophical literature generally, and it is by no means
certain that the Sartre of *La Nausée* has solved it. There is even a
sense in which the skill with which he describes Roquentin's
symptoms rebounds against him and is counter-productive. The
more convincingly Roquentin is made to feel ill by the sight of such
harmless objects as chestnut trees and tramway seats, the less
persuasive is Sartre's assumption that this is how we all ought to
feel. All it does is to invite the comment that David Hume could
think exactly the same thoughts as Roquentin, Mathieu Delarue or
Sartre's Baudelaire, recognising himself in *A Treatise on Human
Nature*, in 1735, as

> nothing but a bundle or collection of different perceptions,
> which succeed each other with an inconceivable rapidity, and are
> in a perpetual flux and movement

without ceasing to be, as he described himself,

> a man of mild disposition, command of temper, of an open and
> cheerful humour, capable of attachment but little susceptible of
> enmity, and of great moderation in all his passions.[39]

So long as *La Nausée* is read as the portrait of a French provincial town at a particularly depressing period of French history, seen through the eyes of a man combining a caustic tongue with a set of strange sensations, it works splendidly. If Roquentin is detached from Sartre's other work and looked at as an example of how somebody of a particular background and peculiar temperament might react to the realisation that there is no God, the ideas he expresses about contingency are fascinating and convincing. The novel satisfies the readers who like their literature to evoke the spirit of place, and presents a situated observer with whom not everybody is expected to identify. The fact that Roquentin is so thoroughly disillusioned an observer makes him exactly the person through whose eyes we want to see a town like Bouville, though without wishing to resemble him in other respects. Problems arise only when the reader becomes aware of the fact that he is expected to think that Roquentin's way of seeing things is one that everybody ought to adopt.

La Nausée is indeed a much better novel from a literary point of view if looked at in isolation from Sartre's other works. It is, in this respect, a little like Camus' *L'Etranger*, which is also about a man who sees the world as absurd, and which is a much more satisfying read if taken in isolation from Camus' theory of the absurd in *Le Mythe de Sisyphe* as well as from the moralising preface in which Camus claimed, in 1955, thirteen years after the book's original publication, that Meursault was 'the only Christ whom we deserve'. From this point of view, both books bring out a central problem of what Iris Murdoch called 'the *genre* of the philosophical novel'.[40] Rightly or wrongly, philosophers are expected to deal with ideas which are universally applicable. Novelists, on the other hand, have traditionally dealt with emotions rather than with ideas, and have presented characters who are interesting precisely because it is very difficult to use their experience to prove universal maxims. Novels of ideas work best if there are a number of different characters presenting contrasting ways of seeing the world, as there are in Dostoievski's *The Brothers Karamazov*, André Malraux's *La Condition humaine*, or Aldous Huxley's *Point Counter Point*. Sartre's major attempt at philosophical fiction, *Les Chemins de la liberté*, does present enough characters for the reader to see that more than one approach to experience is possible. *La Nausée* does not. Only one point of view is admitted, and to pretend that Roquentin is a philosophical Everyman is to make claims for both him and the novel itself which cannot be satisfied.

Sartre's more unconditional admirers naturally have a reply to this kind of criticism. If you tell a Christian that you do not have a sense of sin, he will reply that your very denial is the best possible proof that you do. Only somebody steeped in the pride and self-satisfaction which are the inevitable concomitants of sin would make such a claim. All men sin through their presumption to do without God, and you have just proved it. If you tell a Marxist that you have already taken account of your own class interests in formulating a particular judgement, he will make a similar reply: your very claim to be free of class prejudice is the clearest possible indication that you are still dominated by the false consciousness typical of the bourgeoisie. A Freudian will reject with comparable scorn any claim that you had perfectly good reasons for acting in a particular way, and were in no way the victim of subconscious urges. Such a refusal, he will tell you, is irrefutable evidence of the terror which your repressed awareness of your unconscious desires inspires in you. The existentialist, especially one sympathetic to the detestation which Sartre and his admirers feel for the bourgeoisie, will point out that only somebody wrapped around in the blind self-satisfaction which characterises this class would be smug enough to deny that he too feels exactly as Roquentin does if he thinks honestly about himself.

There is no point in trying to refute these arguments. You only end up by annoying the people putting them forward, especially if you are also perfectly prepared to agree that there is no God but insistent that this does not particularly worry you and certainly does not make you feel sick. It is best to behave as Camus' Meursault ought to have done when the examining magistrate waved the crucifix in his face: nod agreeably and let him get on with it. This is especially true when there are many more interesting ideas to talk about, such as the curious fact that our own society keeps its greatest honours for the writers who most contradict its official values. For while this society endorses what the American Declaration of Independence calls the 'right to the pursuit of happiness', the authors it most admires are those who, like Graham Greene, T.S. Eliot, Samuel Beckett or Sartre himself, tell people how unhappy they are.

Both the contents of Sartre's books and the popularity which he still enjoys are an interesting historical and social phenomenon. One of his principal reasons for writing was to tell people what it was like to be alive in the middle of the twentieth century. Although he undoubtedly succeeded, he also bore unconscious as well as conscious witness to his time. He did so in his presupposition that religious belief had disappeared so completely that it was no longer necessary to rehearse the arguments for not believing in God. His many admirers gave very much the same kind of evidence about how people knew that they were expected to react to certain works of art. Very few of them pointed out how odd it was to assume that everybody ought, literally as well as metaphorically, to feel sick at the very thought of their own existence. Almost nobody has argued that the experience described in *La Nausée* is far too unusual to be used as the basis for a general world view. The presupposition has tended to be that because Roquentin is hostile to bourgeois society, he must be right. This, for the historian of twentieth-century attitudes, is a significant pointer as to how fashion dictated that one should react to certain kinds of books and ideas.

There have naturally been many attacks on Sartre's ideas, either from writers committed to a philosophy such as Marxism or Christianity, or from people who, like the Henri Troyat of *La Tête sur les épaules*, thought it was very wicked to point out how awkward it was for conventional morality to try to 'draw all the consequences of a consistently atheist stand-point'. Most of Sartre's ideas in his early philosophy are right. It is very unlikely that God exists, at least in the form given to Him by Christian theology, and this does create problems when you try to find a rock hard foundation for moral judgements. Sartre is also right to insist that human beings are free. What is odd is the tendency not to question the emotional reaction which he tries to persuade people to have towards these facts of life, and especially towards the death of God. In Somerset Maugham's *Of Human Bondage*, Philip Carey reflects triumphantly on the intoxicating joy which he feels as the 'degrading superstitions' of religious belief fall away from him, and he feels the whole world spread out for him for his enjoyment. When he then 'thanks God that he no longer believes in Him',[41] his reaction is just as justifiable, logically and emotionally, as either Roquentin's or Sartre's; as well as rather healthier.

Satire and Politics

For the reader who does not share all Sartre's philosophical and
political presuppositions, it needs only a slight shift of angle to see
Roquentin as funny. He is an intelligent, well-educated man, and
yet he can find nothing satisfying to do with his life. He despises
virtually everybody he meets, loses interest in a book that he has
spent four or five years trying to write, fails to come to the help of
the one man in the novel who needs him, and finally has to give up
seeing the only person in the world who comes near to understanding the nature of his problems, his girl friend Anny. Sartre would
nevertheless not have sympathised with any reader who saw
Roquentin as involuntarily comic. The only time he suggests that
Roquentin's attitude is not perfect is in *Les Mots*, the account of the
first ten and a quarter years of his life which he published in 1963.
There, looking back on the first twenty-five years of his literary
career, he remarks:

> *J'étais* Roquentin, je montrais en lui, sans complaisance, la trame
> de ma vie; en même temps, j'étais *moi*, l'élu, annaliste des enfers,
> photomicroscope de verre et d'acier penché sur mes propres
> sirops protoplasmiques.[42] (I *was* Roquentin; pitilessly, I showed
> in him the very warp and web of my own life; at the same time, I
> was *I* myself, the chosen one, the keeper of the archives of hell, a
> photomicroscope of glass and steel trained on my own protoplas-
> mic juices.)

In his essay in favour of politically committed literature, 'Qu'est-
ce que la littérature?' (1947; 'What is Literature?') Sartre criticises
writers who try to take a bird's eye view of events. The Sartre of *Les
Mots* echoes this view in regretting that the Sartre of *La Nausée* tried
to place himself above and beyond the hell of contingency which he
describes. But the Sartre of *Les Mots* is not calling into question the
truth of Roquentin's experience, and even gives himself a little pat
on the back for writing about it so well:

> Je réussis à trente ans ce beau coup: d'écrire dans *La Nausée* –
> bien sincèrement on peut me croire – l'existence injustifiée,
> saumâtre de mes congénères et mettre la mienne hors de
> cause.[43] (At thirty, I had a major achievement to my credit: I
> described, in *La Nausée* – in all sincerity, believe me – the

unjustified, brackish existence of my fellow human beings, while
leaving my own untouched.)

But if Sartre sees nothing else wrong either with Roquentin or
with himself, he sees plenty wrong with French provincial life,
especially in a place like Bouville. For it is a town dominated by the
people Sartre most dislikes, the French provincial middle class. It is
they, more than anybody else, who are guilty of refusing to
acknowledge their contingency, and there is a philosophical as well
as a political basis to Sartre's attack on them. The satire is also
sometimes quite funny, as in the description of the ceremonies
which mark the Sunday morning walk:

Sur l'autre trottoir, un monsieur, qui tient sa femme par le bras,
vient de lui glisser quelques mots à l'oreille et s'est mis à sourire.
Aussitôt, elle dépouille soigneusement de toute expression sa
face crémeuse et fait quelques pas en aveugle. Ces signes ne
trompent pas: ils vont saluer. En effect, au bout d'un instant, le
monsieur jette sa main en l'air. Quand ses doigts sont à proximité
de son feutre, ils hésitent une seconde avant de se poser
délicatement sur la coiffe. Pendant qu'il soulève doucement son
chapeau, en baissant un peu la tête pour aider à l'extraction, sa
femme fait un petit saut en inscrivant sur son visage un sourire
jeune. Une ombre les dépasse en s'inclinant: mais leurs deux
sourires jumeaux ne s'effacent pas sur-le-champ: ils demeurent
quelques instants sur leurs lèvres par une espèce de rémanence.
Quand le monsieur et la dame me croisent, ils ont repris leur
impassibilité, mais il leur reste encore un air gai autour de la
bouche.[44] (On the opposite pavement, a gentleman who is
holding his wife by the arm has just whispered a few words in her
ear and has started smiling. She promptly and carefully wipes all
expression from her cream-coloured face and takes a few steps
blindly. These signs are unmistakable: they are going to greet
somebody. Sure enough, a moment later, the gentleman shoots
his hand into the air. When his fingers are close to his felt hat,
they hesitate for a second before settling delicately on the crown.
While he is gently raising his hat, bowing his head a little to help
the operation, his wife gives a little start and fixes a youthful
smile on her face. A shadow passes them, bowing as it does so;
but their twin smiles do not disappear straight away. They
remain for a few moments on their lips, a sort of residual

magnetism. By the time the lady and gentleman pass me, they have regained their passivity, but an expression of restrained cheerfulness still lingers about their mouths.)

But Sartre's intention is not merely to amuse his readers. His satire has political as well as philosophical overtones, and these are particularly noticeable when he describes the local worthies whose portraits hang in the municipal art gallery. People like le docteur Rémy Parrottin, or the businessman and politician Olivier Blévigne are presented as the legitimate targets of Roquentin's anger primarily because they thought they had rights. This, in Sartre's world, is an impossibility. Only somebody who had the metaphysical right to exist in the first place, in that he had been created for some divine purpose, could have any personal or social rights at all. It is, in the view of the Roquentin who looks at the portraits of the self-confident members of the upper-middle class in the Bouville museum, a mark of the pretentious folly characteristic of this class that they should also think of themselves as having the right to own property.

For these men – there are only three women among them, none described in detail – are not only wrong philosophically. They are also wrong politically. Not only are they, as Hamlet puts it, 'arrant knaves all, crawling between heaven and earth'. Their political behaviour has shown them beyond peradventure to be members of the species which Swift condemned as 'the most pernicious race of little odious Vermin that Nature ever suffered to crawl upon the surface of the Earth'.[45]

Like Swift's pernicious insects, they have defended their social rights with a brutality which Sartre presents by ironic understatement when he makes Roquentin quote from a description of how, when the discussions intended to end the dockers' strike of 1898 broke down, 'une intervention discrète de la troupe fit rentrer le calme dans les esprits' (a discreet intervention by the military restored an atmosphere of calm).

In 1971, Sartre said that he had based this incident on what had actually happened at Fourmies, near Paris, on 1 May 1891, when the army fired on a demonstration organised by a group of striking miners, killing nine people and injuring sixty others.[46] The reader acquainted with the even more violent episodes in the class war in France which took place in Paris in 1848 and 1871, also has little difficulty in recognising what Roquentin is really talking about

when he mentions 'l'échaffourée de Jouxtebouville' (the scuffle at
Jouxtebouville). Although apparently a minor episode, it evokes
the much more violent battles whereby the French nineteenth-
century bourgeoisie kept the working class in its place. The Second
Republic, established after the uprising of February 1848 had
driven Louis-Philippe from the throne, began by trying to solve the
problem of unemployment by setting up national workshops in
Paris. These could find no work for the thousands of workers who
had flocked to Paris, and who were costing the taxpayer a great
deal of money, so in June 1848 it was decided to disband them.
When the workers refused to go, 10,000 of them were shot.

Twenty-three years later, after the crushing defeat by Prussia in
the summer of 1870, the siege of Paris, and the signature of the
peace treaty which handed Alsace and Lorraine over to the newly
united Germany, the working and lower-middle classes in Paris
established the *Commune*. It lasted eleven weeks, from 18 March to
28 May 1871, and was put down in the second of the great *semaines
sanglantes* (bloody weeks) of nineteenth-century France. This time,
20,000 Parisians were killed by their fellow citizens from the
provinces, and the working-class population of Paris were subjected to a further and more obvious ideological humiliation.
Because it was assumed that the events of *l'année terrible* of 1870–1
had been brought about by a spirit of rebellion displeasing in God's
sight, it was decided to do penance by raising a public subscription
to build the Eglise du Sacré Coeur, arguably the most hideous
imitation of a wedding cake to disgrace the skyline of a capital city.
Not to be outdone, the citizens of Bouville spent 14 million francs
constructing the church of Sainte-Cécile-de-la-Mer.[47]

The French readers of the 1930s, coming to Sartre as a still
relatively unknown author, would have immediately seen what
Roquentin was talking about, and situated Sartre as a man politically on the left. They would have been right to do so, and no writer
has ever taken a more political stance on the issues of his day. *La
Nausée* itself, however, is only incidentally a political novel.
Although his posthumously published letters to Simone de
Beauvoir show Sartre to have been keenly aware of the international politics of the 1930s – and to have been capable of trying to
reassure one of his temporary mistresses, Louise Védrine, by
writing to her on 31 August 1939, that Hitler 'cannot possibly go to
war with German public opinion in its present state'[48] – he was, at
that time, far from being a political animal. Neither he nor Simone

de Beauvoir bothered to vote, not even in the election of March 1936, which brought the Popular Front to power. The satire in *La Nausée* has an anarchistic rather than a consciously committed air. It nevertheless provided the emotional tone for Sartre's more active political career after the Second World War, and his detestation of the bourgeoisie grew more intense with old age, leading him to describe the student rebels of 1968 as people who

> Découvrirent que la vieille société bourgeoise était foutue et ne se protégeait de la mort que par la matraque des flics[49] (discovered that the old bourgeois society was done for and was protecting itself from death only by the truncheons of the police).

La Nausée was well reviewed. All the critics, including André Rousseaux in the Catholic *Figaro*, the Academician Edmond Jaloux in the equally conventional *Nouvelles Littéraires* and André Thérive in the even more conservative *Le Temps*, greeted Sartre as a highly gifted and extremely original writer. Jaloux, it is true, found Roquentin's visit to the art gallery rather boring, and pointed out that attacks on the bourgeoisie had been par for the course in French literature since Octave Mirbeau in the nineteenth century.[50] But the basic relationship between Sartre and his middle-class readership was established in 1938 and remained unchanged until his death in 1980: he insulted them; they praised him and bought his books. In Stella Gibbons's *Cold Comfort Farm*, Cousin Amos preaches a sermon at the Church of the Quivering Brethren. He looks triumphantly down on his expectant congregation and thunders: 'You're all damned'. His listeners then settle themselves more comfortably into their seats in order to enjoy hearing the worst.

It is easy to see why Roquentin is so angry with the middle-class models of the portraits in the art gallery at Bouville. While they may not have formulated their right to exist with quite the eloquence which Roquentin attributes to them, they have patronised their wives, used emotional blackmail to bully their children into sacrificing their lives to their parents' interests, and massacred the working class. All the poor Autodidact, the only other male character to occur more than once or twice in the book, is trying to do is to improve himself. He is a lawyer's clerk who spends all his spare time in the public library, diligently reading his way through all the books in its collection. Unfortunately, as Roquentin discovers, he is doing so in strict alphabetical order according to author; and his motives for spending so much time in the library are not always those of pure scholarship. A major climax in the plot of *La Nausée* occurs when the Corsican librarian, one of Sartre's most successful minor characters, catches him trying to seduce two schoolboys who are doing their homework at the same table.

Roquentin, as his name implies, has red hair. He is also a big man[51] and his first reaction on seeing the little Corsican librarian venting his righteous indignation on the unfortunate Autodidact is to lift him up by his jacket and hold him spluttering with rage up in the air. But then, to the reader's considerable disappointment, he is overwhelmed by one of his frequent attacks of indifference and puts him down. The Autodidact is turned out into the street and goes off alone, rejecting the offer of help which Roquentin makes him. It is a very well managed and moving episode, but it does not prevent Roquentin – and, through him, Sartre himself – from remaining something of an intellectual snob in the way that the Autodidact is treated in the rest of the novel.

In France, this does not matter. The French language does not even have a term to designate people who look down on those less well educated than themselves. English does, and it seems gratuitously cruel on Sartre's part to make fun of man whose principal failing is a passion for self-improvement. French society has never done much for its intellectually ambitious but socially modest citizens, and there was no more opportunity for the Autodidact to develop his potentialities in the Bouville of the 1930s than there had been for Emma Bovary to find something other than adultery to occupy her mind in the Normandy of the 1840s. But the satire directed at the poor Ogier P..., the 'real name' of the Autodidact, does more than add to the value of *La Nausée* as an unconscious as well as a conscious portrait of French society. It emphasises another aspect of Sartre's work which has limited his appeal anywhere but in the most intellectually advanced areas of the English-speaking world, and that is his rejection of what he calls Humanism.

In England, the terms 'humanist' and 'humanism' are still what the linguistic philosophers of the 1930s and 1940s used to call 'Hurrah words'. They evoke qualities such as tolerance, a concern for living individuals rather than abstract ideas or bureaucratic systems, an open-minded attitude to experience and a readiness to consider the possibility that you might be wrong. In France, they tend to describe those whom Camus describes in *La Peste* as being 'enfoncés dans la stupide confiance humaine' (sunk in stupid human confidence), blind to the tragedy of existence, over-confident in the ability of reason and science to find an answer to social problems, ignorant of the events epitomised by the place names of Auschwitz and Hiroshima, wilfully blind to the existence of the class war, and incapable of appreciating that the reign of the middle classes is over. This is the sense that Sartre gives to the word 'humanist' when he satirises the Autodidact for using it to describe the faith which gives him confidence to face the future, and his intellectual influence has been more permanent in this context than in almost any other. All the thinkers who succeeded and replaced him as leaders of intellectual fashion in France – Roland Barthes, Jacques Derrida, Michel Foucault, Philippe Sollers, Julia Kristeva – have followed his example in using 'humanism' as a Boo word, something to be sneered at and rejected.[52]

There are political and historical reasons for this. In 1940, the collapse of the French army was immediately followed by dramatic and depressing political changes. The Third Republic, which had been in existence since 1870 and made France a secular Republic which offered free education to everyone, was replaced by the Vichy régime, which brought the catechism back into the classroom and taught the French, as the Anglican prayer book used in British schools in the 1940s put it, to 'think much of their duties and little of their rights' forgetting all this nonsense about individuals having rights against the state. The optimistic and outward looking Republican slogan of *Liberté, Egalité, Fraternité* was abandoned in favour of the cautious and repressive conservatism of *Travail, Famille, Patrie*, and a corporatist society established from which class conflict was officially banned. Faced with a crisis in which the humanism officially inspiring its version of bourgeois democracy was put to the test of deciding between collaboration and resist-ance, between Pétain and de Gaulle, the French middle class went for order and self-interest, rejecting justice and self-sacrifice as unnecessary luxuries. By a majority of 569 to 80, the *députés* and *sénateurs* of the Third Republic voted on 18 July 1940 to give the 84-year-old Marshal Pétain full powers to abolish the régime under whose laws they had been elected. The House of Commons, like the English middle class in general, was not required to make a comparable choice. The Spitfire and Hurricane ensured that humanism in England was not put to any serious political test, and was able to retain its intellectual respectability.

No event could have been more nicely calculated than the defeat of 1940 to bring out how accurately *La Nausée* had satirised the defects of the French bourgeoisie. The modern equivalents of the Pacômes, the Parrottin and General Aubry flocked around Marshal Pétain with the same enthusiasm that their ancestors had shown in 1871 for the Adolphe Thiers who had plotted the repression for the *Commune*, and the General Gallifet who had carried it out. The political party to which the Autodidact was so proud to belong, the *Section Française de l'Internationale Ouvrière*, was so divided as to whether or not to vote in favour of giving full powers to Marshal Pétain that its leader, Léon Blum, did not even suggest what they ought to do. The French reader of *La Nausée* is clearly expected to react with hostility to the Autodidact's announcement that he had joined the *SFIO* in 1920, the year in which it split from the more militant and aggressive French Communist Party. The enthusiasm which Sartre was later to show for the hard rather than the soft left is already there in the satire of the Autodidact's political attitude, just as his theory of liberty underpins the attack on the Autodidact for having sold his intellectual freedom for the ready-made ideas associated in contemporary French with the word humanism.

The principal target for the satire in *La Nausée* is thus the French middle class, in its humbler as well as more successful manifestations, and Sartre is in this respect in a well-established French tradition. This aspect of *La Nausée* did nothing to reduce either its or Sartre's popularity with the French reading public, and Cousin Amos enjoyed his customary success. But the account of Roquentin's misfortunes in the last third of the novel also shows him in a satirical rather than a flattering light. It is understandable that he should be able to do nothing to help the Autodidact, who will always feel ashamed of having being caught out trying to seduce the schoolboys. Unlike André Gide, who confidently used biology and ancient history in *Corydon* to justify his liking for boys, the Autodidact will never develop the self-assurance which Gide also drew from the fact that he was very rich. But Roquentin is equally unsuccessful in a relationship which he sees as much more important than his accidental friendship with the Autodidact. He totally fails to re-establish contact with his former mistress Anny, who comes back to see him in Bouville and with whom he presumably has, at some time in the past, been 'in love'.

The term seems inappropriate for Roquentin, and there is no sign that any tenderness which he might have felt for Anny was ever reciprocated. On one occasion, he remembers, when she was living in Djibouti and he in Aden, and they had only 24 hours together, she would be as awkward and as difficult with him as she could until there were exactly 60 minutes before he had to leave. Then, as she took his hand and squeezed it hard, he could see that she was crying. It was, he says, 'a job well done'.[53]

In a way, this kind of behaviour makes her a very suitable partner for Roquentin. Her quest for perfect moments, in which she will be acutely conscious of the passage of time and really feel that she exists, corresponds to Roquentin's ambition to have what he calls 'adventures': periods of time in which every moment and every event fit into a meaningful pattern. The irony of the relationship is that when they meet again towards the end of *La Nausée*, she refuses to recognise that her present disillusionment corresponds exactly to Roquentin's attacks of nausea. The reader of *La Nausée* can see this. Her statement that

> Je croyais que la haine, l'amour ou la mort descendaient sur nous, comme les langues de feu du Vendredi saint (I used to think that hate, love or death descended on us like tongues of fire on Good Friday)

but has come to realise that

> il n'y a que moi, moi qui hais, moi qui aime. Et alors ça, moi, c'est toujours la même chose, une pâte qui s'allonge . . . ça se ressemble tellement qu'on se demande comment les gens ont eu l'idée d'inventer des noms, de faire des distinctions[54] (I am the only one, I am the one who hates, I am the one who loves. And this 'I' is always the same, a dough which goes on stretching and stretching . . . indeed, it looks so much like itself that you wonder how people got the idea of inventing names and making distinctions)

is a kind of paraphrase of what Roquentin has gone through. But she either cannot or will not recognise that this is the case, so that when she proceeds to dismiss as nonsense Roquentin's attempt to tell her that they have had the same experience, she seems gratuitously perverse. She and Roquentin would be capable of making each other so splendidly unhappy by spending the rest of their lives together that it is a pity to see Sartre yielding to the 'failure to communicate' cliché and dismissing her from the novel. He has already made one major technical blunder by bringing her in far too late. To send her away again so soon does more than suggest that he can, for all his versatility, occasionally be a very poor craftsman. It is, naturally, highly improbable that Sartre wanted the reader to see the relationship between Anny and Roquentin as a satirical account of what happens when two equally clever and equally intolerant people get together. This is nevertheless what happens.

This is not to say that the Sartre of *La Nausée* fails in his depiction of Roquentin and Anny. They are, on the contrary, extremely well-drawn and believable characters. But they are not people whose attitudes and experience have a generality which enables them to be used as models. Roquentin's denunciation of the men he calls *salauds* (bourgeois swine) at the end of his visit to the Bouville art gallery is more of a blunderbuss than a rapier. It is simply not true that members of the ruling class in modern society justify their position by the claim that they have been born with certain rights. Sartre certainly thought they did, and wrote his own commentary on Roquentin's visit to the art gallery in Bouville when he argued in his 1947 essay 'Materialisme et Révolution' that

Tout membre de la classe dominante est homme de droit divin. Né dans un milieu de chefs, il est persuadé dès son enfance qu'il est né pour commander et, en un certain sens, cela est vrai, puisque ses parents, qui commandent, l'ont engendré pour qu'il prenne leur suite.[55] (Every member of the ruling class is a man by divine right. Born in a class of leaders, he is convinced from childhood that he is born to rule, and in a sense, this is true, since his parents, who rule, have brought him into this world so that he can follow in their footsteps.)

The short story 'L'enfance d'un chef' (Childhood of a Leader) in the 1939 collection *Le Mur* is a portrait of just such a leader, and the notes to the *Pléiade* edition of Sartre's fiction describe the passage from 'Materialisme et Révolution' as 'une excellente définition générale'[56] (an excellent general definition) of the psychology and attitudes of a ruling class. This may have been how Sartre's stepfather, Joseph Mancy, saw things, though he had himself risen from quite humble origins to be managing director of the docks at Le Havre. He apparently saw Sartre, with whom he had a number of lively discussions on politics in the 1930s, as the 'représentant patenté du Parti Communiste'[57] (the official representative of the Communist Party), and Sartre had grown up in a very conservatively minded middle-class household. But any claim which the modern ruling class may put forward to justify its 'right to rule' is nothing like the attitude described by Sartre. His diagnosis suggests a serious belief in the ideas satirised in a little poem that Simon Templar pens at one point about a man who was

> Trained from his earliest youth to rule
> At that immortal Public School
> Whose playing fields have helped to loose
> Innumerable Waterloos,

or in the social background to Hilaire Belloc's Cautionary Tale about Lord Lundy, who was too freely moved to tears and ruined his political career. When, at the end of the poem, Lord Lundy is told by his father that

> We had intended you to be
> The next Prime Minister but three
> The stocks were sold, the press was squared,
> The middle class was quite prepared.
> But as it is, my poor heart fails,
> Go out and Govern New South Wales[58]

it is almost as though Belloc had read the account of Roquentin's visit to the art gallery in Bouville and decided to show how easily some of the narrator's political views could be satirised. The claim of the members of the modern ruling class is that they are cleverer and more competent than other people. Sir Humphrey Appleby has a first-class honours degree – almost certainly in classics – and it is now the norm in France for senior civil servants to go through the even more rigorous selection and training characteristic of the Ecole Nationale d'Administration.[59]

Neither is it true that the notion of rights is particularly connected with conservative modes of thought. In the eighteenth century, it was very revolutionary, and modern trade union leaders are just as keen on ensuring that their members' rights are recognised and extended as left-wing politicians are to defend the rights of the working class to a share in the nation's wealth. It may

well be that Anny's way of giving value to every minute in the last
hour you are going to spend with somebody you love is a very good
one. But there is no sign that she ever behaved any differently, or
thought that a loving relationship could also sometimes be a
relaxed one. Like the American philosopher Brand Blanshard,[60]
Sartre believed that in philosophy, the place of common sense
should be in the dock, not in the witness box, and certainly not on
the judge's bench. He might have done better to choose a less
eccentric pair of prosecuting counsels.

Literature and Autobiography

In Marcel Proust's *A la recherche du temps perdu*, the book which the
narrator says that he is now going to write turns out to be the book
that the reader has just finished reading. It has been suggested[61]
that *La Nausée* is a kind of down-market version of Proust's novel,
and that by deciding to look for a reply to contingency in the
creation of a work of art, Roquentin is behaving exactly like
Proust's Marcel. As the title indicates, the narrator in *A la recherche
du temps perdu* has wasted his time – on love affairs, on trying to get
on in society, in conversations about literature – but is now going to
win this time back by making it into the material for a book.
Roquentin, having wasted his time trying to write a biography of
the eighteenth-century adventurer Monsieur de Rollebon, is now
going to redeem his life by making it into the substance of a work of
art.

   This is an interesting way of looking at *La Nausée*. *Les Mots*
describes how Sartre's childhood virtually predestined him to
become a writer, and inculcated into him something very like the
Proustian idea of salvation through literature. The comparison is
not, however, a very satisfactory one, mainly because *La Nausée* is so
very far from having the qualities of the book which Roquentin
hopes he is going to write. It is not 'beautiful and hard as steel', and
if it is going to make people 'ashamed of their existence', it will not
do so by any contrast between the lack of order in their lives and
the mathematical perfection of its finish. The first page has a
quotation from Louis-Ferdinand Céline's *L'Eglise*:

> C'est un garçon sans importance collective, c'est tout juste un
> individu (He is a fellow without any collective significance, barely
> an individual).

This contradicts the impression given elsewhere in the text that Roquentin's experiences have a philosophical importance which applies to the whole of mankind. It also invites the reader to see *La Nausée* as belonging to quite a different literary tradition from Proust. Louis-Ferdinand Céline's 1933 novel, *Voyage au bout de la nuit*, was a highly realistic, sombre account of life in post-war Europe and North America, written in prose which broke with literary tradition in France by being an almost direct transcription of the way ordinary people spoke. Many of the best passages in *La Nausée* show strong traces of Céline's influence, and the book is like *Voyage au bout de la nuit* in giving a portrait of the tawdriness and squalor of French society between the wars. This is certainly not what Roquentin's promised book would set out to do. Unlike *A la recherche du temps perdu*, *La Nausée* is not itself the book which has enabled the narrator to work out his salvation. It is nevertheless a novel which comes to the same conclusion that Proust does: art is the only means by which we can give meaning to life. Indeed, as with Proust, the impression is that the slogan of 'Art for Art's sake' becomes 'Life for Art's sake'.

When seen in this context, *La Nausée* invites the reader to look at the whole of Sartre's work as forming one single book: the intellectual biography of a writer. There sometimes seems to be an unwritten rule that great French writers should begin by losing a parent, generally their father, sometimes their mother, and in the case of one of the greatest, Jean Racine, both mother and father, when they are still very young. Like Albert Camus, Roland Barthes, Charles Baudelaire, Alexandre Dumas *père*, André Gide, François Mauriac, Charles Péguy, Antoine de Saint-Exupéry and Emile Zola, Sartre lost his father when he was very young. He was only 15 months old on 17 September 1906, when Jean-Baptiste Sartre, a naval officer, died of a fever he had caught in what was then the French colony of Cochinchina. His mother, *née* Anne-Marie Schweitzer, having 'ni argent ni métier' (neither money nor a job), had no choice but to go back home to her parents. They, according to Sartre's account of the first ten and a quarter years of his life in *Les Mots*, exploited her shamefully.

'Les familles, bien sûr', he comments, 'préfèrent les veuves aux filles mères; mais c'est de justesse'[62] (Families, of course, prefer widows to unmarried mothers; but only just).

There is no independent evidence to say whether Sartre's grandparents really illustrated this maxim and showed all the selfishness and hypocrisy which the rest of Sartre's work presents as typical of the French bourgeoisie. It is sometimes tempting to treat the autobiographical fragment, which ends when his mother remarried in 1916, as fiction, and see it as the most entertaining and perhaps the best of his novels.[63] His grandfather, Charles Schweitzer, is indistinguishable from one of the *salauds* in the Bouville art gallery, and his grandmother, *née* Louise Guillemin, very like one of their downtrodden but resentful wives. *Les Mots* is also like all Sartre's other fiction in that it tells a story which illustrates an idea.

This is that Freud was wrong to maintain that our basic character is formed before we are four years old, and in unconscious response to the tensions set up in us by the Oedipal situation. For Sartre, there is no such thing as unconscious motivation, and our character is a result of the choices we make, not of the forces acting upon us. In *L'Etre et le néant*, Sartre offers an alternative to Freudianism in what he calls 'existential psychoanalysis', and tried it out in his studies of Jean Genet and Charles Baudelaire before applying it to himself in *Les Mots*. In his view, the child becomes conscious, round about the age of seven or eight, of its basic family situation. It then makes a choice which enables it in some way or other to make sense of its experience. This is what Baudelaire does when his mother remarries when he is still only six, choosing to be the misunderstood and rejected child and to base the whole of his character on this choice. It is what Jean Genet does when accused, at the age of eight, of being a thief, deliberately assuming the personality which other people had projected on to him. *Les Mots* tells how Sartre made his own first 'existential choice', and why he became a writer.

In Sartre's recollection, Charles Schweitzer was too selfish in his love for his only grandson to share him with other people, and found a series of excuses not to send him to school. This, coupled with the fact that Sartre had no brothers or sisters, and lived in a fifth-floor flat with his widowed mother and elderly grandparents, gave him a very lonely childhood, in which he found his main consolation in books. To begin with, he just read them, concentrating on adventure stories. But when he began what *Les Mots* calls 'another pretence', and started to write his own books, an incident or series of incidents took place which set him on a path which he subsequently realised had determined the whole of his life: his grandfather, for once, took him seriously.

Everybody in the Schweitzer household play-acted, Grandfather Schweitzer more than anyone. His favourite role was that of adoring grandfather, and Sartre maintains that his own delight in playing the adored grandson might in different circumstances have led to no permanent ill-effects. But one day, seeing the seven-year-old Sartre writing earnestly away, Charles Schweitzer took him on one side and spoke to him seriously, as a real father might talk to his son. Literature, he told Sartre, was a very chancy profession. You had to be careful before going into it. Poets got drunk, left their wives, ruined their lives, think of Verlaine, think of Rimbaud. But, in return, poets were more than the 'unacknowledged legislators of mankind'. They were the true defenders of culture, the men who kept the light of civilisation burning in a brutal and selfish world, the sole priesthood of true believers and the only genuine heroes of the modern world. A man who was going to be a writer – as the young Sartre obviously was, no two ways about it, you're very gifted my boy, you're not my grandson for nothing – had to accept the idea of living in an ivory tower. There, he would watch over the true values of civilisation, occasionally adding to them by using his personal sufferings to create works of pure, stern, formal beauty. Writing was a dangerous profession, but the only one worth taking seriously. Albert Thibaudet once said that French nineteenth-century literature 'began with the poetry of religion and ended with the religion of poetry'. According to the Sartre of *Les Mots*, the 'religion of poetry' was exactly what his grandfather believed in; and he so inculcated a belief in it into his grandson that Sartre never quite recovered.

The obsession which Sartre has with the nature of literature does suggest that there is some truth behind what he said happened to him when he was still quite a small boy. The publication of *Les Mots* was a major event in the French literary world of the early 1960s, and its 200 or so pages perhaps the best thing Sartre ever wrote. Its account of the literary ideas instilled into him in his childhood nevertheless came as something of a surprise to the French literary world. Ever since the establishment of his review, *Les Temps Modernes*, in 1945, and more particularly since the publication in 1947 of 'Qu'est-ce que la littérature?', Sartre had been famous for a theory of literature which completely contradicted the one described in *Les Mots*. It was a theory which said that what mattered most of all was the writer's commitment to the social issues of the day. The vigour with which Sartre had put this theory forward had helped to make him one of the most widely discussed and controversial writers of the twentieth century. Indeed, for much of his adult life, there was only one Frenchman better known than he was, and that was General de Gaulle. The publication of *Les Mots* suggested that the person with whom Sartre had really been arguing with was himself; or, at least, with the self that still bore the imprint of the ideas which Charles Schweitzer had instilled in him during his lonely and unhappy childhood.

Les Mots also suggests that there was something autobiographical on Sartre's part about Roquentin's decision to try to escape from contingency by writing a book. It was not until after the Second World War that Sartre began to insist on the need for the writer to take sides, and his first concept of a literary vocation was very like Roquentin's. Just as the denunciation of the *salauds* in the art gallery at Bouville looks forward to the more politically conscious Sartre of the post-war period, so Roquentin's dream of making sense of his experience through writing a book is a tribute to the impact made on the infant Sartre by his grandfather. This is especially so since the book which Roquentin intends to write will have nothing of real life about it. It will be very much the kind of work which his grandfather presented to the infant Sartre as most desirable.

There is an intriguing contrast, within the overall structure of *La Nausée*, between the book that Roquentin finally decides to write and the one on which he has been working until his discovery of contingency makes everything change. This is a biography of the eighteenth-century adventurer Adhémar de Rollebon, a totally invented character, and one of Sartre's most successful creations. Roquentin gives up trying to write a book about him because of his realisation, as he says, that

> jamais un existant ne peut justifier l'existence d'un autre existant.[64] (An existent can never justify the existence of another existent.)

What this means is that he cannot, by writing about Monsieur de Rollebon, make either his own existence or that of the Marquis any less absurd. In the past, before the onset of his nausea prevented him from believing in the reality of any human project, Roquentin had found a reason for living in writing this particular book. As he puts it:

> Monsieur de Rollebon était mon associé: il avait besoin de moi pour être et j'avais besoin de lui pour ne pas sentir mon être. Moi, je fournissais la matière brute, cette matière dont j'avais à revendre, dont je ne savais que faire: l'existence, *mon* existence. Lui, sa partie, c'était de représenter. Il se tenait en face de moi et s'était emparé de ma vie pour me représenter la sienne. Je ne m'apercevais plus que j'existais, je n'existais plus en moi, mais en lui. C'est pour lui que je mangeais, pour lui que je respirais, chacun de mes mouvements avait son sens au-dehors, là, juste en face de moi, en lui ... je n'étais qu'un moyen de la faire vivre, il était ma raison d'être, il m'avait délivré de moi. Qu'est-ce que je vais faire à présent?[65] (Monsieur de Rollebon was my partner: he needed me in order to be, and I needed him in order not to feel my being. I furnished the raw material of which I had far too much, so much that I didn't know what to do with it, existence, *my* existence, while his task was to perform. He stood in front of me, and he had taken over my life so that I could live out his life for him. I had stopped noticing that I existed, I didn't exist anywhere but in him. It was him that I ate for, him that I breathed for, everything I did had its meaning out there, there, in front of me, in him. ... I was nothing more than a means of bringing him to life, he was my *raison d'être*, he had freed me from myself. What am I going to do now?)

It is disappointing that Roquentin should give up writing his biography of Monsieur de Rollebon. While the book which he intends to write at the end of *La Nausée* would probably be very boring, any biography which put together the tantalising glimpses that we have of the Marquis could not fail to be a good read. Monsieur de Rollebon is completely different from all the other characters in *La Nausée*. When he wishes to do something, he succeeds, a gift illustrated by an anecdote about a bet he once made to bring about the deathbed conversion of a convinced atheist. When he emerged triumphant and announced that the dying man was ready to take the sacraments, the witnesses were amazed.

'Etes-vous si fort dans l'art de la dispute?' demanda le curé, 'vous l'emportez sur les nôtres!' – 'Je n'ai pas disputé', répondit M. de

Rollebon, 'je lui ai fait peur de l'enfer'.[66] ('Are you so strong in argument?' asked the local priest, 'you completely outclass our people.' – 'I didn't argue', replied M. de Rollebon, 'I terrified him with the torments of hell'.)

The technical reason for Monsieur de Rollebon's presence in *La Nausée* is to give Roquentin something to do, and to explain why he is in Bouville. Most of the documents about Monsieur de Rollebon's life, Roquentin explains, are in the municipal library at Bouville, and without his visits to the library Roquentin would not have met the Autodidact. But Rollebon also provides a contrast between the enlightened scepticism of the eighteenth century and the sadder agnosticism of the twentieth. Diderot's remark that human beings would begin to be free and happy only when the last king was strangled in the bowels of the last priest presupposed that happiness is possible, even at a high cost to kings and priests. When *La Nausée* was published, in 1938, France had not had a king for 90 years, and had been a secular republic since 1905. This had not, however, made people very much happier, and the death of God seemed to have produced more problems than it had solved. As Sartre was to point out in 1946, in 'L'Existentialisme est un humanisme',

L'existentialiste . . . pense que c'est très gênant que Dieu n'existe pas, car avec lui disparaît toute possibilité de trouver des valeurs dans un ciel intelligible; il ne peut plus y avoir de bien *a priori*, puisqu'il n'y a pas de conscience infinie et parfaite pour le penser; il n'est écrit nulle part que le bien existe, qu'il faut être honnête, qu'il ne faut pas mentir, puisque nous sommes sur un plan où il y a seulement des hommes. Dostoievski a écrit: 'Si Dieu n'existait pas, tout serait permis'. C'est là le point de départ de l'existentialisme.[67] (The existentialist . . . finds it extremely awkward that God does not exist, because this removes all possibility of finding values in an intelligible heaven. There can no longer be anything which is good *a priori*, since there is no infinite and perfect mind to contain such an idea. Nowhere is it written down that goodness exists, that we ought to be honest, that we ought not to tell lies, because we all live on a level at which there are only other men. Dostoievski wrote: 'If God does not exist, everything is permitted'. That is the starting point for existentialism.)

The figure of Monsieur de Rollebon thus reminds us of the contrast between the optimism which the Enlightenment had about the future and the reality which Roquentin finds everywhere around him now that this future has arrived. Rollebon underlines the difference between the eighteenth century, where it was still possible for a man to order his life on rational principles, and the 1930s, where it was not. For although Rollebon was not particularly successful in any of his undertakings, and in fact ended his life in disgrace, his attitude is very much that of the most attractive and successful of all French politicians, Maurice de Talleyrand, who is not mentioned in the text but whose career comes to mind at almost every turn.[68]

Talleyrand began his political career at the age of 35 by proposing in 1789 that France should solve its economic problems by nationalising the Church lands, while nevertheless remaining sufficiently the Bishop d'Autun to celebrate mass for the revolutionaries on 14 July 1790; helped Bonaparte to seize power in 1799; worked as his Foreign Minister until it was obvious that he was going to be defeated; changed sides in 1814 just in time to organise the return of Louis XVIII; represented France at the Congress of Vienna with such skill that only Napoleon's return from Elba prevented it from acquiring all its natural frontiers; served the Restoration monarchy until the revolution of July 1830 interrupted it and replaced Charles X with Louis-Philippe; served Louis-Philippe as Ambassador to London – as he took his oath of allegiance, he whispered 'Sire, c'est le treizième' (Your Majesty, this is the thirteenth) – and ended his life reconciled with the Church. From time to time, as a change from the Rendez-vous des Cheminots, Roquentin enjoys going to the café Mably. What he likes there is the way the manager's face has 'un air de canaillerie bien positif et rassurant' (an air of down-to-earth and reassuring dishonesty). The evocation, through the portrait of Monsieur de Rollebon, of the personality and achievements of Maurice de Talleyrand produces a comparable effect: in a world of nauseating physical reality, ineffectual literary men and disagreeable women, the presence of a successful rogue quite restores one's faith in human nature.

Sartre liked the eighteenth century. He described it in 'Qu'est-ce que la littérature?' as 'le paradis bientôt perdu des écrivains français'[69] (the rapidly lost paradise of the French writer), and looked back at it with almost equal nostalgia eleven years later in *Questions de Méthode*, the essays he published in 1957 as part of his

attempt to reconcile Marxism and existentialism. There, he argued
that a philosophy was first and foremost a means whereby a rising
class made sense of its experience. Eighteenth-century rationalism
was the ideological weapon whereby the French middle class
overthrew the old aristocracy in the revolution of 1789, and Sartre
envied writers such as Voltaire and Diderot for having played what
he saw as so important a part in history. In contrast, Sartre rarely
had a good thing to say about anybody in the nineteenth century.
He accused Flaubert and the Goncourt brothers for having been
responsible for the repression which followed the *Commune* in 1871
'parce qu'ils n'ont pas écrit une ligne pour l'empêcher'[70] (because
they did not write a single line against it), and criticised writers such
as Maupassant for passively accepting to become hired entertainers
for the bourgeoisie. In *La Nausée*, this dislike also comes out in the
attack on the literary conventions of nineteenth-century fiction.

Roquentin's objection to the traditional nineteenth-century
bourgeois novel is linked to his realisation that what he calls
'adventures' are impossible. This is not because interesting and
unusual things do not happen. Sartre gives Roquentin a livelier
and more exotic past than he had enjoyed himself, making him
refer to the time when he was involved in what sounds like a rather
shady business deal in Indochina, and endowing him with memor-
ies of a period spent with a girl who made her living among the
criminals in Hamburg. Roquentin, we are given to understand, has
been around, and there is no sense in which his disillusionment can
be dismissed as sour grapes. Neither do his problems have anything to do with sexual frustration. The owner's wife at the Café
des Cheminots needs a man a day, and Roquentin is happy to
oblige. His inability to experience what he calls 'adventures' is a
subjective matter, not the result of a lack of interesting things
happening to him. It is a result of the fact that he can see his
experience only as a series of equally meaningless, undifferentiated
moments.

In T. S. Eliot's *Murder in the Cathedral*, the Third Priest describes
the same experience but does so in a very different way. He agrees
with Roquentin when he says that

> One moment
> Weighs like another. Only in retrospection, selection,
> We say, that was the day.

But because the Priest's life is ordered in the light of God's Providence, what would otherwise be meaningless is lit up with the perpetual possibility of spiritual significance. He can talk, as Roquentin cannot, of

> The critical moment
> That is now, and here,

and say that 'Every day is the day we should fear from or hope from', adding that

> Even now, in sordid particulars
> The eternal design may appear.[71]

Roquentin cannot have a belief like this, and the contrast with Eliot's world is absolute. Nowhere else, perhaps, does Sartre's vision more fully contradict the Christian viewpoint. In a literary context, Roquentin is also talking about something more important than the fact that you never realise the importance of what is happening to you until afterwards. He is not interested in mundane experiences such as deciding not to do something only to realise, with infinite regret, that the door of opportunity swings open only once. He is also a cut above the normal run of humanity in not feeling constant shudders of embarrassment whenever he looks back at his past life. What worries him is the fact that nobody can ever give a true account of any experience. By the time the moment arrives at which people get round to describing what has happened to them, the meaning of the events has completely changed. Nobody can ever 'tell it like it is'. Not only does the act of telling totally change what is being told. Nobody can ever put themselves back in the mood where they didn't know how it was going to end.

Roquentin explains what he means by inventing a typical example of narrative from a French nineteenth-century novel:

On a l'air de débuter par le commencement: 'C'était par un beau soir de l'automne de 1922. J'étais clerc de notaire à Marommes.' Et en réalité c'est par la fin qu'on a commencé. Elle est là, invisible et présente, c'est elle qui donne à ces quelques mots la pompe et la valeur d'un commencement. 'Je me promenais, j'étais sorti du village sans m'en apercevoir, je pensais à mes ennuis d'argent'. Cette phrase, prise simplement pour ce qu'elle est, veut dire que le type était absorbé, morose, à cent lieues d'une aventure, précisément dans ce genre d'humeur où on laisse passer les événements sans les voir. Mais la fin est là, qui transforme tout. Pour nous, le type est déjà le héros de l'histoire. Sa morosité, ses ennuis d'argent sont bien plus précieux que les nôtres, ils sont tout dorés par la lumière des passions futures.[72] (It sounds as though you are beginning at the beginning: 'It was on a fine Autumn evening in 1922. I was a lawyer's clerk at Marommes.' In fact, you have started at the end. The ending is there, unseen and present, and it is this ending which gives these few words the pomp and value of a beginning. 'I was walking along, I had left the village without noticing it, I was thinking about my money problems.' This sentence, taken by itself, means that the chap was absorbed, gloomy, miles away from an adventure, exactly in the sort of mood when you let things happen without noticing them. But the ending is there, transforming everything. For us, the chap is already the hero of the story. His gloomy state of mind, his money worries are much more precious than ours, they are bathed in the golden light of the passions that are to come.)

It is fair comment, a reminder that even the most innocent looking narrative has something in it of the detective story, where you must never read the text without losing sight of the possibility that the apparently accidental dropping of a teaspoon might turn out to be an important clue. Sartre illustrates the point further by having Roquentin read Balzac's *Eugénie Grandet* while eating his Sunday lunch in a restaurant. Whenever he opens the novel and reads a snatch of conversation, both he and the reader of *La Nausée* immediately understand what is happening in Balzac's novel. Balzac is not reporting what people actually said. He is using conversation as a means of telling the story. The contrast is obvious when Roquentin reproduces the conversation of the couple sitting next to him. Like most married couples, they talk elliptically, referring to people and events which they both know well enough not to need to spell out who is who. The remarks they make are thus virtually incomprehensible to an outside listener, and neither Roquentin nor the reader of *La Nausée* can make out what they are on about.

The books that Sartre published after *La Nausée* do not follow up this notion of the artificiality of prose fiction. He was, in the late 1930s and early 1940s, much more interested in using literature to talk about moral and philosophical questions. Although his ideas in *La Nausée* are an intriguing anticipation of the attitude towards fiction underlying the French 'New Novelists' of the 1950s and 1960s, he himself began to adopt a much more utilitarian attitude towards literature. He wrote books in order to express certain moral and political ideas, many of which are given a trial run in *La Nausée*, albeit in a negative and not always immediately recognisable form.

Freedom and Responsibility

Roquentin's decision to give up writing his book about Monsieur de Rollebon is immediately followed by one of the best scenes in the novel, his lunch with the Autodidact. It is a set piece of determined cynicism on Roquentin's part and of desperate, embarrassingly good intentions on that of his host. In what sounds suspiciously like a parody of some of the more positive aspects of Sartre's later existentialism, the Autodidact tells Roquentin about a book he has just been reading by an American author, called *Is Life Worth Living?* The author concludes, he explains,

> en faveur de l'optimisme volontaire. La vie a un sens si l'on veut bien lui en donner un. Il faut d'abord se jeter dans une entreprise. Si ensuite l'on réfléchit, le sort en est jeté, on est engagé.[73] (in favour of deliberate optimism. Life has a meaning if you choose to give it one. First of all you must act, you must throw yourself into some enterprise. If you think about it later on, the die is cast, you are already committed.)

Roquentin's experience with the book he was going to write on Monsieur de Rollebon has just shown that this is not true. The nature of existence is such as to make all projects purely provisional. Since they can always be called into question, they are nothing more than temporary expedients for hiding the pointlessness of existence from ourselves. It is only, Roquentin learns, by a constant effort of will power that we can keep our projects alive, and a moment is bound to come when we see that these projects are simply undertakings which we have quite gratuitously imposed upon ourselves.

In the books that Sartre wrote in the 1940s, it is man's permanent ability to call himself and his values into question which makes people free, and which provides the only possible way in which we can give meaning to our own and other people's lives. Roquentin is not the kind of person to put forward the more positive side of existentialism, and the reader who approaches Sartre's work chronologically first comes across his theory of liberty in its most negative form. This freedom stems from the fact that we are always conscious of what we are, and consequently always able to change. There is nothing we can do to abolish our awareness of ourselves and of our freedom. This is a point made in the short story 'La Chambre', and what Sartre sees as the self-evident nature of human freedom is what explains the sub-title of *L'Etre et le néant*: 'essai d'ontologie phénoménologique'. These words are less obscure than they seem. The opening sentence of *L'Etre et le néant* reads:

La pensée moderne a réalisé un progrès considérable en réduisant l'existant à la série des apparitions qui le manifestent.[74] (Modern thought has made considerable progress in reducing the existent to the series of appearances which show it to be there.)

What this means was summed up in one of the Quotable Quotes in *New Woman* in August 1989, and which is a virtual translation of Roquentin's observation that 'les choses sont tout entières ce qu'elles paraissent – et *derrière* elles ... il n'y a rien':[75] 'Things are entirely what they appear to be,' read the quotation in *New Woman*, 'and behind them there is nothing.'

Phenomenology is the study of things as they are, and dismisses as pointless any speculation as to what might 'lie behind them'. When told that our freedom of choice is an illusion, because we are all the time controlled by forces we cannot see, the phenomenologist will reply that it does not matter whether it is an illusion or not so long as it is a consistent one. A world in which we seem to be free is, for the phenomenologist, exactly the same as a world in which we are free. There is nothing lying behind the objects we see or the sensations we experience, nothing either guaranteeing that they are what they seem to be or showing that they are, in some mysterious way, quite different from the way they look.

Sartre does not discuss in any great detail the argument that our freedom is severely limited by the physical and psychological features we inherit from our parents. He refers to limitations of this kind only by implication, and his reply is that of the Stoics: we may inherit a particular physique, just as we may find ourselves in a situation that severely limits our freedom of movement. What matters is the approach we take to these limitations. Since this approach depends on what is in our mind, and since Sartre considers that the mind can always rise above bodily factors, the atttitude we adopt is the result of a totally free decision. This is a much more invigorating approach than the atmosphere of *La Nausée* would lead one to expect, and Sartre's first novel is not the best of introductions to all the ideas which made him so powerful an intellectual force in the France of the 1940s and 1950s.

He emerged from the war with a series of very clear messages about man's duty to himself and to other people. The death of God, he argued, means that human beings are not cast into a pre-ordained mould. The human condition remains grim, and there is still no ultimate point in our being here. But because it makes freedom both possible and necessary, even contingency is a good thing, and Sartre is very scornful of anyone who tries to pretend that they are not free. This is the offence known as Bad Faith, and just as the basic idea of phenomenology was usefully summarised in the quotation from *New Woman* about things being 'entirely what they appear with nothing behind them', the ambition of someone enjoying their 'mauvaise foi' was given succinct expression when a cartoon in the London *Star* for 26 March 1959 depicted a woman saying to her friend: 'I want to be swept off my feet by somebody I can bend to my will.'

The concept of bad faith is easy to understand and describes the way we are all sometimes tempted to behave. If, for example, I am driving along an English motorway, and trying to choose between stopping for coffee at the service station just coming up, or pressing on for another twenty miles, I am conscious that this is a decision that I and I alone have to take. But if I stop at the next service station, I run the risk of finding that there is a long queue, or that the coffee is awful. I don't want to blame myself for doing the wrong thing, and should therefore be quite happy if the decision were to be taken out of my hands. Then, suddenly, it is: I realise that I am being overtaken at great speed, on my left, by one of those enormous lorries with TIR and MAXIMUM SPEED 80 KILOMETRES AN HOUR on it. I cannot now go into the left-hand lane in readiness to turn into the service station, so that my terror at the prospect of imminent annihilation is accompanied by a blessed feeling of relief. *Force majeure* has taken the decision out of my hands. If the coffee at the next service station but one turns out to be awful, it is not my fault. I cannot be held responsible for a decision forced upon me by circumstances beyond my control.

Although the term *mauvaise foi* does not occur in *La Nausée*, the novel contains plenty of people guilty of it. When Roquentin sees two old ladies gazing rapturously at the statue of the late-nineteenth-century scholar Gustave Impétraz, he comments that their adoration comes from the fact that Impétraz has provided them with all the certainty that they need, acting like a father to them so that they will never have to think for themselves.[76]

Impétraz has taken the responsibility for these ideas off their shoulders, and they are duly grateful. But they are quite wrong to let somebody else do their thinking for them, and it is in his insistence that only we can make up our own minds that Sartre shows another aspect of his work, the links it has with Protestantism. The Autodidact is guilty of having sold his freedom and independence of mind for the mess of pottage offered by nineteenth-century humanism. The Pacômes, Aubrys and Wakefields of this world have run away from their freedom and responsibility into the stereotyped concept of Rights.

It is curiously tempting, though a denial of everything Sartre stood for, to suggest that there was a genetic factor in his desire to use literature to tell people what he thought was wrong with them, and what they ought to do about it. So much of his work nevertheless has so strongly Protestant a flavour that it is impossible to forget that he is the descendant of a long line of Protestant pastors. It is true that there are some marked differences. His great uncle was Albert Schweitzer of Lambaréné, the incarnation of the Protestant conscience in action, but there is no way of reconciling his famous remark: 'The African is my brother, yes. But my younger brother' with Sartre's insistence that the victims of Western imperialism can liberate themselves only through violence. Not even the most fervent supporter of liberation theology could underwrite Sartre's remark in his 1961 preface to Franz Fanon's *Les Damnés de la terre* (*The Wretched of the Earth*) that,

Car, en ce premier temps de révolte, il faut tuer: abattre un Européen, c'est faire d'une pierre deux coups, supprimer en même temps un oppresseur et un opprimé: restent un homme mort et un homme libre; le survivant, pour la première fois, sent un sol *national* sous la plante de ses pieds.[77] (In the first stage of rebellion, killing is essential. To shoot a European is to kill two birds with one stone, eliminating an oppressor and a member of the oppressed race at one and the same time. What remains are a dead man and a free man. The survivor, for the first time, feels a *national* soil beneath the soles of his feet.)

There is also a gap between Sartre's readiness to speak more than frankly about sex and the reticence traditionally associated with Protestantism. Neither is there any question of any belief in the doctrines of Predestination characteristic of the Calvinist tradition. His work is nevertheless very Protestant in its insistence on personal responsibility, in his tendency to denounce the sins of the flesh even more vigorously than he describes them, and in his refusal ever to see literature as entertainment. The books that Sartre is interested in writing are intended to fulfil some useful purpose: either they will save one person by the creation of a perfect, albeit artificial world; or they will improve the human lot by helping to bring about social change. There is no question of their simply telling a tale that will keep children from play and old men from the chimney corner. It is also unlikely that they will be very absorbing to anyone not already interested in ideas.

Even in *La Nausée*, a book written before Sartre had got fully into his stride as the apostle of atheistic existentialism, there is more than a touch of the enthusiasm with which John Knox denounced sin. The invective which concludes Roquentin's visit to the art gallery in Bouville,

Adieu beaux lys, tout en finesse dans vos petits sanctuaires peints, adieu, beaux lys, notre orgueil et notre raison d'être, adieu Salauds[78] (Farewell, you beautiful lilies, elegant in your little painted sanctuaries, farewell, you beautiful lilies, our pride and our reason for living, farewell, you filthy swine)

is stronger in tone than the reproofs normally addressed to members of the Free Presbyterian Church, but the idea is the same. The bourgeoisie has clothed itself in the iniquitous concept of

Rights, and refused to see that salvation is possible only through the humbling recognition of their own contingency. The young couple whom Roquentin sees in the restaurant, identified by the Autodidact as the incarnation of Youth and Love, are nothing more than two lechers telling lies to each until it is time to make the beast with two backs. The old men whose stories illustrate the wisdom stemming from the passage of years are merely fools, wise in their own conceit. Their wisdom is worthless, since all it does is seek to explain the present by the past, and the past by even more distant events

> comme ces historiens qui font de Lénine un Robespierre russe et de Robespierre un Cromwell français[79] (like the historians who make Lenin into a Russian Robespierre and Robespierre a French Cromwell).

Roquentin himself is more than a secular Everyman whose recognition and rejection of the false gods by which he had earlier tried to hide his contingency is going to put us all back on to the straight and narrow path. He is a brand snatched from the burning, the chosen soul who ends his misadventures among the heathen by the resolve to work out his own salvation with diligence, writing a book whose hardness and metallic perfection will make it shine out like a good deed amid the encircling gloom of the universal absurdity of the world. Sartre is also, like many another preacher before him, quite prepared to give useful advice. Since freedom is the only value, people must use it properly. This is one of the ideas linking together the short stories in *Le Mur*.

3

Le Mur

Advice

The five stories in *Le Mur* (*Intimacy*) do not offer a set of ready-made solutions. They all end unhappily, and it is only by seeing each one as a kind of photographic negative that the reader can understand how Sartre is presenting one way of behaving as better than another. Artistically, this is a good rather than a bad thing. Improving anecdotes had already gone out of fashion before Saki wrote the story in which Bertha was found and eaten by the wolf because her medal for obedience clinked against her medals for good conduct and punctuality.[1] Three of the stories in *Le Mur* nevertheless have a cautionary note to them, with 'Intimité' and 'L'Enfance d'un chef' even going so far as to suggest a definite line of action to take.

In October 1939, when Sartre was serving as a private soldier in the French army during the first months of the Second World War, Simone de Beauvoir wrote to describe how she had just finished reading the French translation of Arthur Koestler's *Spanish Testament*, adding that some scholar in 200 years time would doubtless claim that Sartre had used Koestler's book as a basis for the first story in the collection, 'Le Mur'.[2] Arthur Koestler was a contemporary of Sartre, a Hungarian journalist born in Budapest on 5 September 1905, who had been sent by the left-wing London paper the *News Chronicle* to cover the Spanish civil war. This had begun on 1 July 1936, when General Franco brought his soldiers from Spanish Morocco to overthrow the Republican government by what he had originally hoped would be a bloodless *coup d'état*. He encountered more opposition than Mussolini had done in the supposed 'March on Rome' in 1922 – in fact, Mussolini arrived by train – or than Hitler when the Nazi party won enough votes in the 1932 elections to enable him to take power with some appearance of legitimacy on 30 January 1933. It took Franco almost three years to defeat the left – in its various forms – and declare himself *Jefe del Estado Espanol* (ruler of the Spanish state) on 1 April 1939; and even then he won only because the Germans and Italians sent their air force to help him.

Whether Franco's régime was quite so much a disaster for Spain as both the democratic and the Marxist left maintained is open to question. On 24 October 1940, four months after the collapse of France, Franco met Hitler at Hendaye, and raised so many objections to the possible passage of German troops through Spain to take Gibraltar by land that Hitler commented that he would, next time he wanted a difficult interview, visit his dentist. One of the traditionally weak Spanish Republican governments might not have been able to resist a German invasion. A left-wing one with a strong Communist membership would probably not have wanted to do so. Since 23 August 1939, Germany and Russia had been allies, and in August 1940 the French Communist Party had quite happily accepted German permission to start republishing its newspaper *L'Humanité* in Paris. But it was by no means clear, in the 1930s and 1940s, that Franco would later appear as the man who made one of the biggest involuntary contributions to Hitler's defeat. Franco was a Fascist who murdered his political opponents with the same ruthlessness as Hitler or Mussolini; and he had little regard for the welfare of foreign journalists either.

For on 2 February 1937, Koestler was arrested and sentenced to death. He spent 102 days in prison, most of them in the condemned cell, hearing his fellow inmates being taken out and shot, and not knowing whether or not the same thing might happen to him the next morning. After his release, he returned to England, and late in 1937, published *Spanish Testament*. It appeared as a volume in Victor Gollancz's Left Book Club, with a preface by the Duchess of Atholl. It was the second part, *Dialogue with Death*, which Simone de Beauvoir had read when it had been published in translation as *Un Testament Espagnol* in 1939, and the theme of a man sentenced to death by Franco's forces was sufficiently close to the plot of 'Le Mur' for Simone de Beauvoir's remark to be justified. The first-person narrator and main character in 'Le Mur', Pablo, is a Spanish Republican who is taken prisoner by the Fascists and sentenced to death. However, the officer in charge of the execution squad is anxious to capture a more important left-wing activist in the area, Juan Gris, and promises Pablo to spare his life if he will tell him where Gris is hiding. Pablo, intending to play a joke on the officer, and knowing that Gris is in a safe house belonging to one of his cousins, tells the Fascists to go and look in the cemetery. There, they find Gris. Without Pablo knowing, he has quarrelled with his cousin, left his house and gone to hide behind a gravestone. The story ends with Pablo in fits of hysterical laughter at the absurdity of it all.

The main interest of the story is not in its rather contrived ending, with its demonstration that the world is so absurd that you can't make predictions of any kind. Pablo tried, as Hilaire Belloc put it in his Cautionary Tale about

John Henderson, an unbeliever
Who lately lost his *joie de vivre*

to 'monkey with the creed'. He was consequently caught, rather as the son in Camus' 1944 play *Le Malentendu* is caught when he tries to give a pleasant surprise to his mother and sister after having spent several years abroad. What he does not know is that during his time away, they have been making a living by murdering the travellers who stay at their inn. He does not tell them who he is and they do not recognise him, so they kill him for his money and find out who he is only when his wife arrives looking for him the next day. Camus' play was not copied from Sartre's story. 'Le Mur' also has a number of qualities lacking in *Le Malentendu*, which was not one of Camus' more successful works.

One of the German existentialists whose ideas Sartre discusses and rejects in *L'Etre et le néant* is Martin Heidegger, who argued that human beings could achieve some kind of authenticity by living towards or for death (Sein zum Tode). German grammar may give this idea advantages which it does not possess in English or French, and there is excellent precedence for Heidegger's advice in the behaviour of the monks of the Cistercian and Jesuit Orders, who used to sleep every night in their coffins. Although Heidegger was not a believer, his idea of 'Sein zum Tode' resembles a number of ideas in atheistic existentialism by having strong Christian resonances. The aim of 'Le Mur' is to show that Heidegger is wrong. Far from being able to live 'towards their death', human beings simply cannot think constructively of their death at all. As Koestler put it in *Dialogue with Death*: 'The virtue of the word lies in the sphere of abstractions; before the concrete and the tangible, language pales.

It becomes a completely useless instrument when it is question of describing such horrible, ordinary and naked facts as the fear of a human being in the face of death.'³

Thus when waiting in prison, knowing that he is going to be shot the next morning, Pablo gazes at his hand and cannot imagine that tomorrow it will not be there at all. He cannot forget that he is going to die in a few hours time – as Dr Johnson sardonically observed, 'when a man knows he is going to be hanged in a fortnight, it concentrates the mind marvellously' – but his mind does not have the ability to think the unthinkable. It is only in the way he sweats in terror and feels his pulse beating that he realises what is going to happen, and even then he fully grasps his situation only when he sees another person looking at him.

In Oscar Wilde's *The Ballad of Reading Gaol* there is a 'coarse-mouthed doctor' who comes to witness the hanging and

> gloats, and notes
> Each new and nerve-twitched pose
> Fingering a watch whose little ticks
> Are horrible hammer blows.

Pablo's captors also send a doctor, a Belgian, to take notes about what is happening, and it is Pablo's fury at the way he knows the doctor is watching him which makes him act so foolishly. In *L'Etre et le néant*, Sartre argues that our relationships with other people always involve conflict. If I am sitting in a park looking at the trees, and become aware of the fact that somebody else is looking at them as well, I immediately feel that he is robbing me of some of my pleasure.⁴ This is not a convincing argument. It is much more fun to watch a football match in a crowded stadium, or a play in a theatre in which every seat is occupied, than to be virtually alone where there ought to be a lot of other people. But it is true that we experience feelings such as embarrassment or shame only if we know somebody else is watching us, or think that they might be.

The incorporation of this idea into 'Le Mur' helps to make it one of the best things that Sartre ever wrote. It adds a note of philosophical originality to a story which is already on the same level as the one reached by three other French authors who have written on death: La Rochefoucauld, with his maxim that 'Ni le soleil ni la mort ne peuvent se regarder fixement' (Men can look directly neither at the sun nor at death); Camus, with the realisation that he gives to Meursault, as he lies in his condemned cell and thinks about his coming execution, that he cannot imagine how the little sound of his heart beat, which has been with him for so long, can ever end; and Perken's realisation, at the end of Malraux's *Les Conquérants*, that

> il n'y a pas de ... mort. ... Il n'y a que moi ... moi ... qui vais mourir (there's no such thing as ... death. ... There's only ... me ... me ... who is going to die).

Whatever echoes of Christianity there may be in Heidegger or Sartre, it is hard to imagine a less Christian way of looking at death than the one described in 'Le Mur'. It is Sartre's 1946 definition of existentialism as

> un effort pour tirer toutes les conséquences d'une position athée cohérente[5] (an attempt to draw all the conclusions of a thorough-going atheism)

with a vengeance, applied to an immediate and very real situation. It reminds us that there is no way in which an atheist can make sense of death. To do so involves trying to think of one's own body as an object. Since this is impossible, death is a biological event which is at one and the same time real and unthinkable.

In *La Nausée*, Roquentin thinks briefly about trying to escape from contingency by committing suicide, only to realise that his death will be just as absurd as his life. He will no more abolish the absurdity of his existence than a man who has hurt the person he loves by something he has said can make the word unspoken. Francis Jeanson, the interpreter of his work who Sartre most agreed with, reproduced in his 1956 *Sartre par lui-même* a cartoon by Robert Lapalme in which Sartre is depicted as a bespectacled, modern Hamlet, gazing straight at the spectator with Yorick's skull held challengingly between his hands.[6] Hamlet is not only, like Sartre, much preoccupied with death. He is also obsessed by the idea of self-awareness, and uses other people in a very Sartrian manner. By comparing himself, as he does, to Claudius, to Polonius, to the Player King, to Laertes, and finally to Horatio, he hopes to find out what kind of person he is. Like Hume – or Roquentin – he knows that he cannot do this by looking inside himself, because every time he looks he finds something different.

Hamlet's similarity to Sartre does, however, stop there. He is at least prepared to think that there may be an afterlife, to the point of not committing suicide because he is afraid of what he might find in 'the undiscovered country from whose bourn no traveller returns'. Sartre had no such thoughts. The hell in *Huis Clos* is merely a nastier version of real life. The three characters – Garcin, the coward; Estelle, the child-murderer; Iñes, the Lesbian who killed herself and her lover – torture one another because they are deprived of the most valuable quality that life has to offer: the possibility of changing what they have become by new and different actions.

Between the completion of *La Nausée* in 1936 and the publication of *Le Mur* in February 1939, history moved very quickly. The Versailles Treaty of 1919 had specifically forbidden the *Anschluss*, or reunification between Germany and Austria. On 15 March 1938, German troops marched into Austria with as little impunity as when they had taken over the demilitarised area of the Rhineland on 7 March 1936. At the Munich conference of 30 September 1938, Great Britain and France surrendered the German-speaking areas of their ally Czechoslovakia to Hitler. The military support which the Germans and Italians were quite openly providing for Franco's rebellion, like Mussolini's conquest of Abyssinia and the victories of Japan over China in the Far East, were all events that were steadily leading to the Second World War. In a letter to Simone de Beauvoir in July 1939, Sartre describes this as a wall separating his life into two parts, and making him into a different kind of writer. In particular, it led him to put forward his doctrine of committed literature, and to play a much more active part in politics. This has given the impression that he changed fundamentally in the early 1940s, and there was certainly a much more openly political content to the books which he published after his return to France from his prisoner-of-war camp in 1941.

There is nevertheless a marked continuity in his political attitudes. Neither before nor after 1940 did he have any sympathy with the form that parliamentary democracy had taken or was to take in France, and he had even less liking for the Fifth Republic of Charles de Gaulle than for the Third Republic of Edouard Daladier or the Fourth Republic of Georges Bidault and Antoine Pinay. But if he showed more enthusiasm for trying to overthrow the régimes which came into being in France after 1945, and played a leading and honourable role in trying to make France decolonise, this did not inspire him to write fiction which had as openly political a tone as certain passages in *La Nausée* or a short story such as 'L'Enfance d'un chef'. This is what the theory of commitment set out in 1947 in 'Qu'est-ce que la littérature?' would have required him to do, but he put his own precepts into practice in the theatre and the essay, not in novels or short stories. As will be seen, he did not even finish *Les Chemins de la liberté*, and he had already written his best attacks on the middle class before he seriously entertained the idea that literature ought always to side politically with the left. His earlier work has nevertheless taken on with the passage of time a number of qualities which make it immune to the more obvious objections to the theory of committed literature that he began to develop after 1945.

Sartre was very conscious of the limitations inseparable from political literature. In 1946, he wrote:

J'ai toujours considéré les bananes comme des fruits morts dont le vrai goût vivant m'échappait. Les livres qui passent d'une époque à l'autre sont des fruits morts. Ils ont eu, à leur époque, un autre goût, âpre et vif. Il fallait lire *L'Emile* ou *Les Lettres Persanes* quand on venait de les cueillir.[7] (I have always considered bananas as dead fruit, whose real taste escaped me. Books which pass from one period to another are like dead fruit. In their day, they had a sharp, pungent taste. The time to read Rousseau's *Emile* or Montesquieu's *Lettres Persanes* was when they had just been picked.)

This remark suggests that once the immediate purpose for which a book was written has been fulfilled, it will have no interest for a new generation of readers. This has happened to some of Sartre's books, and the world has also changed in such a way as to make a number of his political ideas look rather silly. In 1957, for example, his play *Nekrassov* was based on the assumption that the criticisms of the Soviet Union appearing in the French press were simply capitalist propaganda. In the 1990s, these criticisms have become the staple diet of the press in the Soviet Union, and are even occasionally mentioned in *L'Humanité* as well. Everyone in the 1947 thriller *Les Mains Sales* assumes that economic and political problems can be solved only by socialism, and they disagree with one another only as to how a socialist régime can most speedily be established. In the 1990s, when all that the countries of Eastern

Europe forced into socialism after 1945 by the Red Army want to do is to get rid of it as quickly as possible, only its construction and characterisation prvent *Les Mains Sales* from being as comically dated as *La Dame aux Camelias*.

Les Mains Sales still remains a very good play. Nothing can take away the excitement of its plot, and it gives in the character of Hugo an excellent portrait of the kind of youthful idealist attracted to Communism in the 1930s and 1940s. A number of Sartre's other works, and especially the short stories in *Le Mur*, have also aged much better than the strict application of Sartre's theory of committed literature would have allowed, and offer a portrait of France in the 1930s which is all the more interesting for being at least partly accidental. Something similar happened in English literature, albeit on a different level, with the Sherlock Holmes stories by Sir Arthur Conan Doyle. Because Doyle was interested primarily in illustrating the art of detection, the portrait at the turn of the century is much better than that of Napoleonic France in the 'Brigadier Gerard' series or of medieval Europe in *The White Company*. All forms of literature are spoiled by too obvious an intention, and had Sartre deliberately set out, either in *La Nausée* or in *Le Mur*, to write an accurate account of French society in the 1930s, he would probably not have succeeded. As it is, with his eye in both books mainly on a number of philosophical ideas which he was anxious to communicate to readers unlikely to read *L'Etre et le néant*, he wrote two of the best examples of historical fiction in twentieth-century French literature.

It is, in this respect, significant and appropriate that *Le Mur* should begin with a story about the Spanish civil war. This dominated political life in the France of the late 1930s as the Russian threats to West Berlin dominated European politics between 28 November 1958 and 26 October 1962, or the Vietnam War did in the USA between 1965 and 1973. This, everyone felt as they read about the bombing of Guernica, is what is going to happen here, and the French had the additional disadvantage of knowing that a lot of their fellow countrymen would be only too happy to have a Franco take over in Paris. On 6 February 1934, an enormous crowd of extreme right-wing sympathisers marched down the Champs Elysées, determined to put an end to the Third Republic by taking the Palais Bourbon by storm and throwing the *députés* physically into the Seine. The contemporary newsreels showing the demonstrators sweeping down the Champs Elysées are a terrifying reminder of how powerful the right was at the time. The *Chambre des Députés* was saved only by the readiness of the police to open fire into the crowd. Seventeen people were killed and over a thousand wounded. Right-wing attempts to overthrow the republic were a permanent feature of French politics in the 1930s and finally succeeded with the vote that gave full powers to Marshal Pétain to install the Vichy régime on 10 July 1940. It was a good piece of planning on Sartre's part, as well as on that of his publisher, to conclude a collection which began with the Fascists winning an episode in the Spanish civil war with the portrait of a young French Fascist in the story entitled 'L'Enfance d'un chef' (Childhood of a leader).

Lucien Fleurier is an only child, the son of a small Paris industrialist who insists that there is no such thing as the class war.

Je fais vivre cent ouvriers avec leur famille. Si je fais de bonnes affaires, ils sont les premiers à en profiter. Je n'ai pas le droit de faire de mauvaises affaires.[8] ('I provide a living for a hundred workers', he tells his son. 'If I do good business, they are the first to benefit. I don't have the right not to make a profit.')

Sartre is already sufficiently of a Marxist by 1939 to present ideas like this satirically and to see Fascism as a specifically bourgeois or petty bourgeois phenomenon, denying that it occurred in the working class. Indeed, in the 'Réflexions sur la question juive', the 1946 essay which provides the same kind of commentary on 'L'Enfance d'un chef' as *L'Etre et le néant* does on *La Nausée*, Sartre goes so far as to contend that anti-semitism is not to be found either in the working class or among engineers. He does not say why the former should be immune, but does make a remark about engineers which suggests that he may occasionally, in spite of his later remark 'J'ai vécu dix ans sous la coupe d'un ingénieur'[9] (I spent ten years of my life at the beck and call of an engineer), have seen the occasional glimpse of virtue in Monsieur Mancy, an old admirer whom his widowed mother married in 1916, and with whom Sartre did not get on very well. Engineers, he explains, are required by their calling to try to solve problems in a rational manner. They are therefore unlikely to be tempted by anti-semitism, which is an emotional attitude rather than an opinion based on evidence. Because their work requires them to use rational techniques, engineers are not likely to fall into the trap which man's nature offers him in the form of his emotions.

Nowhere in his work is Sartre more obviously a product of Cartesian rationalism than in the analysis of the emotions which he presented in his 'Esquisse d'une théorie des emotions' in 1939. It is never true, he argues, to say that we are carried away by our emotions. They are not natural forces like the wind and tide, or even physical urges like the desire to sneeze or go to the loo. They are ways of behaving which we adopt when problems become too difficult for us to be able to solve them by rational means. The fox cannot reach the grapes and scornfully declares them green, the child cannot solve a mathematical problem so tears up his book in disgust, I am so furious that the car won't work that I kick it. When we laugh, cheer or burst into tears, it is so that we can achieve in a short time the feelings of delight or grief which can only be fully experienced by living through the full consequences of an event.

The self-portrait of Sartre which emerges from the 'Esquisse d'une théorie des emotions' is that of a totally rational man entirely in control of what he thinks or feels. This is so depressing that it comes as a relief to discover that he could occasionally get quite cross if he lost at chess,[10] and there is something slightly off-putting about the way he lays down the law on matters which are surely more complicated than he suggests. It soon becomes clear that Sartre is in fact writing about the emotions in order to analyse a set of political attitudes of which he very strongly disapproves. He wants to prove that the anti-semite is the person who is angry and vice versa. He does not talk very much about any other emotions, and it would have been interesting to have a more detailed account of what he thought about the delight which we can take in the achievements of our children and the successes of our friends. He is mainly interested in anger. It is the main emotion accompanying anti-semitism, and he also sees it as offering a very convenient solution to the problems of contingency.

Lucien Fleurier is not only like Roquentin in being an only child. He also experiences his own body in very much the same way. Throughout his childhood, he never stops feeling embarrassed by his life,

ce cadeau volumineux et inutile, qu'il avait porté dans ses bras sans savoir qu'en faire ni où la déposer[11] (this useless and voluminous present which he had carried in his arms without knowing what to do with it or where to set it down).

When he is introduced to the ideas of *L'Action Française*, one of the main Fascist groupings in the France of the 1930s, he obtains the reassuring awareness of being a true Frenchman with rights, and is filled with the passionate indignation irresistibly inspired in him by the Jews. He even feels, when he thinks of himself, the same hardness and steel-like certainty which Roquentin associates with the book that he decides to write at the end of *La Nausée*.

Sartre may be describing his own sensations, or he may merely be using a convenient set of images in order to make his point. He is nevertheless assuming that his audience is going to be led by other details of the story, as well as by its general atmosphere, to realise that they know people like Lucien Fleurier, and thus see that the satire of French right-wing attitudes in 'L'Enfance d'un chef' is accurate. Sartre certainly knew what he was talking about as far as French adolescents were concerned. Between coming first in the *Agrégation*, in 1929, and finally giving up teaching to become a full-time writer in 1945, he spent some ten years as a schoolmaster. He had an unconventional approach to teaching, which the authorities quite liked. In April 1937, he was honoured by a 'special inspection', and was required to teach only three years in the provinces before obtaining an appointment to the rather smart Lycée Pasteur, in the Parisian suburb of Neuilly. But like other schoolmasters before and since, he was not always happy in his job, and developed a healthy dislike for adolescents. It is not solely because he grows up into a Fascist beast that Lucien Fleurier is so unpleasant. His obsession with sex, like his habit of licking his finger and moistening the spots on his face, belongs to pubertal schoolboys of any political persuasion, and is clearly modelled on reality.

The closing line of the story describes Lucien's decision to grow a moustache. This was a sign used by the Fascists of the 1930s to tell themselves and other people how virile they were, and Roderick Spode, founder of the Black Shorts of Britain in the world of P. G. Wodehouse, has grown a moustache when Bertie meets him in *The Code of the Woosters* in an antique shop on the Brompton Road in the late 1930s, virtually at the same moment that Lucien is deciding to grow his. Spode is prevented from making too much of a nuisance of himself by Bertie's ability to tell him that he knows all about Eulalie. This is not, as Bertie and Aunt Dahlia had earlier suspected, the Christian name of an unfortunate girl whom Spode has seduced and betrayed, but the trade name of the emporium in

Bond Street, *Eulalie Soeurs*, of which Spode is the proprietor, and on whose account he exercises his considerable talent for designing ladies' underwear. As Bertie puts it to Jeeves, you have to choose: 'You can't be a successful dictator and design women's underclothing. One or the other. Not both' and Jeeves agrees that the knowledge of Spode's profession, if bruited abroad, would 'unquestionably jeopardise his authority over his followers'.[12]

The humour of *The Code of the Woosters* makes it more effective as committed literature than the fiercer satire in 'L'Enfance d'un chef'. It is nevertheless unlikely that either Wodehouse or Sartre actually influenced anyone. Few readers of *Le Mur* would have been interested in *L'Action Française*, just as not many people sane enough to admire P. G. Wodehouse would have felt any enthusiasm for Sir Oswald Mosley and his Black Shirts. One of the disadvantages of committed literature is that it almost always involves preaching to the converted, and the military defeat of Fascism in 1945 made sermons on the subject superfluous. In spite of the 'Sartre. Sois clair. Sois bref'[13] (Sartre. Speak clearly. Make it short), which he found waiting for him when he addressed the students occupying the Sorbonne in May 1968, Sartre probably had a greater impact later in his career, when he had virtually ceased being a creative writer, than he had done in the 1930s and 1940s, when he was at his most productive. His anti-Americanism, his opposition to middle-class society, his anarchism and cult of violence exactly fitted the mood of the 1960s. But although Michel-Antoine Burnier was probably wrong in his claim in his book, *Les Existentialistes et la politique*, that 'L'Enfance d'un chef' 'stopped a number of Lucien Fleuriers from growing their moustache',[14] it remains very readable as a portrait of a peculiarly unattractive French adolescent; or, as the *Pléiade* edition of Sartre's fiction quotes Sartre as saying in 1971, 'de tout ce que pouvait contenir de merde un coeur bourgeois'[15] (of all the shit that can be found in a bourgeois heart). It also has some interesting links with Sartre's ideas on the emotions and with the debate about whether we are what we are as a result of heredity, of environment, or of a free choice.

Like 'L'Enfance d'un chef', 'Réflexions sur la question juive' also concentrates on the anti-semite rather than on the Jew. It is, Sartre maintains, the anti-semite who creates the Jew as the object that he needs to hate. The Jew himself, he argues, is simply a man whom other people think of as a Jew, and he has no time for definitions based either on religion or on race. This is fully consistent with a number of other ideas in Sartre's early work, and especially with his definition of existentialism as the philosophy in which existence precedes essence. Simone de Beauvoir showed how this idea worked in a feminist context by arguing that 'On ne naît pas femme. On le devient'. (You are not born a woman. You become one.) There is, she maintained, no such thing as the 'essence of femininity' as expressed in a liking for pretty dresses, an intuitive rather than an analytical approach to social or intellectual problems, or an irresistible biological urge to have babies. These are aspects of 'the female condition' that women have been forced to accept by the way in which men, the dominant sex, have thought of them, and tricked women into thinking of themselves. They are the result of the social role which women have been compelled to perform, not of their physical constitution. If there have not so far been any women chess champions, this is due to the fact that women have always been placed in a position where they had to interrupt whatever they were doing to look after some domestic crisis: stop the baby crying or the pot boiling over, greet the men on their unexpectedly early return from the hunt, look after an aged parent. Their breeding consequently never selected out those qualities of concentration which enabled men to excel at the one game from which the element of chance is totally excluded.

This is not an example that Sartre or Simone de Beauvoir puts forward. Although less indifferent to science than the man whose ideas she presented in so convincing a form, she was no more interested than he was in illustrating her views with examples from mankind's most successful intellectual activity. Neither she nor he would have been interested in an example which so nicely illustrates the point at which the idea of the inheritance of acquired characteristics almost ceases to be nonsense. In the case of the Jew, Sartre argues, there is nothing racial in the expertise in finance which Jews are said to possess. It is the result of the fact that lending money for interest was forbidden to Christians during the Middle Ages but not to Jews. Even the inheritance of certain genetic diseases, if you follow Sartre's argument to its logical conclusion, is a result of the situation in which one group of human beings has been placed by another. The higher incidence of diabetes among Jews stems from the in-breeding forced upon them by the insistence of the Christians that they live in ghettoes.

Not all Jews have been entirely happy with Sartre's rejection of

race and religion as a basis for their identity. There is nothing
self-contradictory about Sartre's advice to anyone persecuted because of the colour of their skin. In 1948, Sartre wrote a preface to
a collection of poems by black African writers, *Orphée Noir* (*Black
Orpheus*). In it, he praised the negro who,

> ramasse le mot de 'nègre' qu'on lui a jeté comme une pierre ... et
> ... qui se revendique comme noir, en face du blanc, dans la
> fierté[16] (picks up the word 'nigger' thrown at him like a stone,
> and proudly proclaims himself black in face of the white man).

After all, he is black, and the values of 'negritude' which Sartre's
ideas helped to develop can be used to build up a culture which has
an independent, objective existence. But it is logically very odd to
try to achieve some kind of 'Jewish authenticity' by defining the Jew
as 'a man whom other men have decided to call a Jew'. If Jews are
not to think of themselves as belonging to a particular race, and are
not going to find a basis for their cultural identity in the practice of
their religion, it is hard to think how they are going to face their
persecutors with any sense of group identity.

In the 1960s and 1970s, when the foreign policy of the Soviet
Union led it to support and arm those Arab states and organisa-
tions whose sole objective was the destruction of the State of Israel,
an impressive number of American, British and European left-
wing thinkers swung over, like iron filings following a powerful
magnet, to an attitude of hostility towards the Jewish state. Sartre
did not do so, and the special number of *Les Temps Modernes*
published in 1967 at the time of the Six Day War tried to hold the
balance between the two sides. So, too, did a special issue on the
problems of Northern Ireland in 1972, and the review which
Sartre founded in 1945 has often been more even-handed in its
approach to social and political problems than he personally has
been sometimes.

One of the advantages of 'L'Enfance d'un chef' is that it cuts both
ways politically. In the 1930s and 1940s, it was axiomatic that
anyone on the left would support the Jews and be unconditionally
in favour of free speech. In the 1960s, 1970s and 1980s, this
changed. At the same time that Israel became, in the eyes of a
number of men and women of the left, an agent of American
imperialism, it became fashionable to say that there should be 'no
liberty for the enemies of liberty'. This is a very Lucien Fleurier-

like attitude to adopt, and when Sartre also said, in 1956,

> on ne répond pas à Rousset. On lui laisse gagner sa vie comme il
> peut[17] (you don't reply to Rousset nowadays. You let him earn
> his living as best he can)

it sounded as though he was putting into practice one of the pieces
of advice that he satirised in 1939. For when describing the changes
that come over Lucien as a result of his conversion to anti-semitism,
Sartre actually says that he 'apprit à refuser la discussion'[18] (learnt
how to refuse to discuss matters) and it is uncanny to see a man
becoming so impossible to distinguish from one of the least
attractive characters satirised in one of his own books.

'L'Enfance d'un chef' links up with more of the issues which
ordinary people face in their daily lives than any other book which
Sartre wrote. At the same time that it sets out to analyse the roots
and nature of intolerance, it also talks about the problems of
growing up and raises many of the issues involved in the debate
about nature and nurture. Although published six years before
Sartre's plea for committed literature in 'Qu'est-ce que la littérature?', it is a good example of how some of his theories work out in
practice. Its links with the 'Esquisse d'une théorie des émotions'
emphasise how profoundly rational the early Sartre was in some of
his attitudes. Nothing could be more in keeping with the European
rationalist tradition than the rejection of the idea that social
problems can be solved by an appeal to the emotions. 'L'Enfance
d'un chef' also suggests, albeit indirectly, a particular course of
action towards the anti-semite who is the cause of all the trouble in
the first place. At one point in the story, Lucien is invited to a party
where he is introduced to a young man whom he immediately
recognises as a Jew. He turns his back on him, disguising what the
reader is clearly expected to see as a free decision in the determinis-
tic phrase:

> C'est plus fort que moi, je ne peux pas les toucher, c'est physique,
> j'ai l'impression qu'ils ont des écailles sur les mains[19] (It's not my
> fault, it's too much for me, I can't touch them, I feel that they
> have scaly hands).

When Lucien discovers that this behaviour, far from shocking
the friend who had invited him to the party, has actually increased

his esteem in his eyes, he is delighted. The way that another person has been compelled to look at him has enabled Lucien to achieve the rock-like solidity which is his aim. It is the pusillanimity of his friend which enables Lucien to become, as Sartre puts it in the 'Réflexions sur la question juive', 'roc impitoyable, torrent furieux, foudre dévastatrice: tout sauf un homme'[20] (a pitiless rock, a ferocious torrent, a devastating thunderbolt: anything but a man) and it is not hard to imagine the advice that Sartre would give to anybody tempted to respect the anti-semite's anger by seeing him in his own terms: tell him not to be so silly, and perhaps even laugh at him. Any anti-semite who happened to read 'L'Enfance d'un chef' would, one hopes, realise the error of his ways, and perhaps also recognise how unattractive anti-semitism makes people.

Sartre's advice in 'L'Enfance d'un chef' is not aimed solely at individuals. It is unusual for any of his books to show the French in a very favourable light, and Lucien Fleurier makes himself even more unattractive than he already is by adopting a very French version of anti-semitism. A number of French writers such as Maurice Barrès, Léon Daudet or Charles Maurras based their anti-semitism on concepts such as race and the 'sense of the soil', and it is they who are depicted as having provided the intellectual framework in which Lucien can give vent to his anger. They went against the whole rational and humanist tradition in French literature, but had an influence over Sartre's contemporaries which became particularly visible when what Charles Maurras called the 'divine surprise'[21] of the defeat of the French armies by the Germans in the summer of 1940 enabled the Vichy government to come to power.

This government led the French, who had already made themselves the laughing stock of Europe in the 1890s and early 1900s by their behaviour during the Dreyfus case, to show themselves almost as bad as the Germans in the way they treated the Jews. Before the Germans had even had time to make their wishes known, Marshal Pétain's government took the initiative in introducing laws banning the Jews from certain professions, and when, in 1942, the Paris police collaborated in rounding up the Jews so that the Germans could send them off to be gassed, Pierre Laval wrote on the bottom of the order the words 'Les enfants aussi' (the children as well). Even nowadays, the readiness of the French to make openly anti-semitic remarks suggests that the portrait of this aspect of their society in 'L'Enfance d'un chef' remains distressingly accurate,

giving *Le Mur* an applicability to French society in general as well as
to the 1930s. Sartre's advice to his fellow countrymen to stop being
so stupid is, in this respect, still timely.

When the collection *Le Mur* was translated into English as
Intimacy, in 1949, Eric Keown wrote in *Punch* that it was 'constructed on the standard Sartre pattern of sadistic violence plus a
nebulous philosophy of despair' adding that its treatment of sex
'left *Lady Chatterley's Lover* sleeping at the post'.[22]

This is a very gratifying remark for any author to have made
about any of his books, and enabled *Intimacy* to appear fairly
quickly in paperback. The collection had already obtained considerable success in France, having won the Prix du roman
populiste in 1939, and has by now sold almost 2 million copies. The
Prix du roman populiste is given

> à toute oeuvre qui peint les gens du peuple et les milieux
> populaires, à condition que se dégage de cette peinture une
> tendresse humaine vraie (to any book depicting ordinary people
> in working-class surroundings, on condition that there emerges
> from this depiction a true human tenderness)

and a purist might object that *Le Mur* does not really qualify.
'L'Enfance d'un chef' and 'La Chambre' are both set in middle- or
upper-middle-class surroundings, and you have to look pretty hard
to find any human tenderness in any of the stories. They are all,
however, overflowing with human interest, and there are other
compensating factors as well.

'L'Enfance d'un chef', in particular, has quite a lot of sex in it. It
describes how Lucien obtains 'une petite démangeaison acidulé' (a
small, acid-like itch) when masturbating, descibes his seduction of a
working-class girl called Maud, and gives an account of a sordid
and unenjoyable homosexual relationship which he has with a
surrealist called Bergère. These details suggest that the Protestant
tone which characterises Sartre's early work also had something of
the horror of the flesh associated in French literature with the
Jansenist movement. Although one of the stories, 'Erostrate', was
republished in a collection of erotic books, there is nevertheless not
a single page of *Le Mur* which contains anything likely to make
anyone more interested in sex than the austerest Jansenist would
think they ought to be.

This is particularly true of the longest story in the collection,

'Intimité', whose rather ironic title was chosen for the English translation of the whole collection. Like 'Le Mur' and 'L'Enfance d'un chef' it offered the reader some advice, even perhaps of the kind which D. H. Lawrence might have been happy to underwrite. The moral of Lawrence's novel is that the inappropriately named Constance Chatterley is right to leave her husband Clifford, made impotent by a war wound, for his virile gamekeeper Mellors. The Sartre of 'Intimité' would also like to argue that the claims of the flesh take precedence over the bonds of marriage. If he fails to do so, it is partly because he was unable, as a writer, to show sex as enjoyable. It is also because he was describing a society in which few people had access to reliable contraceptive techniques.

The dispiriting manner in which Sartre wrote about sex did not reflect his personal experience. Just as the obsessional images about sickness which recur throughout his early work were not accompanied by any loss of appetite, so he was able to depict the sexual unhappiness of his characters while enjoying a varied and interesting sex life himself. From 1929 to his death in 1980, he had an 'open relationship' with his mistress, Simone de Beauvoir. They justified the affairs they had with other people by quoting Ernest Dowson's line, which they do not seem to have entirely understood, about being 'faithful to thee Cynara in my fashion'.[23] Sartre had several mistresses, and she a number of lovers. They lived in a narrow circle of acquaintances, and she liked women as well as men. In the 1930s, this led to the situation where they occasionally shared the favours of the same woman and wrote to each other about it. There is no record or even rumour of Sartre having been sexually interested in other men, and little evidence to support seeing any of the episodes in 'L'Enfance d'un chef' as autobiographical. 'Intimité' is even more obviously an invented cautionary tale.

The story is divided into four parts. In the first we see events from the point of view of Lucienne Crispin, otherwise known as Lulu, who is being tempted to leave her semi-impotent husband Henri for her more virile lover Pierre. Parts II and IV are told from the standpoint of her friend Rirette, who would rather like to manoeuvre Lulu into going off with Pierre. Sartre was not fond either of the name Lucien or its female version of Lucienne. In *Le Sursis* (*The Reprieve*), the second volume of *Les Chemins de la liberté*, there is reference to a Lucien who has turned out to be a coward. When the woman making the reference is called Maud, it is tempting to wonder if this is Sartre's old enemy Lucien Fleurier, and whether Sartre expects his readers to remember that Lucien once had an affair with a Maud. Sartre takes a very austere view of cowards, and depicts the Lucienne of 'Intimité' as a kind of moral coward in that she is not prepared to 'risk all for love'. Sartre thinks that this is what she ought to do, and his criticism of her shows how some of his ideas on ethics might work in practice.

In the lecture 'L'Existentialisme est un humanisme' Sartre compares Maggie Tulliver, the heroine of George Eliot's *The Mill on the Floss*, with La Duchesse de Sanseverina, in Stendhal's *La Chartreuse de Parme*. Both women act in the same way, in that each sacrifices the man she loves so that he can marry somebody else. But whereas, in Sartre's reading of the story, Maggie Tulliver sacrifices Stephen Guest to 'une jeune oie'[24] (a little goose; Maggie's cousin Lucy Deane) in the name of 'la banalité d'un amour conjugal' (the banality of conjugal love), La Sanseverina gives up her beloved Fabrice del Dongo for rather different reasons. It is so that he can pursue his love affair with the beautiful young Clélia Conti that La Sanseverina – who also happens to be Fabrice's aunt – sacrifices her passion for him.

The title of one of the first books to be published on Sartre in English, Iris Murdoch's *Sartre, Romantic Rationalist*, highlights the rather unexpected affiliation which 'Intimité' shows him to have had with the movement whose members thought that the rights of passion overrode those of society. As Roquentin's attitude to the Autodidact showed, it is not a good thing, in Sartre's world, to be one of the weak or obscure, or to try to do good according to fairly humble lights. He clearly thought that whatever glittering prizes were available in mid-twentieth-century France ought to go to those ruthless enough to trample over other people in order to get them.

This is very clear in the attitude which everyone in 'Intimité' has to the unfortunate Henri. Lucienne has as little regard as Emma Bovary for any promises she might have made to her husband when they were married, and Sartre does not call into question the scorn which the Romantics traditionally poured on deceived husbands. The important person in the story is Lucienne, and her function is to illustrate two points about the nature of freedom set out in *L'Etre et le néant*. The first of these, which Sartre supports by quoting the authority of the Austrian psychiatrist Stekel, is that the origin of our complexes always lies in a conscious choice.[25] The second is that human beings are so constituted as to be unable to escape from their freedom, however afraid of it they may be and however hard they may try. Indulging in bad faith, which Lucienne does in quite an exemplary manner, can be only a temporary expedient. Whatever we do to hide it from ourselves, or us from it, our freedom always resurfaces.

Sartre's thesis that the origin of our complexes is always a conscious one is based upon *a priori* reasoning rather than empirical observation. The Freudian theory of repression, he argues, is based on a logical contradiction. The conscious mind, in his view, can repress unconscious drives only if it knows that they are there in the first place. To argue otherwise would be tantamount to saying that a schoolmaster can tell an unruly pupil to shut up without even knowing that he is there. Since, in Sartre's view, it is one of the defining characteristics of the mind to be conscious, it can be no more influenced by unconscious forces than an oil-fired burner can be made to work by plugging it into a gas main.

Although not an entirely convincing argument, it underlines the attachment to rational modes of thought which inspires the 'Esquisse d'une théorie des emotions'. One of Sartre's intellectual heroes was Descartes, whom he praised for encouraging the growth of democracy by pointing out how social rank disappears when we are faced with a mathematical problem. Sartre would certainly have liked to see everybody behaving with the same rationality which he saw as inspiring his own actions, and this is not an unusual attitude. If the theory of the conscious origin of complexes implicit in the analysis of Lucienne's behaviour in 'Intimité' is not entirely convincing, this is partly because it is so simplistic. As in the case of Sartre's theory of the emotions, it is impossible not to feel that matters are more complicated than he suggests. The story also displays a male chauvinist attitude to female sexuality which is unusually blatant even by the standards of Latin civilisation.

In spite of the obvious debt which Simone de Beauvoir's feminist theory owes to Sartre's ideas, he personally does not seem to have been particularly sympathetic to the women's movement. His one attempt to depict a progressively-minded woman, the journalist Véronique in his 1955 satire on the French right-wing press, *Nekrassov*, is embarrassingly bad, and his other women are even more unattractive than his men. They are either leeches, like Marcelle Duffet in *Les Chemins de la liberté*, bringers of disaster, like Jessica in *Les Mains Sales* or Johanna in *Les Séquestrés d'Altona*, clear-sighted bitches, like Inès Sereno in *Huis Clos* or Anny in *La*

Nausée, real practitioners of incest, like Leni in *Les Séquestrés d'Altona*, or potential ones like Ivich in *L'Age de raison*, pure-minded hockey captains like Hilda in *Le Diable et le Bon Dieu*, or incredibly dim prostitutes like Lizzie in *La Putain respectueuse*. Oddly enough, however, it emerges from the 1986 biography of Sartre by one of his own immediate circle, Annie Cohen-Solal, as well as from the excellent and more neutral account by Ronald Hayman in his 1986 study, *Writing Against: A Biography of Sartre*, that he had relatively few men friends but a large number of women ones.[26]

Lucienne is one of the leeches, and it is made clear early on in her monologue that she is not very keen on sex. She is pleased rather than annoyed by her husband's failure to have an erection, thinks nostalgically of the similarity which the *soutane* of the Catholic priests gives them to women, would like to enjoy Platonic, asexual relationships with men, and remarks: 'le plaisir, il n'y a que moi qui sache me le donner'[27] (only I know how to give myself an orgasm).

Sartre is said to have described himself, in what one hopes was a throwaway remark, as having been 'more a masturbator than a copulator',[28] and he endows Lucienne with the same characteristic. She is enthusiastic about the idea of going away with Pierre, by whom she would prefer to be socially flattered rather than sexually aroused. In *L'Etre et le néant*, Sartre quotes Stekel as saying that every time he had been able to get to the root of a problem of female frigidity, it had 'lain in a conscious choice'.[29] This implies that Lucienne has deliberately decided to be frigid because she is afraid of the disturbance and emotional commitment inseparable from successful sex, and Sartre's presentation of her problems recalls the advice said to have been offered to nervous brides in Victorian England. Instead of being told to close her eyes and think of England, Lucienne is strongly advised to forget all this nonsense about masturbation, make up her mind to be the free girl she really is, and let herself go in what Mellors would have called a good fuck.

It is difficult for Lucienne to do this, and the reader's sympathy is as much with her as it is with the other women in French literature whose sexual problems are no real fault of their own. When describing Thérèse Desqueyroux's lovemaking with her husband Bernard, for example, Mauriac writes that

Comme devant un paysage enseveli sous la pluie, nous nous représentons ce qu'il eût été sous le soleil, ainsi Thérèse découv-rait la volupté[30] (As, looking at a rain-soaked countryside, we imagine what it might be like in the sunlight, so Thérèse discovered sexual pleasure).

The General's wife in Anouilh's *La Valse des Toréadors*, is also very frank about her husband's inadequacies, telling him that what she understands of his behaviour is

ce qu'entendent toutes les femmes inassouvies par de petits coqs vide satisfaits, mon ami. Tu n'as pensé qu'à me tromper toute ta vie et tu veux me quitter maintenant que je suis vieille et malade, pour apaiser quoi, au juste, chapon? Ce terrible tempérament? Apprends d'abord à satisfaire une seule femme, à être un homme digne de ce nom avec elle dans son lit, avant d'aller courir dans le lit des autres.[31] (what every women understands after having been left unsatisfied by an easily contented little cock. The only thing you've thought about for the whole of your life has been to have it off with somebody else apart from me, and now that I am old and ill, you want to leave me. And why, may I ask? To satisfy that tremendous sexual appetite? Learn how to satisfy one woman, to be a real man in her bed, before trying to run off between the sheets with somebody else.)

In Zola's *Thérèse Raquin*, the heroine takes up with Laurent because her husband Camille cannot satisfy her sexual needs, and Bernard Desqueyroux is as inept in bed as all Mauriac's male characters. The actions of Elizabeth Fischer, in Balzac's *La Cousine Bette*, are inspired as much by sexual frustration as by social jealousy, and the number of sexually unhappy women in French literature offers a surprising contrast to the reputation which Frenchmen enjoy abroad for their sexual exploits. In 'Intimité', Lucienne's lack of interest in sex is much more the result of the way her lover treats her than of any conscious or unconscious decision which she may or may not have taken to be frigid. Not only does he take her to a hotel with a creaking bed and thin sheets. At the crucial moment, he withdraws, leaving her with an understandable sense of frustration. This leads her to comment:

Mon Dieu, dire que la vie c'est ça, c'est pour ça qu'on s'habille et qu'on se lave et qu'on se fait belle et tous les romans sont écrits sur ça, et on y pense tout le temps et finalement voilà ce que c'est, on s'en va dans une chambre avec un type qui vous étouffe à moitié et qui vous mouille le ventre pour finir.[32] (My God, to think that that's life, that you dress and wash yourself and make yourself beautiful for that, that that is what all the novels are written about and you think about it all the time and then in the end you go off in a room with a chap who half stifles you and ends up by leaving you with a soaking wet belly.)

What used to be referred to by Catholic priests as the 'pratique funeste' (fatal practice) of *coitus interruptus* is often given as a reason to explain the phenomenon of *la dénatalité française*, the demographic decline which led France, the most densely populated European country in 1789, to have fewer people by the end of the nineteenth century than Germany or the United Kingdom. An anecdote told by Simone de Beauvoir suggests that Sartre regarded *coitus interruptus* as normal practice. When asked by a worthy Swiss lady (*une matrone suisse*) what advice he could give her to avoid the danger of her son getting his unsuitable girl friend (*une créature*) with child, Sartre replied: 'Apprenez-lui à se retirer, Madame'[33] (Teach him to withdraw, madam). The lady replied that she would do as he suggested, adding that she expected advice emanating from such a source to have considerable impact.

There is, unfortunately, no means of knowing whether Sartre was just giving a silly answer to a silly question, or whether he really meant it. Neither he nor Simone de Beauvoir had a well-developed sense of humour, and he may well have been speaking seriously. Between 1920 and 1967, all forms of artificial birth control were officially banned in France, and the other references in his fiction to *coitus interruptus* as the principal method used to avoid having children provide an interesting example of how his books reflect the social realities of his time. In *L'Age de raison*, Mathieu Delarue has made his mistress Marcelle Duffet pregnant by not withdrawing in time, and his friend Pinette is quite specific about what he is going to do when he goes off to seduce the local postmistress while waiting to be taken prisoner after the defeat of the French army in 1940. When Mathieu suggests that he risks making her pregnant, Pinette replies:

Moi? Ah! là, là. Tu ne me connais pas! Je suis le mec régulier. Ma femme n'en voulait pas parce qu'on était trop pauvres et j'ai appris à me surveiller. Non, Non. Elle a eu son plaisir, moi le mien.[34] (Me? Oh no, oh no. You don't know me. I'm a good bloke. My wife didn't want any children because we were too poor and I learnt to be careful. No, no. She came, and so did I.)

Sartre is not deliberately setting out to write novels which show how the absence of efficient contraception made people unhappy and frustrated. If he were, his novels would be much less effective than they are as a portrait of France in the last years of the Third Republic, and it is once again for the information that he gives the reader almost by accident, without realising its importance, that his fiction is so useful a guide to the France of his time. The reader can see, if Sartre cannot, that his implicit advice to Lucienne to stop being a silly girl and let herself go is not very practical. No woman can do this in a cold, creaking bed with thin sheets, especially if she is also worried about getting pregnant if her lover does not withdraw in time.

After the first part of the story, in which we see events solely through Lulu's eyes, we switch to the feelings of her girl friend Rirette. She is delighted when Lucienne comes to tell her that she has gone off with Pierre, but puzzled and annoyed that her friend should go deliberately to a part of Paris where she knows that her husband will intercept her. When the inevitable happens, and the normally placid Henri comes across the two women and seizes his erring wife by the arm, Rirette tries to make matters go her way by grabbing Lulu's other arm. Lucienne lets herself go as 'molle comme un paquet de linge'[35] (limp as a bag of laundry) in the hope that the person who can tug hardest will decide her fate. It is a good example of what Sartre calls 'bad faith', and a neat illustration of the idea that it is only because we know we are free that we think up such complicated subterfuges to pretend to ourselves as well as to other people that we are not.

The behaviour of Lucienne has, in this respect, a more convincing universality about it than Roquentin's nausea. We can all remember occasions when we have acted as she does, finding relief in the genuine accident which deprives us temporarily of our freedom, or even behaving in such a way as to make a comparable accident inevitable. We are all, as the title of Eric Fromm's book *The Fear of Freedom* implies, afraid of our ability to decide to do one thing rather than another. One of the attractions of Sartre's early philosophy is that it explains why this fear exists. If we know that it is by our own free decision that we have performed a particular action, we also know that it is nobody's fault but our own if the results turn out to be less satisfactory than we had hoped. It is always easier to blame our environment or our genetic make up for the folly or cowardice for which we alone are responsible.

As befits a short story by Sartre, 'Intimité' ends in defeat. Lucienne goes back to her husband while Rirette feels a sense of disappointment at her failure to order matters in a way that she thinks appropriate. Sartre is as adept in finding the right detail to characterise Rirette as he is in describing how, in the First World War, Lucien Fleurier's father managed to avoid the unpleasantness to which millions of his fellow citizens were subjected by accepting the argument that he would be more useful looking after his factory in the Paris suburbs than in being exposed to the dangers of trench warfare just like any Tom, Dick or Harry. Rirette likes men who pay attention to their personal appearance, who have a faint smell of English tobacco and eau de cologne about them, who are good with head waiters so that they are served first in restaurants, and who have a signet ring and cigarette case.

In the critical orthodoxy established in France by the influence of Roland Barthes, this accumulation of details would be dismissed as just so many 'effets de réel', or what the Pooh-Bah of *The Mikado* would describe as 'mere corroborative detail to add a touch of verisimilitude to an otherwise bald and unconvincing narrative'. In so far as Barthes is right in his contention that all apparent accounts of what happens are simply part of a 'structure of persuasion', and that apparently realistic details are simply rhetorical flourishes to produce added conviction in the reader's mind, this dismissal is probably justified. Like a number of Barthes's ideas, however, it tends to spoil rather than to increase the innocent pleasure which readers might otherwise derive from fiction, and from such details as Odette, the wife of Mathieu's respectable brother Jacques, laying in a lot of sardines in preparation for the war which seems about to break out in September 1938; as Roquentin, wandering about in the streets of Bouville and noticing Pierre Benoit's *Koenigsmark* in a luxury edition bound in blue leather; or the wives who come to see their husbands after they have been taken prisoner by the Germans in 1940 being tough, hard bitten, solid looking women, leaving 'les jolies poupées au regard tremblant'[36] (the pretty dolls with misty eyes) to bear their grief at home.

These notations do more than provide a pleasure comparable to the one which George Orwell took in the 'unnecessary detail' in

Dickens. They show an ability to enter another person's mind which it would have been agreeable to see Sartre developing and exploiting in a second, third or even fourth volume of short stories. If he did not do so it was because he was interested in bigger game. Like his lifelong enemy François Mauriac, he was not content simply to exploit the literary gifts which the gods had poured upon him. Just as Mauriac was dissatisfied with his marvellous ability to satirise the landowners, wine merchants and lawyers of his native Bordeaux, but felt himself compelled to write novels exploring the mysteries of Catholic doctrine, so Sartre could not rest content with the talents which fate had bestowed on him. He always wanted to do more than entertain his readers, and was not satisfied with his ability to explore interesting ideas, create intriguing characters, tell good stories or explain to his contemporaries what they and their fellows were like. Instead, he felt himself obliged to undertake the uphill task of trying to democratise the French Communist Party, or compelled to try to define the nature of literature.

In 1970, Laurence Peter wrote *The Peter Principle*, arguing that everyone rose to the level of their incompetence: the good sales-man became the unsuccessful manager, the first-rate teacher the inefficient head, the good lecturer the incompetent head of depart-ment. Sartre's career from the 1950s onwards, when he increasing-ly abandoned creative literature in favour of political activism, shows that it can happen to writers as well. What Jules Gaultier called 'le Bovarysme', the tendency to imagine ourselves other than what we are, and to think that we would be better at what we would like to do than at what we are good at, is a very frequent human characteristic.

Like *Les Mots*, 'Intimité' is an attempt to destroy a myth. In the 1963 autobiographical fragment, it is the myth of the Baudelairean 'vert paradis des amours enfantines', of the Wordsworthian 'splen-dour in the grass' of the idyllic childhood which Sartre calls into question and destroys. He restores the balance by describing the kind of childhood which many people actually have, and which Philip Larkin encapsulated in his poem 'I remember, I remember'. Sartre's is even worse than Larkin's conclusion that 'Nothing, like something, happens everywhere'. It is one of loneliness and frustration, of constant dissatisfaction with himself, of guilt and resentment, of a longing to be different that can be satisfied only by daydreams. 'Intimité' and *Les Mots* are both debunking books, the target of the autobiographical fragment being the perfect world of childhood, that of the short story the irresistible chic and sexual adroitness of the Parisian midinette. In *Les Mots*, Sartre notes how the same principles of *realpolitik* which govern relationships between adults also exist for children. When he was at home, his grandfather loved to see him performing the role of the perfect child. But when he was with other children, this didn't work.

Entre eux, les enfants détestent le cabotinage. Ce sont des hommes pour de vrai[37] (Among themselves, children hate play acting. They are real grown ups).

Sartre is excluded from what he sees as the magic, unattainable world of the spontaneous, unreflective friendships which ordinary children have with one another. Like Thom Gunn, he thinks with envy of

> All the toughs from Alexander
> To those that wouldn't play with Stephen Spender,

and the fact that he is not the only person to look back on his childhood with displeasure gives *Les Mots* as universal a note as anything he wrote. In 'Intimité', the Parisian midinette does not have the ready wit, the instinctive elegance and indefatigable sexual generosity attributed to her by legend. Sartre depicts her as one suspects that many of them were: vapid, selfish and constantly afraid of getting pregnant. It is a saving virtue of this particular short story that Sartre's grasp of what people are really like makes it possible to take the advice he has to offer with a strong pinch of salt.

Madness

The other two stories in *Le Mur*, 'La Chambre' and 'Erostrate', do not set out to tell other people how they ought to behave. Both deal with madness, a subject which recurs on a number of occasions in Sartre's work and culminates in the remark made by Johanna in the 1959 play *Les Séquestrés d'Altona*:

Les fous disent la vérité. Il n'y en a qu'une: l'horreur de vivre.[38] (Madmen tell the truth, the only one there is: the horror of living.)

As a philosopher concerned with the nature of the mind, and especially with the workings of the imagination, Sartre was understandably interested in abnormal phenomena such as hallucinations, and in the 1930s became one of the first writers to experiment with mescalin. This did not produce in him the same beatific effect that it later did on Aldous Huxley. His 'doors of perception' were not cleansed and Blake's prophecy was not fulfilled. Everything did not appear to him, 'as it should, infinite'. Instead, he had terrifying hallucinations involving shellfish, and went through a period in which he was convinced that he was being followed everywhere by a lobster. Uncharitable critics have claimed that he invented this particular illusion in order to provide himself with an excuse not to accompany the indefatigable Simone de Beauvoir in her walks up the French mountains, but this is probably not true. His letters to her assure her of his readiness to walk 'as far as she wants'.[39] His hallucinations were probably genuine, and seafood provides images of horror in all his works, reaching a high point as a central theme in *Les Séquestrés d'Altona*. There, the central character is a German officer, Franz von Gerlach, who has tortured partisans on the Russian front in 1943, and tries to justify the crimes he has committed to a 'tribunal of crabs', arguing that they will probably be the only creatures left alive in the thirtieth century.

The image is effective in that it emphasises both the possibility that there will not be a future (we do not know whether crabs think or not, just as we do not know whether we shall all have been destroyed by then) and our inability to imagine by what criteria the future will judge us (even if crabs did think and could understand us, their ideas of right and wrong would almost certainly not be ours). The frequency with which the image occurs nevertheless points to a number of obsessions which Sartre had difficulty in keeping under control, and in the mid 1930s, after his mescalin injection, he did go through a period in which he thought he was going mad. This obviously did not happen. Madmen do not write long-running plays, well-argued works of philosophy and highly successful fiction. However, Sartre did retain an interest in the abnormal which is occasionally slightly suspect. This is noticeable in 'La Chambre', the most moving of the short stories, and makes 'Erostrate' the least successful of the five.

Like Sartre's most successful play, *Huis Clos*, 'La Chambre' is set in an enclosed space. So, too, are a number of the scenes in *Les Séquestrés d'Altona*, where Franz von Gerlach has deliberately locked himself away in a garret, and it is tempting to link Sartre's interest in sequestration with his early childhood, where he was cut off from other children, emerging from a fifth floor apartment only in the company of his mother, and never allowed to escape from the possessive love of grandfather Schweitzer. The situation in 'La Chambre' nevertheless takes matters much further. Eve's husband Pierre has gone mad, and Eve is giving her parents a great deal of worry by refusing to recognise the situation and put him in a home. In the view of her parents, Monsieur and Madame Darbédat, who are presented with the same hostility which Roquentin directs at the portraits in the municipal art gallery in Bouville, the mad are simply people who are being perverse. With a little effort, they could probably be as sane as anyone else. But even if this is not true, they are not suitable company for anyone, let alone an only daughter who could have made a better marriage, and whom Madame Darbédat suspects of still sleeping with her deranged husband.

Two of the English-speaking critics to have written with most sympathy about Sartre, Andrew Cooper and R. D. Laing, in *Reason and Violence in Sartre's Philosophy*, were associated with the 'anti-psychiatry' movement of the 1960s, which argued that it is Western society, rather than the supposedly mad individual, that constitutes a suitable case for treatment. The Sartre of 'La Chambre' is not so explicit about the matter. Monsieur and Madame Darbédat are bourgeois swine, and the reader's sympathy is clearly expected to be with Eve. But there is at least the suggestion that Pierre's condition is genuinely pathological. It is nevertheless not he who is at the centre of the story but Eve, who is a particularly interesting character in that her behaviour totally contradicts the argument in *L'Etre et le néant* that what we call 'loving somebody' can be reduced to the wholly selfish desire to make them love us. She is more sympathetically drawn than any of Sartre's other female characters, with her attitude anticipating that of the father in *Les Séquestrés d'Altona*. When Franz asks old von Gerlach whether he can still love a war criminal, his father's reply takes on a universal quality when he says 'le boucher de Smolensk, c'est toi'[40] (the butcher of Smolensk is still you). Eve may suspect that her husband is sometimes putting it on, that the flying statues by which he says he is so terrified are all an invention, and that the fork which he gazes at with such horror looks as ordinary to him as it does to her. The fact remains that she still loves him, and does so to the point of wanting to live with him in his world and on his terms.

All writers, except perhaps for authors of mathematical and scientific textbooks, try to make the reader see the world in a particular way. There is no such thing as neutral discourse, and even the apparently objective and factual 'The Life and Times of Jean-Paul Sartre' printed at the beginning of this book cannot avoid making the reader see certain aspects of his career as more important than others. But if Sartre differs from other authors only by degree, he does put his cards on the table more openly and more frequently than most. He makes no bones about writing stories in order to illustrate an idea, and is quite obviously trying to prove a point about the nature of the mind when he describes the failure of Eve's attempt deliberately to follow her husband into his mad world. Pierre is having one of his hallucinations, and Eve is almost on the point of believing in his flying statues when she hears footsteps in the corridor outside. Immediately, the thought comes into her mind that it is her charwoman, Marie, to whom she owes money for the gas. Nobody can deliberately go mad, and the awareness which we all have of ourselves is an inescapable fact of life. Neither is there any way for us to leap over the wall which separates human minds one from another. All that Eve is going to be able to do for her husband when madness finally strips him of the last vestiges of humanity is kill him.

It is nevertheless through this love that Eve is going to make whatever sense of her experience she can. In Sartre's view, the two most important things about human beings are that they are free and that they want to give their life meaning. Every one of us is possessed by the longing to avoid the feeling that ordinary experience is just one damn thing after another. We are all driven on by the wish to place ourselves in a position where we can look back at what we have done with satisfaction and forward to what we are going to do with hope. This desire to make sense of our own experience is, in Sartre's view, as essential a characteristic of human beings as the awareness which we all have of our own freedom. We are not what Somerset Maugham called 'creatures of circumstance', the passive victims of heredity and environment. What we call our character is the result of the choices we have made in the situation in which the accident of our birth and upbringing has placed us.

What makes us the kind of person we are is what Sartre calls 'le projet', the desire that we have to act in accordance with our own ideal self image. The way we do this, like the nature of our self image, varies according to our social situation. It depends on the kind of childhood we have had, on the friends we have made and on the body we have inherited. Although it is influenced by the way we earn our living, it is never determined by it. When our project expresses itself through our sexual preferences, these should be seen not as a result of early conditioning but as an integral part of the way we have chosen to live our lives. In Sartre's view, Genet's homosexuality was not determined by his hereditary make up, any more than it was forced upon him by the exclusively male company of the reform schools and prisons in which he spent most of his life between the ages of 15 and 30. It was the result of the way he chose to see himself in relationship to other people. Because of what Sartre depicts as the crucial incident in his childhood, when he was seen from behind at the moment of stealing, he always wanted to be taken from behind.

In his 1946 essay on Baudelaire, which he dedicated to Jean Genet, Sartre maintains that the poet's inability to bring together the two sides of his sexual life was inseparable from his deliberate choice to be an unhappy and misunderstood outcast. The reason why he could not make love to the beautiful Madame Sabatier when she offered herself to him was that he had decided, when still a child, that fate had decided to deny him all worthy relationships. It was not because Madame Sabatier reminded him unconsciously of his mother. If he worshipped Madame Sabatier from afar, and reserved his sexual passion for Jeanne Duval, for whom he had little esteem and no adoration, it was because this was how he wanted to live all his relationships: as a constant proof of the unworthiness to which he claimed to be predestined. This inability to bring together Eros and Agape was, according to Sartre, a result of the way that Baudelaire had chosen to behave at the age of 6 or 7. It was his means of trying to make sense of what he saw as his mother's rejection of him when she escaped from her widowhood to marry the dashing Major Aupick, by whom she was already pregnant. It was a choice that led Baudelaire not only to write a particular type of poetry but also to prefer one kind of food to another, to have a particular relationship with money and to adopt his highly reactionary political attitudes.

Sartre's concept of what he calls 'existential psychoanalysis'[41] makes the very unFreudian assumption that children are capable of a more or less conscious choice from the moment that they reach the age of 7 or 8. There is no evidence for this apart from the essays which Sartre wrote about Baudelaire, Genet and himself, and the speculations about Flaubert's childhood in the opening pages of *L'Idiot de la famille*. The choice of 7 or 8 may be an unconscious reflection on Sartre's part of the view traditionally taken by the Catholic Church about the age at which children make their first communion. What is known, as will be seen later, as 'l'âge de raison' (the 'years of discretion' in the Anglican Church) is the age at which children are seen as being able to distinguish between good and evil, and this is also the age at which Sartre, perhaps by a cultural coincidence with the France still seen by some people as 'la fille aînée de l'Eglise' (the eldest daughter of the Church), thinks that we all begin to decide on the kind of person we are going to be.

Existential psychoanalysis is also based on what Sartre calls a holistic concept of the human personality. This is one in which you cannot detach one aspect of a person's behaviour from all the others, or see the individual as nothing more than the sum of his parts. In Sartre's view, not even the concentration camp commander who murdered Jews in the daytime and devoted himself with exemplary care to the well-being of his budgerigar in the evenings can be seen as an exception to this rule. His total brutality in one context is merely the other side of an excessive and irrational concern in another. Moreover, and in most cases, the different aspects of our personality are organically connected in a very visible and understandable manner.

This is very much the case with the story in *Le Mur* called 'Erostrate'. This describes a clerk, Paul Hilbert, whose project is one of which Roquentin would have approved, and which seems at times to attract more than a clinical interest from Sartre himself. Hilbert is a fierce opponent of what he calls 'Humanism', and elects as his hero the legendary Greek figure of Herostratus, who achieved by burning down the temple of Diana at Ephesus an immortality denied to its unknown architect. Hilbert intends to demonstrate the impossibility of humanism in a very public manner. First of all, he will write a letter of violent denunciation to 102 French writers famous for their love of mankind. Then, he will show them that there is at least one person who hates his fellow men sufficiently to put his feelings into practice. He will do this by performing what the French writer André Breton described, in the second manifesto of surrealism, as 'l'acte surréaliste le plus simple' (the simplest surrealist act): going down into the street and firing at random into the crowd.

While it is hard to see that this definition proves anything apart from the fact that Breton could not distinguish between literary posturing and criminal insanity, it is Hilbert's chosen way and there is some satisfaction for the bourgeois reader fond of his own skin in the fact that Hilbert fails to carry out more than part of his plan. He bundles the letters into the postbox in such haste that he crumples them up and cannot finally get them all in, and succeeds in shooting only one person, whom he probably kills. He then panics and seeks refuge in the lavatory of a café. There, he is too terror-striken to behave as he intended and does not use the last bullet in the revolver to kill himself. At the last minute, he chickens out and surrenders.

Considerable enthusiasm has been expressed for the letter which Hilbert sends to his 102 humanist writers. Michel Rybalka, writing in the 1982 *Pléiade* edition of Sartre's fiction, says that the letter

> nous fait penser à ceux qui, comme Beckett et Camus, on développé en littérature les grands thèmes du pessimisme philosophique (brings to mind the writers who, like Beckett and Camus, have used literature to express the great themes of philosophical pessimism).

These literary qualities, he argues, make the story seem

> moins comme l'étude d'un cas psychopathologique que comme un voyage aux bords du nihilisme et un témoignage personnel sur la misère de l'homme (less a study of a psychopathological case than a voyage to the frontiers of nihilism and an act of personal witness to human misery).[42]

Like Roquentin's outburst against the civic worthies of Bouville, Hilbert's letter relies on passion and rhetoric rather than example and argument. It refers neither to man's unique capacity to organise the systematic murder of his own species, nor to the ingenuity visible throughout the ages in the invention of new instruments of torture. Neither does it describe the extraordinary ability of human beings to invent religions which encourage them to persecute one another, and to sacrifice their own and other people's capacity for happiness in order to appease imaginary gods. It might, had it done so, have been more than an expression of the way a madman sees the world. However peculiar some of its implications may be, Roquentin's denunciation of 'les salauds' is explicable in rational terms by reference to the political behaviour of the French middle class. There is no such guide to Hilbert's wrath. Instead, he is made to write with disgust about his hatred of men, the revulsion he feels on watching them 'mastiquer avec mesure en gardant l'oeil pertinent' (chew away in moderation with an alert expression in their eyes), or 'passer sans relâche de la sérénité à la surprise pleurarde[43] (passing without interruption from indignation to tearful surprise), and about the resentment which he feels at finding every door barred to him by the notice 'Closed to everyone who is not a humanist'.

These descriptions of Hilbert's persecution mania give every sign of being an accurate notation of the state of mind of a madman. It is very difficult to take them as the viable expression of a defensible intellectual attitude, and Michel-Antoine Burnier's remark in his *Les Existentialistes et la politique* to the effect that Hilbert, like Roquentin, seemed to him to be a 'positive hero'[44] is an indication at one and the same time of poor literary taste and of the fact that Sartre owed a good deal of his popularity to his ability to crystallise a rebellion against bourgeois society which was fashionable, un-thinking and dangerous.

In his satire of Lucien Fleurier, as in his later presentation of Franz von Gerlach, Sartre knows exactly what he is doing and why. If he exploits his own obsessions, it is to produce a very deliberate effect on the reader. This is not the case in 'Erostrate', where even as well-informed a commentator on Sartre's work as Michel Rybal-ka clearly had difficulty in telling where Sartre's opinions end and Hilbert's madness begins.

'Erostrate' was a very early story, completed in the spring of 1936, only a year after Sartre's experiments with mescalin had made him feel that he might be going mad himself. Annie Cohen-Solal suggests that there is a strong autobiographical ele-ment in it, describing Hilbert as 'almost the double of the writer',[45] and linking it with the enthusiasm that Sartre felt in the 1930s for Violette Nozières, a girl accused of murdering her parents. Sartre was, argues Annie Cohen-Solal, who had the advantage of knowing him personally and belonging to his intellectual circle in the Paris of the 1970s and 1980s, inspired in much of his early work by a strong personal resentment against society, and it is easy to explain why this should have been so. After being adored as a child, he felt himself rejected when his mother remarried. This feeling of rejection was made worse by his dislike of Joseph Mancy, and the unsuccessful efforts which his stepfather made to prepare him for the only career which he regarded as suitable, that of an engineer, did nothing to improve the situation. Ronald Hayman goes so far as to write that: 'If the whole of Kafka's work was a love-letter to his father, the whole of Sartre's was a declaration of hatred to his step-father'.[46]

Until he came to Paris to study at the Lycée Henri IV in 1920, Sartre had had a particularly unhappy adolescence, and even after his idyllic years at the Ecole Normale Supérieure de la rue d'Ulm, from 1924 to 1928, he had a difficult time establishing himself as a writer. He consequently looked forward gloomily to a life spent teaching in the French provinces. One of his earliest stories was called 'Jésus la Chouette' (Jesus the Owl), and rivalled Hugh Walpole's *Mr Perrin and Mr Traill* as an account of an unhappy and inadequate schoolmaster. Sartre was in fact very good at his job, but he clearly had difficulty throughout his adolescence and early manhood in shaking off a number of complexes, chief among them the terrifying experience, brilliantly suggested in *Les Mots*, of discovering how ugly he was, and of how difficult it was for him to make certain people like him.

This discovery had been all the more overwhelming in that he had been told, in his early childhood, how very handsome he was, and clearly never managed to reconcile the way in which he was adored by everybody at home while remaining an object of total indifference, or even hostility, in the eyes of the people whom he regarded as his true judges, the other children of his own age. Yet while 'Erostrate' becomes more understandable if read as an exercise in imaginative autobiography, this does not make it a good story. Like a number of other books, by other writers apart from Sartre, it shows how badly people write when they yield to the temptation of providing a direct description of their own unhappiness. Even more than *La Nausée*, it is an account of a number of attitudes and obsessions which it would be tempting to describe as peculiar to Sartre himself were it not for one important fact: the popularity which it derived from the obvious echoes which it aroused in large sections of the French reading public. For it was not only his skill in handling words and creating interesting characters which won Sartre such immediate recognition in the late 1930s. It was the fact that his unhappiness, together with his resentment against society, led him to express a set of attitudes that other people found intellectually valid as well as emotionally attractive. From the very beginning of his career, Sartre's success as a writer had strong sociological overtones. This, clearly, was how many intellectuals in France – represented in 1966 by Michel-Antoine Burnier, and as late as 1982 by Michel Rybalka – saw the world.

'Erostrate' nevertheless links up with the saner and more intellectually convincing side of Sartre's work by the way it anticipates the argument in 'L'Esquisse d'une théorie des émotions'. Like 'L'Enfance d'un chef', it illustrates how we use emotion in order to try to make sense of our experience when rational solutions are beyond our reach. Hilbert is unmarried, has no friends, works at a very humdrum job in an office, and has no interest in politics or religion. If he reads a book, it is solely to find examples in history or mythology to justify the hatred which is the only means he has of giving some kind of meaning to his life. His project is explicable in Adlerian terms as an attempt to compensate for a fully justified feeling of inferiority.

Hilbert hates men with the same unthinking enthusiasm that l'Autodidacte loves them, and like Ogier P..., he has some weird sexual habits. In the context of the typology of sexual attitudes set out in *l'Etre et le néant,* he is the Sadist, the person who attains the most satisfying awareness of himself by using pain to imprison another person in her or his body. What Hilbert likes to do is pick up a prostitute, make her strip naked by threatening her with a revolver, and then force her to walk up and down in front of him while he sits fully clothed in an armchair. He thus compels her to become fully conscious of what he sees as the ridiculous heaviness of her own flesh, and there is a passage in *L'Etre et le néant* which suggests that Hilbert reflects some of Sartre's own personal feelings:

La vue d'un corps nu, de dos, n'est pas obscène. Mais certains dandinements de la croupe sont obscènes. C'est qu'alors ce sont les jambes seules qui sont en acte chez le marcheur et la croupe semble un coussin isolé qu'elles portent et dont le balancement est pure obéissance aux lois de la pesanteur. Elle ne saurait se justifier par sa situation; elle est entièrement destructrice de toute situation, au contraire, puisqu'elle a la passivité de la chose et qu'elle se fait porter comme chose par les jambes. Du coup, elle se découvre comme facticité injustifiable, elle est de trop, comme tout être contingent. Elle s'isole de ce corps dont le sens présent est la marche, elle est nue, même si quelque étoffe la voile, car elle ne participe plus à la transcendance transcendée du corps en acte.[47] (The sight of a naked body is not obscene. But certain involuntary waddles of the rump are obscene. This is because the legs alone are being deliberately moved by the walker, and the rump looks like an isolated cushion which they are carrying, and whose movement is pure obedience to the laws of gravity. It cannot be justified by its situation. On the contrary, it is entirely destructive of any situation, since it has the passivity of a thing and is carried like a thing by the legs. Immediately, it reveals itself as unjustifiable facticity, it is de trop like all contingent beings. It is isolated in the body whose present meaning lies in moving forward, it is naked even if veiled by some cloth, for it no longer participates in the transcended transcendence of the body in motion.)

What Sartre calls 'certains dandinements de la croupe' are what other people would describe as a wiggling bottom. Marilyn Monroe and Jayne Mansfield both had one, and only the most austere representatives of the women's movement would describe the innocent pleasure which male audiences derived from *The Seven Year Itch* or *The Girl Can't Help It* as 'obscene'. In spite of the implicit recommendations of 'Intimité', Sartre has a puritanical attitude towards the body which sometimes makes his analysis of the human condition unconvincing. To judge from his novels and plays, he clearly preferred thin women: Anny, in *La Nausée*, disappoints Roquentin by the fact that she has allowed herself to get fat, and a comparable fate overcomes Ivich in the third volume of *Les Chemins de la liberté*; Marcelle, in *Les Chemins de la liberté*, is a plump, fertile girl, and it is not an accident that Hilbert particularly chooses a fat woman to humiliate. Iñes, in contrast, in *Huis Clos*, like Johanna in *Les Séquestrés d'Altona*, was always played in Sartre's lifetime by an actress who was rather thin. This puritanical attitude towards the body nevertheless did not prevent Sartre from allowing the account of Hilbert's treatment of the prostitute to be reprinted in 1953 in René Varin's *L'Erotisme dans la littérature française*.[48]

Hilbert is so delighted by the feelings provided by the spectacle of the prostitute walking up and down naked in front of him that he has a spontaneous orgasm. Nobody reads pornography by accident, and there were probably enough people in the France of the 1950s interested in the same kind of sex as Hilbert to make it worth Monsieur Varin's while to include 'Erostrate' in his collection. The description of Hilbert's visit to the prostitute also gives the story something of the same interest as Jean Genet's play *Le Balcon*. There, the action takes place in a brothel, appropriately referred to in the slang term of 'une maison d'illusions' (House of Illusions). A bank clerk impersonates a Bishop, an electrician a General and a milkman a High Court Judge, each aided and abetted by prostitutes considerably more intelligent and co-operative than the girl unfortunate enough to be picked up by Hilbert. The point that Genet is making – indirectly, since his principal aim was to show that the whole of society is based on illusion – is that prostitutes are rarely used to provide straight sex. In a society as liberated as our own, this is not difficult to obtain. What is more difficult, because it is embarrassing to ask for, and because few people enjoy being cast in a supporting role for somebody else's private fantasies, is the satisfaction of sexual tastes of which Hilbert's are by no means the most unusual.

The point that Sartre was making in including 'Erostrate' in a collection of short stories aimed at illustrating a number of serious philosophical ideas is to remind his readers of the holistic principle underlying the concept of existential psychoanalysis. It is because Hilbert is so inadequate in every other area of his life that his sexual behaviour is so peculiar. Sexual tastes, in Sartre's view, are not a kind of conditioned reflex left over from the forgotten traumas of early childhood. However odd they may seem to an outside observer, they are an integral part of the way in which some human beings try to make sense of their experience. This may make things uncomfortable for other people, and one feels even sorrier for the prostitute than for Lulu or Lucien Fleurier's Maud. This is another reason to feel that any intellectual sympathy which we may feel for Hilbert is misplaced.

One of Sartre's great virtues as a writer is the challenge he offers to disagree with him. Once Hilbert is seen as a pathological case, and not as a down-market version of a Beckett or a Camus, 'Erostrate' is a good short story, just as *La Nausée* is a marvellous novel when Roquentin is seen not as someone undergoing an experience we all ought to have but as a man made ill by a particular philosophical discovery. But just as 'Erostrate' describes the way we all hope we will never be, so some of the ideas associated with it are more intriguing than convincing. Practitioners of unorthodox sex do behave as one of the main theories in *L'Etre et le néant* says that everybody behaves, and as Genet depicts the characters in *Le Balcon* as behaving. They play at being what they are not, temporarily achieving a particular mode of existence in the way that Hilbert does. They do not all play his same role of tyrannical master. They like to be returning heroes, devoted slaves, innocent victims or inexhaustible studs. But not all practitioners of unorthodox sex are social inadequates in search of the same kind of consolation for their inferiority as Hilbert. Indeed, if there is only a grain of truth in the mythology of British prostitution, the oddity of sexual behaviour actually tends to increase with the wealth and social rank of the practitioner.[49]

The fact that most of these practitioners are men also suggests that there is a fundamental imbalance between the sexual needs of men and the emotional behaviour of women. No woman, one feels, would expose herself to the ridicule directed at any users of 'special services' who happen to be found out, and would in any case not need to do so. Since most pornography is also aimed at men rather than at women, there may well be an important difference between male and female sexuality which helps to explain why Sartre treats women so differently from men, both in his fiction and plays and in his philosophical essays. The women in his work do not have projects. When Anny makes the same discovery as Roquentin, she goes off to be the kept woman of a rich Egyptian. She does not set out to write a book, and none of the women in *Les Chemins de la liberté* actually tries to do anything unless forced into a particular line of action by a man. Even if this is an accurate description of the way women tend to behave, the unflattering portrait of women in Sartre's work makes it understandable that Simone de Beauvoir should have become so ardent a feminist. The main argument in *Le Deuxième Sexe* is that the principal defect of male-dominated society had been to refuse women the opportunity of going beyond their own immediate experience towards something which they themselves would like to do. In so far as this is based upon the idea of the all-importance of the project, this is a very Sartrian argument. It is also one which Simone de Beauvoir turns very neatly against the impression which Sartre gives in his fiction, philosophy and plays of the passive way in which his women tend to act.

Discrepancies

'Erostrate' is nevertheless not primarily about sex but about madness. Like 'La Chambre', and like some of the passages in *La Nausée* and *L'Etre et le néant*, it underlines a central dichotomy running through the whole of Sartre's work. On the one hand, there are the various views of what literature ought to be; and, on the other, there is his practice as a writer. It may well be true that he did, in the course of the Second World War, abandon the concept of 'life for art's sake' which Roquentin presents as a solution to his problems, and replace it by the notion of committed literature with which his name is more generally associated. But this did not produce any change in the texture of his prose, his use of imagery, his pessimistic view of human beings, or the various kinds of depressing experience which he chose to describe.

Literature, Sartre argued in his major theoretical text, 'Qu'est-ce que la littérature?' ought to become 'la subjectivité d'une société en révolution permanente'[50] (the self-consciousness of society in permanent revolution). The final aim of art, he maintained, is to take

> ce monde multicolore et concret, avec sa lourdeur, son opacité, ses zones de généralité et son fourmillement d'anecdotes, et ce Mal invincible qui le ronge sans cesse sans jamais pouvoir l'anéantir. L'écrivain le prendra tel quel, tout cru, tout puant, tout suant, tout quotidien, pour le présenter à des libertés sur le fondement d'une liberté.[51] (this multicoloured concrete world, with its weight and opacity, its zones of generality and its multifarious anecdotes, and this invincible evil which gnaws away at it without ever being able to destroy it completely. The writer will take this world as it is, with its rawness, its stink and its sweat, in all its humble details, to present it to other liberties on the basis of one individual liberty.)

Moreover, argues Sartre, 'l'oeuvre d'art, de quelque côté qu'on la prenne, est un acte de confiance dans la liberté du lecteur' (the work of art, however you look at it, is an act of confidence in the freedom of the reader) and the art of prose 'est solidaire du seul régime où la prose garde un sens,: la démocratie'[52] (belongs to the only régime where prose can have a meaning: democracy). The aim of the contributors to *Les Temps Modernes*, whose first number appeared in October 1945, was to 'contribute to bringing about certain changes in society'. Sartre's own declared ambition, like that of the people writing in his review, was to ally himself

> du côté de ceux qui veulent changer à la fois la condition sociale de l'homme et la conception qu'il a de lui-même[53] (with those who want to change both man's condition and the conception he has of himself).

This is all very worthy, as Roquentin observes when flicking through the books L'Autodidacte has been reading in the public library at Bouville and finding in them 'rien que d'élevé'.[54] But it is a far cry from the world of La Nausée, with its sagging café seats and lukewarm beer, and the Corsican librarian spitting into his handkerchiefs and spreading them out to dry on the radiator, and it is just as far from the stories in Le Mur, with their vapid shop girls, wheezing prostitutes, inadequate adolescents, madmen and murderers. If one accepts his own view of how Sartre's concept of literature developed, this is perhaps understandable. In the 1930s, when he was writing La Nausée and Le Mur, he had not yet gone through what he described on a number of occasions as the crucial experience of discovering what he called his own 'historicité'.[55] He had not, in other words, come to appreciate the all-pervasive and all-important nature of politics. But the situation does not change very much with the three and a quarter volumes which Sartre published between 1945 and 1949 of his projected four-volume novel, Les Chemins de la liberté. The plot centres round a projected abortion, and the predominant atmosphere is the same mixture of physical sickness and mental anguish which still strikes so powerful a note in his pre-war fiction. The characters are just as unhappy as everybody is in La Nausée or Le Mur, and human experience is just as sordid, miserable and frustrating.

What Sartre thinks literature should do is make people more aware of the possibilities inseparable from human freedom. What he excels at is the description of how men and women are prevented from achieving their full potential. What sticks in the reader's mind after she or he closes one of Sartre's novels is not the evocation of human beings as free and responsible adults trying to make sense of their experience in a godless universe. It is the details he gives of the sordidness of human life. What we remember is Lulu noting that her husband never changes his underpants often enough, so that they always become slightly but visibly soiled; Hilbert looking at the naked, ample flesh of the prostitute as it bounces up and down at his command and saying to her: 'Tu te rends compte?' (Do you realise?); together with the vision of a pregnant Marcelle Duffet vomiting into the sink, producing a 'une eau mousseuse et trouble' (a foamy, turbid liquid) that looks rather like the beaten white of an egg, clutching at the porcelain rim, smiling wryly as she thinks that it looks rather like sperm, and murmuring to herself 'souvenir d'amour'.[56] There is a good deal to be said for a really depressing read, and Sartre is the best of writers to offer it, more entertaining than Beckett, less complex than Kafka, less repetitious than Kierkegaard, cleverer and nastier than Camus. But traditionally, writers of the left have given a more cheerful account of experience than their colleagues on the right. They have taken the view that happiness was possible, and that it was therefore worthwhile trying to organise society on a fairer and more efficient basis. Right-wing authors, in contrast, especially in France, have tended to argue as Pascal did that since human beings were going to be unhappy anyway, there was no point in trying to carry out any changes in society at all. Sartre offers the curious example of a man who was profoundly pessimistic about human nature, who was very good at describing how unhappy people were, and yet who still believed that society could and should be improved.

4

Les Chemins de la liberté

Characters, Ethics and Plot

Two problems of translation help to define Sartre's intentions and achievements in his most ambitious undertaking as a novelist, the proposed tetralogy, or four-volume work, to which he gave the overall title of *Les Chemins de la liberté*. Should this be rendered, as it was in the 1970 BBC television adaptation, as *The Roads to Freedom*, a title implying a successful arrival, or would a less optimistic version such as *The Paths of Freedom*, with the idea that people following them might not necessarily get anywhere, be more appropriate? Should one retain the original title for the translation of the first volume, *L'Age de raison*, and continue to call it *The Age of Reason*? Or would it be more appropriate to pay attention to what the term 'l'âge de raison' normally means in French, and refer to it as *The Years of Discretion*?

A translation back into French of *The Age of Reason* would give 'le siècle des lumières', the phrase normally used to refer to the eighteenth century *Aufklärung* or Enlightenment. It is very unlikely that this was what Sartre had in mind. The expression 'l'âge de raison' is used to describe the age, round about 7 or 8, at which French children are deemed to be able to distinguish between right and wrong, and are therefore able to take their first communion.[1] In the Anglican Church, which is less optimistic about the speed of human development, this happens when children attain what the prayer book calls the 'years of discretion', sometime in their early teens. Since the main character in *L'Age de raison*, Mathieu Delarue, has constant difficulty in knowing whether he is doing the right thing or not, the French title has ironic connotations which are only partly there in the English title of *The Age of Reason*. Since, however, the 'years of discretion' has a slightly old-fashioned sound in modern English, and is not an expression widely used or recognised, it would be better to stick to the original translation. After all, there is still a wide gap between the way all the characters in the *Age of Reason* behave and the ideals of the Enlightenment.

There is less doubt as to what the second volume of the series, *Le Sursis*, should be called in English. It is *Suspended Sentence*, not *The Reprieve*. The subject matter of this volume is the Munich crisis of September 1938. The outbreak of the Second World War a year later shows that the conflict which Chamberlain had sought to avoid by handing over parts of Czechoslovakia to Hitler had only been postponed. The world had not been granted a permanent reprieve. The disaster which led to over 20 million deaths had merely been put off. There is no problem about the translation of the third volume, *La Mort dans l'âme*. *Iron in the Soul* exactly renders the state of mind of everyone – except, of course, the victorious Germans – who witnessed the defeat of France in the summer of 1940. *La Mort dans l'âme* is a magnificent historical novel, well up to the high standard set by Zola's account of the defeat of the French armies in the 1870 war against Prussia, *La Débâcle*. George Orwell commented in *England, Your England* that the most famous battle poem in English literature – *The Charge of the Light Brigade* – is about a cavalry charge that went the wrong way. There is a touch of irony in the fact that the two most famous novels about warfare in the adopted language of Napoleon 1 – *La Débâcle* and *Le Sursis* – should be about crushing defeats.

The actual events in *Les Chemins de la liberté* suggest that it would be better to translate the whole title as *The Paths of Freedom* rather than *The Roads to Freedom*. The more neutral version echoes the line in Gray's *Elegy in a Country Churchyard* that 'Paths of Glory lead but to the grave' and emphasises the fact that nobody in the novel succeeds in transforming the potential freedom which all human beings possess into a more positive and active form. For Sartre, this is achieved only by those who deliberately commit themselves politically, and do so in such a way as to give their fellow human beings greater political freedom. In his original concept, Mathieu Delarue was to do this through his activity in the resistance movement. However, the impression left by *La Mort dans l'âme* is that Mathieu is killed in the battle of France in 1940, and Sartre completed and published only two episodes of the proposed fourth volume, *La Dernière Chance*. These appeared in the November and December 1949 numbers of *Les Temps Modernes* under the title of 'Drôle d'amitié' (Strange Friendship). Neither of them tells us anything about any of the characters in the earlier volumes except for the Communist, Brunet, and both concentrate on what he saw as his betrayal by the Nazi-Soviet pact of 23 August 1939.

The problem created for men and women of the left in the 1940s by the foreign policy of the Soviet Union was one of the major factors which prevented Sartre from finishing *La Dernière Chance*. This heightens the interest of *Les Chemins de la liberté* as an unconscious as well as a conscious account of the social and political atmosphere of the 1930s and 1940s, and in this respect all three volumes, like *La Dernière Chance*, have the same double interest as *La Nausée* and *Le Mur*. They are what they set out to be, a series of very deliberate attempts to write philosophical novels about mid-twentieth-century French society. But at the same time, by the information they.unconsciously contain about what Sartre thought himself, and how he expected his readership to respond, they are something more: a testimony about how men and women of the left thought it was axiomatic to see the world in the period between the coming to power of Hitler in 1933 and the outbreak of the Cold War. Like his other fiction, and like a number of his plays, the volumes in *Les Chemins de la liberté* are often all the more interesting if looked at in a framework which Sartre did not wholly understand, and which he would have rejected on political grounds if he had been able to do so. Like a number of other writers, Sartre was sometimes at his best when he did not quite know what he was doing.

All books offer the same kind of double interest. They are all, at one and the same time, a conscious attempt to make the reader react in a particular way, and the unconscious expression of the attitudes which are so much a part of the way the author sees the world that he often does not even know they exist. This study of Sartre tries first and foremost to explain why he was so interesting a writer.

But it cannot avoid also being the expression of the self-confidence in his own culture which enables an elderly, sceptically-minded member of the English middle class to write about a foreign author, and show how he went wrong. Any historian interested in how the English middle class saw the world in the 1990s will find in the conscious and unconscious assumptions governing this study of Sartre the substance of a useful footnote. For just as there were aspects of Sartre's books of which he was not always entirely conscious, the same is true of mine.

Throughout his career as a political writer, which he saw as beginning with the impact on him of the Second World War, Sartre saw the only way to social progress as lying in some kind of alliance with the Communist Party. This stemmed from the fact that the Communist Party, in the France of the mid-twentieth century, was the only one to receive the support of the organised French working class. It was also because Sartre thought – like many other people at the time – that the only desirable society was one in which the means of production, distribution and exchange would cease to be owned by individuals and became instead the property of the whole community. Since the aim of the Party was to bring about just such a society, it enjoyed, in the eyes of Sartre and of those who thought like him, an immensely privileged position. This means that the idea running through the whole of *Les Chemins de la liberté* is that commitment means joining the Communist Party. Nobody maintained that the Party was perfect, and many joined for the same reasons for which Sartre offered it his support in the 1950s: because they thought they could make it into a more democratic organisation, and France into a more egalitarian society. There also seemed to be no other party in France which offered anything like the same chance of bringing about a classless society.

The hindsights of the 1990s suggest that Sartre was wrong to have the faith he did in the ability of socialism to bring about a fundamental improvement in human society, and seriously misled in the hopes he placed in the French Communist Party. He did not set out to illustrate how deep the illusion from which he was suffering was, and would have vigorously rejected any suggestion that it was an illusion. What *Les Chemins de la liberté* show is how deeply rooted this illusion was, and their value as an historical novel is all the greater precisely because this demonstration was not deliberate. For Sartre, as for his admirers, it went without saying that liberal democracy was a snare and a delusion; that a system based even partly on private enterprise could do nothing but exploit and oppress the working class; and that, as he wrote in his essay 'Matérialisme and revolution', in 1947:

Je sais qu'il n'y a pas d'autre salut pour l'homme que la libération de la classe ouvrière: je le sais avant d'être matérialiste et sur la simple inspection des faits; je sais que les intérêts de l'esprit sont avec le prolétariat.[2] (I know that there is no salvation for man except in the liberation of the working class: I know this before accepting materialism, simply by looking at the facts. I know that the interests of the mind are on the side of the proletariat.)

This may still be true, however much the affluent societies of the industrialised West may now offer a large number of their citizens a standard of living as yet unattained by any socialist society, and inconceivable when Sartre wrote these words. The fact remains that the Marxism which Sartre considered to be, as he put it in 1957,

> la philosophie de notre temps ... indépassable parce que les circonstances qui l'ont engendrée ne sont pas encore dépassées[3] (the philosophy of our time, one which we cannot go beyond because we have not gone beyond the circumstances which gave it birth)

has not proved a successful basis for organising a modern society. This gives the presupposition about the decline of capitalism and its inevitable replacement by socialism which runs through *Les Chemins de la liberté* – as it does through all Sartre's other work – a kind of old-world charm, akin to the presuppositions about class running through Victorian fiction.

Novelists have always been realistic in two ways: on the one hand, they have consciously told their readers what they thought that the society of their time was like; but at the same time, they have provided details about how people thought, felt and acted which they regarded as so natural as to be mentioned without comment. The very title of the first volume of Galsworthy's *The Forsyte Saga*, for example, speaks volumes about the attitude of even the richest members of the upper-middle class in late Victorian England towards housing. Soames Forsyte is regarded as highly eccentric by other people – and very enterprising by himself – by having his own house built and thus becoming 'A Man of Property'. At a time like ours, when it has become the norm to own one's house, it is people who content themselves, as most of the Forsytes did, with rented property, who are seen as very odd. Now that the virtually universal assumption is that the way to economic prosperity lies through a free market economy, and that the newspapers describe how the Soviet Union is opening not only a McDonalds' but a Pizza Hut and a Stock Exchange as well, the presuppositions running through Sartre's work speak volumes to the modern reader; but in a way that Sartre never intended.

The half million or so words which make up *L'Age de raison*, *Le Sursis*, *La Mort dans l'âme* and 'Drôle d'amitié' also have another advantage: they make you realise what an entertaining novelist Sartre could be when the mood was on him, and regret the problems which prevented him not only from bringing his tetralogy to an end but also from writing any other novels.

In 'Qu'est-ce que la littérature?' Sartre wrote with amusing hostility about the contract linking the nineteenth-century, bourgeois writer to his public. In return for the money which they paid him by buying his books, argues Sartre, such a writer offered his readers entertainment, amusement, and the occasional insight into human behaviour. It is hard to see what is wrong with this, and a great pity that Sartre's own vision of the author's calling prevented him from accepting a similar contract with his readers. The talent which runs through *Les Chemins de la liberté* shows what an enviable gift he had to amuse and entertain, but which he despised to the point where he simply could not be bothered to fulfil the basic duty which any novelist owes his readers: that of telling them what happened next, and how it all ended.

In this respect, as I shall argue in more detail later on, it does seem that Sartre was telling the truth when he talked about the peculiar vision which his extraordinary upbringing gave him of the essentially religious nature of literature. His failure to finish *Les Chemins de la liberté* reinforces the case for seeing the whole of his work as a kind of intellectual biography, a working out of the problems about the nature of literature to which, like a 7-year-old child being told about the sexual problems of his divorced parents, he was introduced at an unnecessarily early age. To the reader coming to fiction in search of the insights which it has traditionally offered into human behaviour, this autobiographical aspect of his work narrows rather than widens Sartre's appeal. Everybody is interested in other people, and what literature has to tell us about them. Reflections on the nature of literature, in contrast, have a minority appeal.

Another reason why Sartre's failure to complete *Les Chemins de la liberté* is so unfortunate is that it denies the reader the opportunity of seeing how Mathieu Delarue redeems himself in the final volume, and consequently how it might be possible to translate the title as *The Roads to Freedom*. In the first and second volumes, Mathieu is very much what Sartre referred to as 'un pauvre sire',[4] a bit of a drip. Like Sartre himself at the time when the first volume was written, between 1938 and 1940, Mathieu teaches philosophy in one of the major lycées. The custom of requiring French girls and boys to study philosophy as part of the *baccaulauréat*, the examination which they take at 18 and which qualifies them for direct entry into a university, goes back to the early nineteenth century, and is still in existence. All teachers responsible for pupils over the age of 11 are referred to as *professeurs*, and it is a mistake to talk about Mathieu as though he taught in a university. Mathieu nevertheless has a good deal in common with some of the university teachers in the novels of Malcolm Bradbury or David Lodge: he has a number of sexual problems, is bad at managing his money, and can neither make up his mind about what he ought to do nor put any decision into effect once he has made it. He has not, in other words, really reached 'l'âge de raison'. Mathieu Delarue is a man who is growing old without growing up.

All these failings are highlighted by the crisis which sets the action of the novel in motion. This happens in the first chapter when his mistress, Marcelle Duffet, tells him that she is pregnant. Mathieu has been clumsy in his use of *coitus interruptus* – he imagines her as thinking to herself that 'il s'était laissé aller en moi comme un gosse qui fait dans les draps'[5] (he let himself come inside me like a boy having a wet dream) – so that what the couple have been trying to avoid since the liaison began seven years earlier has finally happened. Mathieu does not beat about the bush. He immediately proposes an abortion, and Marcelle, with a readiness later revealed as misleading, agrees. This aspect of the novel caused some scandal when *L'Age de raison*, originally completed in 1940, was finally published in October 1945, and laid Sartre open to the taunt by François Mauriac about being 'un romancier célibataire dont les personnages sont si curieusement obsédés de l'abortion'[6] (a bachelor novelist whose characters have so strange an obsession with abortion). What also seems strange is that a man in his early thirties, as Mathieu is, and who earns his living by teaching the discipline which Kant defined as trying to answer the three questions What can I know? What should I do? What dare I hope? does not even stop to consider the moral issues raised by abortion. Mathieu certainly knows what he is doing, and his reflections on Marcelle's pregnancy are an unexpected bonus in a book written by a man whose other work shows such little sympathy with procreation:

On aurait dit qu'il y avait quelque part un enfant tout fait qui attendait l'heure de bondir de ce côté-ci du décor, sous ce soleil, et que Mathieu lui barrait le passage. En fait, c'était à peu près ca: il y avait tout un petit homme pensif et chaffouin, menteur et douloureux, avec une peau blanche, de larges oreilles et des grains de beauté, avec une poignée de signes distinctifs comme on en met sur les passeports, un petit homme qui ne courrait jamais dans les rues, un pied dans le trottoir et l'autre dans le ruisseau; il y avait des yeux, une paire d'yeux verts comme ceux de Mathieu ou noirs comme ceux de Marcelle qui ne verraient jamais les cieux glauques de l'hiver, ni la mer, ni jamais aucun visage, il y avait des mains qui ne toucheraient jamais la neige, ni la chair des femmes, ni l'écorce des arbres: il y avait une image du monde, sanglante, lumineuse, maussade, passionnée, sinistre, pleine d'espoirs, une image peuplée de jardins et de maisons, de grandes filles douces et d'insectes horribles, qu'on allait faire éclater d'un coup d'épingle, comme un ballon du Louvre.[7] (You would have said that there was a child already in existence somewhere, waiting to leap into life and that Mathieu was stopping him. And, in fact, that was the case: there was a little man, thoughtful and weasel faced, devious and glum, capable of suffering, who would never run along in the street with one foot on the pavement and the other in the gutter; that there were eyes, a pair of green eyes like Mathieu's or dark eyes like Marcelle's, which would never see the vitreous skies of winter, never see the sea or anybody's face, that there were hands which would never touch snow, or women's flesh, or the bark of trees, that there was a vision of the world, full of blood and light, sullen, passionate, gloomy, overflowing with hope, a vision of the world peopled with gardens and houses, with tall, gentle girls and terrifying insects, and which was going to be pierced by a pin, like a toy balloon.)

Although the text of *Les Mots* dismisses Sartre's father with the remark that he had 'versé les quelques gouttes de sperme qui font le prix ordinaire d'un enfant' (spilt the few drops of sperm necessary to produce a child), parts of his work are shot through with a longing for a father-son relationship which is as intense as the feelings which bring Stephen Daedalus and Mr Bloom together in *Ulysses*. In *Les Mains Sales*, Hugo is in search of a new, political father to replace the biological one he has rejected, and finds him in Hoederer, who seems equally happy in turn to treat Hugo as an adopted son. This adds to the atmosphere of the play as a personal as well as a political tragedy, while in *Les Séquestrés d'Altona*, the relationship between Franz and his father produces the most moving scenes in the play.[8] *L'Age de raison* nevertheless stops short before showing Mathieu as a man who might later come to regret what he is proposing to do. Mathieu's problems are strictly financial ones, and it is these and these alone which preoccupy him.

Abortion was illegal in the France of 1938, the year in which the action of *L'Age de raison* is taking place, and remained so until 1974. But it was always possible to find what was ironically referred to as 'une faiseuse d'anges', and Simone de Beauvoir defended the plot of *L'Age de raison* against accusations of immorality on the grounds that Sartre was merely talking about the kind of things that happened. In 1938, according to the figures she quoted, there were almost as many abortions in France as there were live births – about half a million – and one of the arguments in the campaign for the legalisation of abortion which she led in the 1970s was that since women were going to have abortions anyway, these might as well be carried out under hygienic conditions. But illegal abortions were expensive, and in order to save Marcelle from going to some back-street practitioner, Mathieu has to find 4000 francs. This corresponded, in 1938, to roughly six weeks' salary for a *professeur agrégé de l'Université*, the rank that Mathieu, like the Sartre of 1938, held in the teaching hierarchy, and is not therefore all that large a sum. But although Mathieu has been teaching for some years, he has no savings and can find nobody prepared to lend him the money. It is his quest for the 4000 francs which provides the central story line for *L'Age de raison*, and it is impossible to read the novel without sympathising on every page with his predicament. At the same time, it is equally impossible not to wish that Sartre had refrained from giving the name Delarue, with its implications of Everyman, to somebody quite so incapable of knowing what he wants or of doing anything to get it.

Mathieu has other problems apart from the need to find the money before the specialist, a German Jewish refugee found for him by his friend Sarah, leaves for America. He is obsessed with Ivich – pronounced Ivik – Serguine, the sister of one of his ex-pupils, Boris, and Sartre echoes the experience of every man over 25 who has tried to have anything to do with a girl of 18 when he notes: 'Si peu de choses intéressaient Ivich'[9] (so few things

interested Ivich). It is a remark comparable in accuracy to Holden
Cauldfield's observation, in *Catcher in the Rye*, that in every school
he had ever been to, 'the athletic bastards always stuck together', or
to the comment by Shelly Thomas in Tom Wolfe's *The Bonfire of the
Vanities* that in New York, 'a girl always has to listen to two or three
hours on My Career first'. But Ivich also has other reasons apart
from the age gap for refusing to be interested by anything that
Mathieu can offer. She is worried by the idea that she has almost
certaily failed the *Physique Chimie Biologie* examination which she
has to pass if she is to carry on at medical school. If she fails, she will
have to go back to live at home with her parents in Laon, a town
that Sartre learned to dislike when he taught there between 1937
and 1939.

Ivich is not, as Marcelle observes with the perception often
shown by older women when talking about the girls whom they
suspect their man of fancying, particularly suited to a medical
career, since she hates all reminders that people have bodies and
will almost certainly faint when she sees her first operation.
Whether intentionally or not, Sartre creates in Ivich one of the
most convincingly disagreeable adolescents in twentieth-century
literature – *ce qui n'est pas peu dire*; quite an achievement in itself – so
much so that it is hard to resist the thought that she rather deserves
the fate she brings upon herself by her behaviour at the time of the
Munich crisis. Ivich is so convinced that war is inevitable, and that it
will destroy civilisation completely, that she goes to bed with a
young man, Georges Sturel, who has been urging her to do so for
some time. She gets pregnant, has a miscarriage, and is last seen in
the expensive, chauffeur-driven motor car of the Sturel family,
complaining of how boring her mother-in-law is, and totally
different from the beautiful, unpredictable young girl whom
Mathieu saw as the incarnation of his liberty.

It is through Ivich that Mathieu is linked to a set of characters
markedly different from his respectable, middle-class brother
Jacques, the rather pi and poker-faced Communist Brunet, and the
passive, leech-like Marcelle. Boris Serguine is unenthusiastically
having an affair with an ageing night-club singer, Lola Montero,
who is the only character in *Les Chemins de la liberté* whom the
reader actually sees working. Boris is fond of Lola, since he finds
the company of all older people restful and reassuring, but dislikes
having to sleep with her. Having sex always makes him lose
consciousness, something which he detests. In *Le Sursis*, he too

misinterprets what is going to happen as a result of Hitler's threats against Czechoslovakia, and signs on for three years in the army. When, in *La Mort dans l'âme*, he comes back to Lola with all the enthusiasm for sex traditional in members of the brutal and licentious soldiery, she has discovered that she has developed cancer of the womb, and can only think nostalgically of how marvellous all this passion would have been if it had happened a year ago. The only characters in Sartre's work who enjoy making love are the two honest proletarians, Maurice Tailleur and his wife Zézette, who come in as bit-part players in the recreation of the atmosphere of the Munich crisis in *Le Sursis*. The homosexual, Daniel Sereno, is particularly disgusted by his own sexual tastes, and the reader first meets him in a very powerfully written scene in which Daniel, in what proves an unsuccessful attempt to punish himself for what he is, tries to drown the beautiful cats which are the only beings of which he is really fond. This self-detestation makes Daniel into one of the most interesting characters in the novel, and provides the *dénouement* which brings *L'Age de raison* to its melodramatic end.

Boris Serguine is an agreeable young man who exercises an understandable fascination on everybody he meets, especially Daniel, who is introduced to him by Mathieu. Although it later transpires that Mathieu does not know that Daniel is a homosexual, Daniel is convinced that Mathieu warns all his pupils against having anything to do with him. When Daniel happens to meet Boris in a bookshop in the Latin quarter, he consequently interprets the young man's refusal to come and have a drink with him as evidence of Mathieu's hostility, and determines to have his revenge. In fact, he completely misinterprets the situation. Boris likes the verbal fencing involved in having a conversation with Daniel, and would be very happy to spend time with him if it were not for an urgent appointment which he has made with himself. Boris goes in for shoplifting, and has already acquired an impressive collection of stolen objects including seventeen toothbrushes, a score of ashtrays, a compass, a poker and a darning egg. He does not steal for profit, for that would be very vulgar, and it is unlikely in this respect that he is based on Jean Genet, the homosexual thief whom Sartre did not meet until May 1944. A more likely source, unless Sartre had a pupil on whose peccadilloes he smiled with as much tolerance as Mathieu does on those of Boris, is Gide's 1926 novel *Les Faux Monnayeurs* (*The Coiners*), which also has a group of schoolboys who go around stealing books. At the moment when Daniel comes across him, Boris is just about to steal a dictionary of French slang, and has promised himself that he will do so before the bookshop closes that evening. In an action whose consequences he could not possibly foresee, he tells Daniel that he has an urgent appointment, thus snubbing him in a way that confirms Daniel in his suspicions of Mathieu's behaviour and strengthens his appetite for revenge.

For some little time, Daniel has been in the habit of going to see Marcelle Duffet in secret. He enjoys her company, and delights in exercising his charms on Marcelle's widowed mother, who runs true to form as a lady of mature years in finding Daniel a delightful and exquisitely polite young man. Daniel knows that Marcelle is pregnant, since Mathieu has asked him to lend him the 4000 francs, and Daniel, in an act of bitchiness inspired by the feelings of self-disgust which he has for himself for failing to drown his cats, coupled with a particularly bad hangover, has refused. His sur-name of Sereno is a deliberate misnomer. Like the lesbian Iñes Serrano in *Huis Clos*, he is anything but at ease with himself. He nevertheless has a keener awareness of what makes people tick than either Mathieu or Brunet, and successfully manoeuvres events so as to produce the result which best fits what he thinks he needs.

When Mathieu tells him that Marcelle is pregnant, Daniel's reaction reflects the same horror for the constant burgeoning of biological life which one could imagine Roquentin or Paul Hilbert as having:

> Ça pisse du sang tous les mois lunaires, et c'est prolifique comme des raies par-dessus le marché[10] (The creatures piss blood every twenty-eight days, and breed like fishes into the bargain).

Daniel's actions lead to Marcelle being able to keep the child, which was what she had wanted to do all along. Daniel hits upon what he sees as a good way of getting his own back on Mathieu, and one which will also enable him to satisfy his own rather unusual psychological needs. Neither he nor anybody else in the novel is any more interested than Mathieu in the moral aspects of abortion. Mathieu eventually finds the 4000 francs by stealing them from Lola, but when he brings them triumphantly to Marcelle, it is to discover that she has been persuaded by Daniel to think that he,

Mathieu, has changed his mind about the abortion and is going to
marry her. Mathieu throws the money on the bed, and goes back to
his apartment, where Boris and Ivich are waiting for him. Lola
arrives, convinced that it is Boris who has stolen the money, and is
persuaded to think otherwise only when Daniel arrives and drama-
tically hands her the banknotes. He and Mathieu are left alone for
Daniel to release his bombshell: he, Daniel, is going to marry
Marcelle, from whom he has therefore just taken the 4000 francs,
and they are going to keep the child. Daniel adds to Mathieu's
surprise by telling him that although he is a homosexual, he
intends to carry out his marital duties to the full. Oddly enough,
although he has known him for years, Mathieu has never suspected
that Daniel was a queer, and a self-tormenting one at that, and does
not seem to find much consolation in Daniel's reminder of the
well-known fact that homosexuals make excellent husbands. Instead, in a remark which seems almost a parody of the general
atmosphere of *L'Age de raison*, he thinks to himself:

> Et puis, ça lui semblait si naturel, si normal: il était un salaud,
> Daniel était un pédéraste, c'était dans l'ordre des choses.[11]
> (Everything seemed so natural, so normal. He was a selfish
> bastard, Daniel was as queer as a coot, it was just the way things
> are.)

He has, he reflects, finally grown up:

> Il bâilla: il avait fini sa journée, il en avait fini de sa jeunesse. Déjà
> des morales éprouvées lui proposaient discrètement leurs ser-
> vices: il y avait l'épicurisme désabusé, l'indulgence souriante, la
> résignation, l'esprit de sérieux, le stoïcisme, tout ce qui permet de
> déguster minute par minute une vie ratée. Il ôta son veston, il se
> mit à dénouer sa cravate. Il se répétait en bâillant: 'C'est vrai,
> c'est tout de même vrai: j'ai l'âge de raison'.[12] (He yawned: he
> had ended his day's work, his youth was over. Already well-tried
> moral systems were coming to offer their help. There was
> disillusioned Epicureanism, smiling tolerance, resignation, a
> serious belief in moral principles, stoicism, everything which
> enables a man to savour, minute by minute, the fact that his life
> has been a failure. He took off his jacket and began to undo his
> tie. He yawned again and repeated: 'It's true, it's really true. It's
> what they call the years of discretion.)

Identity, Choice and Politics

One sometimes has the impression, on reading the early Sartre, that he is deliberately setting out to prove his versatility. *L'Age de raison* is very obviously the work of the same man who wrote *La Nausée*. Mathieu, thinking about himself, reaches exactly the same conclusions as Roquentin:

> Je suis là, je me déguste, je sens le vieux goût de sang et d'eau ferrugineuse, mon goût, je suis mon propre goût, j'existe: exister, c'est ça: se boire sans soif.[13] (I'm here, I savour myself, I feel the old taste of blood and rusty water which is my own taste. I am my taste, I exist. That is what existence is: drinking yourself without being thirsty.)

At the same time, the careful plotting and the varied, imaginative characterisation of *L'Age de raison* offer a marked and welcome contrast to the use of the introspective, diary form of *La Nausée*, making Sartre the Galsworthy of the French philosophical novel in his mastery of the art of story telling as well as in the unconscious light which he casts upon the social realities of his time. As in *The Forsyte Saga*, you read on because you want to know what is going to happen next. You admire the way it all fits together, and envy the skill of a writer so apparently in control of his material. But at the same time, both Sartre and Galsworthy offer the additional satisfaction of a character who takes over the book in a way that the author almost certainly had not originally intended. Galsworthy thought that Soames Forsyte was an unattractive character, and that the reader ought to admire his sensitive wife Irene, her lover, the architect Bosinney, and the man she eventually marries, Soames's cousin Jolyon. As the novel develops, however, Soames becomes by far the most interesting character, Bosinney is revealed as a complete incompetent who cannot even arrive at a correct costing for the house which he has designed, Irene becomes unbearably priggish, and Jolyon an agreeable nonentity tied to his wife's apron-strings.

Something rather like this happens in *L'Age de raison*, though in a way which does not lead to quite such a gap between intentions and achievement as in Galsworthy. Mathieu is obviously the character who embodies Sartre's own preoccupations and world view, especially in the way he illustrates the Sartrian concept of the absence of fixed moral values. It is easy for the comfortably-situated bourgeois reader to say that Mathieu had a clear duty to marry Marcelle, and to give up a private freedom which has become increasingly empty and formal. It is just as easy for Brunet to tell Mathieu that he ought to join the Communist Party, and to do so not for the Party's sake but for his own. Mathieu is perfectly aware that one concept of duty would require him to marry Marcelle. But he knows that there is no compulsion upon him to choose that concept of duty rather than another. In so far as he realises that it is he and he alone who has to take that decision, and that the death of God means the disappearance of rock-hard moral values that can dictate his conduct to him, he is indeed a twentieth-century Everyman. He may not be very competent in the practical details of everyday living, but he is more honest with himself than any of the other characters in the book. They live by a self-vision, and a concept of where their interest lies, which may make them more able to act but which also makes them more limited.

Thus Daniel, who is as tormented as Mathieu about the kind of person that he really is, plays a decisive role in the plot precisely because he has hit upon a way which he thinks will provide some kind of solution to his problems. It is not one that is going to make him happier, though it does provide some very pleasant moments for Marcelle. The real reason why Daniel marries Marcelle is to remind himself, by the torment of living with a heavily pregnant woman, of just how much he hates being a homosexual. This, since Daniel is a very Sartrian character, will enable him to come a little closer to his ambition to 'être pédéraste comme le chêne est chêne'[14] (be a homosexual as an oak-tree is an oak-tree). Like all the characters in Sartre's work who have come to an understanding of what it means to be free, Daniel suffers acutely from the fact that he can never coincide exactly with what he is. When Humpty-Dumpty said to Alice 'Explain yourself, child', and she replied, 'I can't, you see, I'm not quite myself to-day' she was anticipating one of the reasons why *L'Etre et le néant* presents human beings as doomed to perpetual frustration. Because I am always aware of myself, or can very soon become so by a quick flick of the mind, I am always doomed to stand a little apart from myself. It is no good telling me to 'Be myself'. There isn't a real self for me to be. Whenever I try to be it, I find one of two things: either that I am not quite the same person that I was yesterday; or that what I am most aware of is my freedom to become a different kind of person.

Daniel is very conscious of how hard it is for him to be exactly what he is, and the means he chooses is the torment which he inflicts upon himself. For him, his marriage to Marcelle has two advantages: since it will be very hard for him to escape from the role of loving husband that this marriage requires him to play, it will make him so perpetually aware of his homosexuality that he will, as it were, almost be able to hold it in the palm of his hand. Certain Christians used to do the same by wearing a hair shirt to remind themselves of their sins. Pascal even had a leather belt specially made for him, with small spikes pointing inwards. When he realised that he was acquiring too good a conceit of himself by winning an argument in mathematics or theology, he would give himself a sharp dig in the ribs. It is not quite the same as Daniel marrying Marcelle in order to ensure that the spectacle of her burgeoning fertility will inspire him with the constant self-awareness which we all derive from self-disgust, but it is near enough to show the emotional continuity between Christian and atheistic existentialism.

At the same time as it provides this parallel, it is also a reminder of a basic tenet of all existentialist thinkers: that the human condition reveals itself to us most clearly not when we are playing cricket, walking the dog or enjoying a glass of claret, but when we are in the extreme situations of loneliness, suffering and despair. It is this aspect of existentialism which helps to explain why it should have enjoyed such a vogue in the middle years of the twentieth century. Human beings do not always want to run away from an awareness of their fate. They often want to become more conscious of what is happening so that they can better understand both the events and themselves. At a particularly gloomy moment in world history, three French writers added to the conscious misery of nations by providing just this awareness. They were André Malraux, Albert Camus and Jean-Paul Sartre. The French critic Pierre de Boisdeffre[15] summed up a widely held opinion in the 1940s and 1950s when he described them as 'des écrivains de la condition humaine' (writers concerned with man's fate). In so far as the human condition is, for North Americans and Western Europeans at any rate, not quite so obviously a source of anguish and despair as it was in the middle of the twentieth century, each of these three writers – like lesser authors such as Antoine de Saint-Exupéry – survives by his literary talent rather than his subject matter, and by the value of his works as historical documents rather than as books which tell the truth about the human condition for all time.

While there is no record of Pascal, often seen by French critics as the father of 'la littérature de la condition humaine', ever thinking about sex, there are other resemblances between him and Daniel which help to explain why Daniel tends to steal the show in *L'Age de raison*. Pascal was very much at home in the real world. He was the first man to wear a wrist watch, the first to think up the idea of a regular public transport system, and one of the first to help lay the foundations of modern science by carrying out the experiment which led to the invention of the barometer. When his father had difficulty, in his role of tax-collector, in working out how much the inhabitants of Rouen owed the royal treasury, Pascal helped him by designing the 'machine arithmétique', the ancestor of the modern computer. Daniel is not up to this level, in spite of his ability to make money on the Paris Stock Exchange in June 1938, an achievement requiring more than native wit. He is nevertheless very different from Mathieu, and in an odd way a more attractive and interesting character. He knows what he wants to do, and is successful at doing it.

Thus unlike Mathieu, whose intellectual activity seems to be limited to an abandoned article on Stendhal, Daniel has a well-stocked library, and there is no reason to disbelieve his remark to the young Philippe Grésigne, in *La Mort dans l'âme*, that he is an expert swimmer and lifesaver. Neither is his remark to Mathieu that 'les pédérastes ont toujours fait d'excellents maris, c'est connu'[16] a mere boutade. The brief glimpses of the couple in *Le Sursis* show him making Marcelle very happy by his constant solicitude for her welfare. Had Sartre completed the tetralogy, Daniel was destined to have almost as glorious a death as Mathieu, whose escape from apparent death in his last stand against the Germans at the village of Padoux in June 1940 was to be followed by heroic activity in the resistance movement.

The defeat of France in 1940 sees Daniel in Paris. Marcelle has given birth to a child whose name and sex remain unknown, and is safely looking after it a long way from the war, in the Pyrenees. 'Marcelle torche son môme à Dax'[17] (Marcelle is wiping her baby's bottom in Dax) is how Daniel puts it, perhaps reflecting how Sartre would have thought of such an event. Daniel walks triumphantly through the deserted streets, glorying in the overthrow of the self-confident, moralistic society which had condemned him for not adhering to its heterosexual norms, delighting in the spectacle of the handsome, blond German soldiers who have gone through the French army like a knife through butter, and waiting enthusiastically for them to hoist the flag of victorious evil on all the public buildings in Paris. Then, as he sees the slender figure of a young man leaning over the pont de Solférino, looking into the Seine, his homosexual rapture reaches new heights.

The characters who inhabit the world of *Les Chemins de la liberté* were not all entirely invented, any more than those in *La Nausée* were. Anny, for example, was partly modelled on Sartre's first mistress, Simone Jolivet, who spent some time as a professional actress and delighted in transposing all the complexities of her stage roles into real life.[18] Mathieu, in spite of his height and broad shoulders, is Sartre himself. Brunet is at least partly modelled on Sartre's closest friend, the Communist journalist and writer Paul Nizan; a fact which becomes important in sections of the uncompleted fourth volume. The original for Ivich was Wanda Kosakiewicz, a close friend of Sartre and Simone de Beauvoir. She later became an actress under the stage name of Marie Olivier, and took the lead in a number of Sartre's plays. *L'Age de raison* is dedicated to her. Boris is modelled on the novelist Jacques-Laurent Bost, a former pupil of Sartre's, and Daniel on another of his friends, Marc Zuorro, who becomes much more intriguing between the covers of a book than he ever seems to have been in real life.

The young Philippe Grésigne, who makes his first appearance in *Le Sursis*, and whose misfortunes provide an important minor theme in *La Mort dans l'âme*, has a more literary origin. Like Maurice Spandrell in Aldous Huxley's *Point Counter Point*, he is based upon the poet Baudelaire. Philippe is a less interesting and much less vigorous version of the author of *Les Fleurs de Mal* than Maurice Spandrell, who carries the hatred of militarism inspired in him by his stepfather to the point of plotting the successful murder of a would-be military dictator, Everard Webley. Philippe does not take his resentment against his widowed mother's second husband, General Lacaze, any further than an unsuccessful attempt to avoid military service on vaguely pacifist grounds. Sartre's attack on Baudelaire for not having had the courage to convert his rebellion against bourgeois conventions into a genuine political revolution is much more convincingly articulated in the long essay which he published on him in 1946.

Philippe Grésigne's main function in *Le Sursis* is to provide a vehicle for Sartre's general dislike of pacifism, and to enable

Mathieu to spend his last night in Paris with Irène, a girl he meets before going off to join the army in September 1938. Irène finds Mathieu very attractive, and suggests they go to bed together. As they are about to make love, she asks him if she should take precautions. Rather surprisingly, in the light of what has happened between him and Marcelle, he says 'Je ne suis pas un salaud'[19] (perhaps best translated as 'Trust me. I'm a gentleman') and tells her not to bother. *La Mort dans l'âme*, Philippe is again there in a subsidiary role, this time to provide a further opportunity for Daniel's character to be more fully developed. After the encounter on the bridge, Daniel follows him through the streets of Paris, enjoying for its own sake the 'longue patience pédérastique'[20] which he has learned to practise on so many other occasions, until he finally captures his prey.

The text of *La Mort dans l'âme* gives only a hint of what could have been one of the best studies of a homosexual relationship in the French novel. Daniel is as complex a character as Proust's Baron de Charlus, as intriguing a creation as l'oncle Alexandre in Michel Tournier's *Les Météores*, and a good deal more interesting than l'oncle Edouard in Gide's *Les Faux Monnayeurs*. Either because the rules of censorship and good taste did not allow Gide to give full vent to his homosexual imagination, or because he did not want to hurt his wife Madeleine's feelings by offering too obvious a self-portrait to his readers, l'oncle Edouard never really comes to life for what he is. Neither Sartre nor Tournier had the same reasons to be as inhibited as Gide, and another reason for regretting Sartre's failure or refusal to finish *Les Chemins de la liberté* is that this prevented the reader from finding out how the meeting between Daniel and Philippe changed both of them. A close relationship clearly developed, which was not wholly sexual. The reader of *La Mort dans l'âme* last sees Daniel preparing to initiate Philippe into the 'dérèglement systématique de tous les sens' which Rimbaud considered as necessary prelude to becoming a poet. This would have made an interesting read in itself, especially since it would have accompanied what Sartre seems to have seen as the logical development of Daniel's homosexuality: the total rejection of all conventional moral norms.

Sartre is, in this respect, at some distance from the aims of the Gay Liberation Movement, just as he does not seem, in his published work at any rate, to have been particularly sympathetic to women. We find out even less about what happens to Marcelle,

Lola and Ivich than we do about the further adventures of
Mathieu, Daniel or Boris, and Sartre's proposed treatment of
Daniel's behaviour during the Occupation implies a curiously
old-fashioned attitude both to women and to homosexuality. On a
number of occasions, Sartre presented the relationship of the
French collaborator to the victorious Germans as that of the
adoring and masochistic woman to the male who has just brutally
raped her. Daniel's behaviour during the Occupation was meant to
illustrate this by bringing out the essentially feminine nature of
homosexual desire, and it is, for once, fortunate for Sartre's
reputation as a novelist that he did not complete this aspect of *Les
Chemins de la liberté*. There was no hint of this rather odd view of
homosexuals as essentially feminine to mar the earlier presentation
of Daniel. The need for him to collaborate is nevertheless necessary
to the plot.

The emotional intensity of Daniel's relationship with Philippe
can be judged by the ending of the novel which Simone de
Beauvoir reports Sartre as having had in mind. In order to prove
to himself that he is not a coward, and to show Daniel that he is not
entirely his creature, Philippe joins the resistance movement. He is
arrested in a general round-up of suspects in the Latin quarter,
and shot. Daniel, crazed with grief, takes one of the bombs that
Philippe has secreted in their apartment, and profits from his
contacts with the occupying authorities to go to a meeting of
high-ranking German officials. There, he commits a rather spec-
tacular act of hara-kiri, blowing himself and the German *Komman-
datura* up at the same time. It is an incident which underlines how
Sartre's imagination, like that of a number of literary men, is easily
attracted by violence, but which might perhaps, had it been
described in detail, have justified calling the tetralogy *The Roads to
Freedom*. If you were interested in making people more free
politically, blowing up Germans in occupied Paris was a very good
thing. As de Gaulle observed in one of his broadcasts, if the
Germans wanted to avoid being killed, all they needed to do was
stay at home.

The kind of liberty implied by Daniel's reaction was not, however, quite what Sartre had in mind when he chose the title of *Les
Chemins de la liberté*. The same is true of Mathieu's 'last man, last
round' defence against the German army in *La Mort dans l'âme*.
Mathieu knows that the Germans have already won, and is not
inspired by anything so old-fashioned as the honour of the

regiment. Like Sartre himself, who had been called up in 1939 and was taken prisoner at Padoux on 21 June 1940, Mathieu is not technically a fighting soldier. Sartre was in the meteorological section, and Mathieu is in communications. His unit has been deserted by its officers, an action which Sartre maintained was the rule rather than the exception in his sector of the front. A group of *chasseurs* arrives in the village where Mathieu's unit is waiting to be taken prisoner, and they belong to a regiment whose traditions require them to carry on fighting. They are also under the command of a determined and conscientious young lieutenant, and decide to make a last stand in the tower of the village church. The Germans show an uncharacteristic inefficiency in attacking this tower in such a way as to make themselves very easy targets, and Mathieu manages to shoot one officer and perhaps two German soldiers before the inevitable happens and the tower collapses under the fire of a small cannon that the Germans bring to bear on it.

Sartre's view, however, was that doing one's duty as a soldier was not enough. In an interview in 1946, he said that Mathieu's last stand was an example of what Hegel called 'terrorist liberty':[21] the assertion of one's own individuality being without regard for the interests of the collectivity. In Sartre's original plan, Mathieu was not intended to be killed. His final destination was to behave in such a way as to indicate that anyone who follows the true road to freedom ends up by taking part in left-wing politics, and Sartre made a beginning at showing what form this participation might take. In a passage which remained unpublished until the appearance of the *Pléiade* edition of Sartre's novels in 1982, Mathieu turns up again in a German prisoner-of-war camp, having made a good recovery after being seriously wounded. There, he organises and takes command of a network which tries to enable prisoners to escape.

This organisation, as he explains to his friend Brunet, has a moral and philosophical aim rather than a purely political one. It does not look too closely at the motives of the prisoners who want to escape. Instead, it ensures that no prisoner can indulge in the bad faith of telling himself that he did not try to escape because there was no means of doing so. By placing his fellow prisoners in a position where they have to recognise that they are still free in spite of their captivity, Mathieu is acting as the ideal existentialist hero, a fact that makes it even more unfortunate that he disappears from

the published text after *La Mort dans l'âme*. This is especially the
case since any attempt to conclude *Les Chemins de la liberté* in the way
that Simone de Beauvoir says that Sartre intended would have
faced him with one of the greatest difficulties confronting any
artist: that of depicting the triumph of virtue. It has always been a
commonplace of Sartre criticism to say that he merely encourages
people to wallow in their own misery, and that his work is
fundamentally unhealthy. It would have been agreeable to see
whether his technical skill would have been up to managing an
elevating ending.

Sartre's intention[22] was that Mathieu should use his own network
to escape from the prisoner-of-war camp and join the resistance
movement. At the same time, he would enjoy a passionate affair
with Odette, the wife of his respectable brother Jacques, who
clearly fancies him in the first two volumes. He would then be taken
prisoner by the Gestapo, and when tortured, refuse to talk. He
would therefore die, as Simone de Beauvoir explains in her
memoires, as a result of having 'made himself a hero', not because
he was 'heroic through his very essence'. This ending would have
been particularly interesting for two reasons: it would have provided a contrast with the behaviour of Garcin, the anti-hero of *Huis
Clos*; and it would have been a prefiguration of the flesh-and-blood
hero celebrated in one of Sartre's best known texts about the
Algerian war, the Communist journalist, Henri Alleg.

When taken prisoner and tortured by French paratroops in
1957, Alleg refused to talk and lived to tell the tale. Sartre
celebrated his achievement in *Une Victoire*, an article whose publication in *L'Express* for 6 March 1958 caused the immediate and illegal
confiscation of the whole issue by the French police. Alleg's
courage in not talking is an illustration of Sartre's contention in
L'Etre et le néant that even a man being tortured still remains free,
since he and he alone decides when the moment has come at which
he can bear the pain no longer.[23] It is clearly to Sartre's advantage
to have this idea illustrated by a real person as distinct from a
fictional character, or by a parallel with an English writer with
whom he had little else in common.

For when the average English middle-brow reader looks at this
aspect of Sartre's theory of freedom, the name which immediately
leaps to mind is that of Kipling, with his injunction in *If* to

> force your heart and nerve and sinew
> To serve your turn long after they are gone

And so hold on when there is nothing in you
Except the Will which says to them 'Hold On'

It is an open question as to whether Kipling had any real
religious beliefs. What is nevertheless certain is that the world he
depicts is very like that of Sartre: man is alone, and can count on
nobody but himself; if things can possibly go wrong, they will do so;
virtue lies in a free decision to do what you see as your duty;
courage lies in making your body subservient to your mind; this is
the essential first step towards overcoming the chaos that otherwise
threatens to reign; it is a man's world.

There are naturally differences. Kipling believed in what he
called; in the title of one of his most famous poems, *The White Man's
Burden*, the need for the Anglo-Saxon races to help the

new caught, sullen peoples,
Half devil and half child

to learn how to rule themselves better and, eventually perhaps, to
reach independence. Sartre thought all forms of imperialism were
wrong. Kipling had an open minded attitude towards literature,
writing that

There are nine-and-sixty ways of constructing tribal lays
And Every-Single-One-of-Them-Is-Right.

Sartre was obsessed with the idea of finding one single, satisfactory definition of literature.[24] But both Kipling and Sartre had a
common detestation of cowardice, and Kipling would have found
the Garcin of *Huis Clos* an even more objectionable specimen than
Sartre does. After having justified all forms of selfishness and
self-indulgence on the grounds that he was 'essentially' a hero and
would behave courageously when the time came, Garcin broke
down and showed the white feather. As the editor of a pacifist
newspaper, it was Garcin's clear duty – which he saw as such – to
stand his ground and mount his protest the moment that war was
declared. Instead, he tried to escape, was arrested at the frontier
and shot.

Neither did the manner of his death offer any consolation for
Garcin's failure to live up to the ideals which he had so optimistical-
ly set himself. Although the text of the play does not say so
specifically, the implication is that Garcin had to be dragged to his

execution in a state of total panic and collapse. It would have strengthened Sartre's claim to be a moral writer as well as a *moraliste* – an analyst of ethical issues – if Mathieu had been described as a viable alternative to Garcin, just as it would have been agreeable if Mathieu's love affair with Odette had been described with the same enthusiasm which Sartre uses to evoke the love-making of Maurice and Zézette. What Simone de Beauvoir calls 'la plénitude d'une passion consentie' might even have led Mathieu and Odette to use a more efficient form of birth control; or even, improbable though this would be in Sartre's world, to try to have children.

As it is, however, the only extracts published in Sartre's lifetime of the intended fourth volume of *Les Chemins de la liberté*, the extracts from *La Dernière Chance* published in *Les Temps Modernes* in late 1949 under the title of 'Drôle d'amitié' deal exclusively with Brunet. Unlike Mathieu – and unlike Sartre himself – Brunet has taken his duties as a citizen seriously enough to accept some responsibility for command. He has become an *adjutant*, the most senior non-commissioned rank in the French army, and one which rather suits his temperament as one of nature's warrant-officers. In an essay written in 1961 in memory of his friend Maurice Merleau-Ponty, Sartre wrote of how he had taken a commission, and commented:

> quand j'ai vu mes officiers, ces incapables, je regrettai, moi, mon anarchisme d'avant-guerre: puisqu'il fallait se battre, nous avions eu le tort le laisser le commandement aux mains de ces imbéciles vaniteux.[25] (when I saw my officers, and realised how incompetent they were, I regretted my pre-war anarchism. Since we were going to have to fight, we were wrong to leave authority in the hands of these incompetent snobs.)

Brunet has fought and stayed with his men for as long as he could, but behaves after being taken prisoner in a manner that would be judged odd in most armies. He cuts off his badges of rank, determined that any authority he is able to exercise shall come not from the official hierarchy of capitalist society but from his energy and prestige as a Communist Party militant. In the long, brilliantly written closing passage of *La Mort dans l'âme* evoking the interminable wait to which the French prisoners-of-war of 1940 were subjected before being told what the Germans intended to do with them, Brunet behaves rather as Oreste in *Les Mouches*. Just as

Oreste believes that 'human life begins on the other side of despair' Brunet does not want his fellow prisoners to be granted their dearest wish. This, as with all soldiers, is to be demobilised and sent home as soon as possible, but Brunet does not think that this would be a very good idea. If they are going to become useful members of the Party, such comforts must be denied them. Only if they are forced to submit to the 'iron discipline' which Brunet sees himself as being able to impose on them when they are denied the comforts of domesticity, will they be able to become sufficiently aware of the class struggle to be able to play a part in it.

Sartre probably did not intend this portrait of Brunet to be satirical. But as happens elsewhere in his work, it is when he is setting out to do something entirely different that he provides his most valuable insights into French society, and especially into the mentality of the French left wing. This happens in *Les Mains Sales*, when his portrait of Hugo leaves the impression that what left-wing intellectuals most want to do is shoot people. His description of Brunet makes one very relieved to have known French Communists as personal friends rather than as superior officers. The apparently uncritical description of Brunet's behaviour in the prisoner-of-war camp looks forward to some of the less attractive ideas developed later in Sartre's career as a political thinker.

Thus in the long essay which he published in 1960, 'La Critique de la raison dialectique', in which he attempted to reconcile existentialism and Marxism, Sartre argued that the only way in which the individual is able to escape from what he calls 'seriality' is by becoming a member of an active group. No other means exists, Sartre maintained, for a human being to cease looking at his fellows with the mixture of isolation, indifference and hostility which characterises people waiting in a bus queue. Only by becoming members of what Sartre called 'le groupe en fusion'[26] could people escape from the impotence and alienation which afflict everybody not engaged in some form of collective action, and his use of the term 'en fusion' implies that this escape will take place at almost as high an emotional temperature as Lucien Fleurier's political activity.

The desire to abolish bourgeois individualism which is clearly Sartre's aim in *La Critique de la raison dialectique* is thus already there in the total lack of irony with which Brunet is presented. Indeed, he is saved from becoming one of the more unpleasant characters in *Les Chemins de la liberté* only by what other people even less tolerant of human weakness than he is are led to do to him. In the prison camp, Brunet moulds his men into a coherent, well-disciplined and self-supporting unit, rather as Colonel Nicholson does in Pierre Boulle's *Bridge on the River Kwai*, particularly insisting on a cold shower every morning as well as on the sharing of food and other comforts. Ignoring the implications of the Nazi-Soviet Pact of 23 August 1939, Brunet stays faithful to the party line inaugurated by the Popular Front of 1936. This leads him to teach his fellow prisoners to think of the armistice signed between France and Germany on 22 June 1940 as merely a temporary measure. Sooner or later, he insists, the USSR will join in the war against Hitler. The pact between Germany and Russia will then be seen as a tactical manoeuvre forced upon the USSR by the need to gain time and prevent the Western democracies arranging for Hitler to attack the Soviet Union first. The inevitable war between Communism and Fascism will then come out into the open, and it will be one in which the French working class will have its part to play.

The 1949 reader of 'Drôle d'amitié' could see that Brunet was right. The invasion of Soviet Russia by Nazi Germany on 22 June 1941 did give the Second World War the meaning which Brunet had predicted. In March 1941, Sartre managed to have himself released from the prisoner-of-war camp in which he had been incarcerated since June 1940. He maintained, quite reasonably in the light of the fact that he was virtually blind in his right eye, that he had never been a soldier in the French army anyway, and was therefore entitled to be repatriated as a civilian. He then joined the resistance movement as a member of a group called 'Socialisme et Liberté' and was probably happier than at any other time in his political life. Between June 1941 and the liberation of France in 1944 there was more unity among men and women of the left than at any time before or since, and it was not until the outbreak of the Cold War in 1945 that the divisions between the Communist Party and the democratic left, in France and elsewhere, began to reappear. But in the period described in 'Drôle d'amitié', the official attitude of the Communist Party created considerable problems for anyone who, like Brunet, still saw the war against Hitler's Germany as a necessary and inevitable part of the general struggle against Facism.

Brunet's almost idyllic existence in the prisoner-of-war camp is brought to an abrupt end by the arrival, in a new batch of prisoners, of a senior party member, Chalais. He is horrified when he discovers what Brunet has been doing, and rapidly explains to him that this is not the correct party line at all. Indeed, it is so far from the correct party line as to be indistinguishable from the policy of Charles de Gaulle, presented by the Communist Party between June 1940 and June 1941 as the tool of the capitalist warmonger Winston Churchill and of British imperialism.[27] Brunet must therefore stop preaching further resistance and tell his comrades that France is well out of an imperialist war which will serve neither the short- nor the long-term interests of the international proletariat.

Brunet is quite prepared to do this. He is a loyal party member, and accepts the need to do what the leadership tells him. If they see the 1939 pact as making any war against Hitler into a crusade in support of international capitalism, then this is the truth, however unpalatable it may be to the French prisoners-of-war whom he has saved from despair by telling them the opposite. To see the worthy Brunet made to twist and turn in this way confirms the value of Sartre's novel as a realistic account of what left-wing politics were like in the 1940s, and there is every sign that this is Sartre's intention. For as was clear to contemporary readers of *Les Temps Modernes*, Sartre had a very specific motive in mind when publishing 'Drôle d'amitié' when he did. He was using it as part of his campaign to rehabilitate the memory of his close personal friend, Paul Nizan.

Like Brunet, Nizan had been a member of the Communist Party in the 1930s, and like Brunet he had been a journalist. While the fictional Brunet writes for *L'Humanité*, the morning newspaper of the French Communist Party, the real Paul Nizan wrote for *Ce Soir*, its evening equivalent. Although the text of 'Drôle d'amitié' does not say how Brunet had reacted when the news of the Nazi-Soviet Pact came over the wires, everyone in the predominantly left-wing readership of *Les Temps Modernes* knew what Nizan had done. He had denounced the pact and left the Party. This had led to his being accused by his erstwhile colleagues of being a traitor in the pay of the French police, and not even his death in action in the defence of Dunkirk in May 1939 had led to any relaxation in the Communist Party's campaign against him. After the war, Nizan's wife, Henriette, was asked to sign a document denouncing her husband as a traitor,[28] and he was regularly accused by the Party itself of having been in the pay of the police.

Sartre's defence of Nizan takes the form of the introduction into the closing section of the third volume of *Les Chemins de la liberté* of the character of Schneider. Like Brunet, and like Chalais, Schneider does not seem to have a first name, and one sometimes has the impression that left-wing circles in France resembled pre-war English Public Schools in that quite close friends addressed one another by their surnames only. In the films in which Sartre and Simone de Beauvoir are seen talking to each other, they also regularly use the 'vous' form, and she always addresses him simply as 'Sartre'. Schneider is a mysterious character, who watches Brunet's proselytising activity on behalf of the Communist Party with quizzical detachment, and does not endear himself to his fellow prisoners by his stand-offish attitude. Chalais's arrival explains why Schneider has been behaving in this way, and brings the plot of 'Drôle d'amitié' to a crisis point.

Schneider, he tells Brunet, is a pseudonym. The real name of Brunet's friend is Vicarios, a journalist expelled from the Communist Party for his opposition to the Nazi-Soviet Pact, and now known to have 'always been a traitor in the pay of the French police and Right Wing, Comrades'. There is, as the notes to the *Pléiade* edition explain, a certain amount of in-house identification by code names here. Schneider is the German for tailor. Sartre, in French, evokes the same trade (because of the Latin, cf. Carlyle's *Sartor Resartus*, or *The Tailor Repatched*). The alert reader is thus invited to see Schneider's reserved but not hostile attitude towards Brunet's enthusiasm for the Communist Party as reflecting the way Sartre himself saw political matters.

Vicarios, as in the English word vicarious, evokes the idea of suffering undergone by a scapegoat. This creates the implication that the Communists who were honest, and refused to accept a new and totally different Party line, were made to suffer in place of the leaders who were really responsible. These leaders did not make up their own minds for themselves, but merely decided without question to do exactly what Moscow told them to do. When things went wrong, they took it out on their subordinates. Most readers of *Les Temps Modernes* were sufficiently familiar with the internal disputes among Communists and ex-Communists to realise that Sartre was identifying himself with the scapegoat Nizan, underlining the injustice done to his friend by the Communist Party's insistence on still seeing him as a traitor, and asking all men and women of good will on the left to think again.

The parochial air which these arguments now inevitably have is a good illustration of what Sartre meant when he said in the interview in 1946 that: 'Books are like bananas. They both taste better when eaten straight off the tree.' Another disadvantage of committed literature, apart from its habit of preaching to the converted, is that it tends to talk about what Wordsworth called 'Old, forgotten far off things/And battles long ago'.

Except for a few eccentrics like Hardial Bains,[29] Secretary of the Communist Party of Canada (Marxist Leninist), there is now widespread agreement that the Nazi-Soviet Pact of August 1939 was a terrible mistake from everybody's point of view except Hitler's, including that of the Soviet Union, and that the Communist parties who fell into line and supported it were behaving very foolishly. In every aspect of the argument put forward in 'Drôle d'amitié', Sartre is pushing an open door. Paul Nizan was about as guilty of being a spy in the pay of the French police as Captain Dreyfus had been of selling military secrets to the Germans. Sartre's presentation of the way Nizan was treated by his former comrades nevertheless adds to the value of 'Drôle d'amitié' as a social document. It shows how the Communist Party, in France and elsewhere, attracted a number of people who would have been more at home in the Spanish Inquisition or the Gestapo. Jean Anouilh's *Pauvre Bitos*, perhaps the best play so far written about the French Revolution, makes exactly the same point about Robespierre. Anouilh, however, was a writer who never made any pretence of being a man of the left.

Chalais tells Brunet to have nothing more to do with Vicarios, whom he arranges to have beaten up by two of the French prisoners-of-war who have accepted the new party line. Brunet, who like Mathieu Delarue is a big, powerfully built man, intervenes in time to prevent this happening, but is so disgusted by Chalais' behaviour that he decides to join Vicarios in his attempt to escape from the camp and go back to France. Vicarios' ambition is to try to clear his name by disproving the accusations made against him, and Brunet wants to discover whether Chalais' views really do represent the new party line. But this attempt takes place before Mathieu has arrived in the camp and set up a proper network for prisoners who want to escape. The honest but intellectually limited Maurice Tailleur, the representative of the French proletariat who recurs from time to time in *Le Sursis*, and is heard by Philippe Grésigne enjoying sex with his wife Suzanne in the next bedroom, has

arrived in the camp in the same consignment as Chalais. He hears
what Brunet and Vicarios are going to do, and runs to tell Chalais.
The moment Brunet and Vicarios get across the barbed wire, the
searchlights come on and the guards open fire. Vicarios is fatally
wounded and dies in Brunet's arms:

> Cet absolu de souffrance, aucune victoire des hommes ne pourra
> l'effacer: c'est le Parti qui le fait crever, même si l'U.R.S.S. gagne,
> les hommes sont seuls. Brunet se penche, il plonge la main dans
> les cheveux souillés de Vicarios, il crie comme s'il pouvait encore
> le sauver de l'horreur, comme si deux hommes perdus
> pouvaient, à la dernière minute, vaincre la solitude.[30] (No
> human victory could wipe out this absolute of suffering. It is the
> Party that has killed him, and even if the U.S.S.R. wins, men are
> still alone. Brunet bent down, plunged his hand into Vicarios's
> filthy hair, and shouted out as if he could save him from horror,
> as if two lost men could at the last moment overcome solitude.)

The text of 'Drôle d'amitié' does not make it difficult to believe
that it was Chalais who told the Germans that Brunet and Vicarios
were going to try to escape. Chalais sums up the basic philosophy of
the Party when he tells Brunet: 'Tu incarnes une déviation. Tu dois
disparaître avec elle.'[31] (You incarnate a deviation, and must
disappear along with it.) Brunet does not think there is anything
wrong in this kind of attitude. Indeed, even before Chalais says
this, he presents Vicarios with an even more rigid view of what true
Party discipline involves when he tells him that the comrades

> n'ont pas trop de toute leur confiance: même si tu es partielle-
> ment innocent, ils ont besoin que tu sois tout à fait coupable.[32]
> (need all the confidence they can get. Even if you are partially
> innocent, they need to believe you are completely guilty.)

Even as late as the 1990s, it is impossible to read a phrase like this
without thinking of Arthur Koestler's *Darkness at Noon*, a novel
which the Communist Party tried to ban when it appeared in
France in 1945 under the title of *Le Zéro et l'infini*, and which set out
to answer one of the great mysteries of twentieth-century politics:
the behaviour of the old Bolsheviks at the Moscow state trials of the
1930s. For in 1936 and 1937, Stalin put on trial virtually every
leader who had been involved in the early days of the 1917

Revolution, and who all seemed to have served the Party faithfully both then and since. Yet when accused of being traitors to the Revolution and the Communist state, and of having always been in the pay of Western reactionaries, the old Bolsheviks all made profuse confessions of guilt. Since they were all obviously innocent, and since it was felt unlikely that even the resources of twentieth-century torture could have produced such unanimity among a group of professional revolutionaries noted for their toughness, nobody could understand what had led them to confess.

The answer, Koestler suggested, lay in the doctrine of the useful lie. His hero, Rubashov, accepts the need to proclaim himself guilty because he has come to believe that this is the best way of serving the cause of socialism. It is better, he thinks, for the masses to think that the economic problems of the Soviet Union are the result of treason and sabotage rather than of mistakes made by the leadership. If the scapegoats selected by the Party were to refuse to accept their guilt, the process of building up socialism could not go on. On the other hand, if the accused were to insist that they were innocent, they would be telling the truth, but they would be doing immeasurable harm to the cause.

In the 1990s, the arguments for the prosecution in *Darkness at Noon* are as dated as the debates in nineteenth-century Oxford about whether earnest young Anglican clergymen ought to go over to Rome because the Papacy's views on the Trinity were sounder than those of the Anglican Communion. Now that almost everybody accepts that the Communist state established by Lenin in 1917 differed from Hitler's Germany mainly by the fact that it lasted longer, Koestler's novel has lost its power to shock. But Koestler knew exactly what he was doing, and the analysis in *Darkness at Noon* exactly matched the opening sentence in the second volume of his autobiography, *The Invisible Writing*:

I went to Communism as one goes to a spring of fresh water, and I left Communism as one clambers out of a poisoned river strewn with the wreckage of flooded cities and the corpses of the drowned.[33]

But when Brunet tells Vicarios that his fellow-prisoners need to believe that he is completely guilty even if he is partly innocent, it is hard to tell what Sartre wants the reader to think, whether he is presenting Brunet as a hero to be admired or a fool to be pitied. To the reader unsympathetic to Communism, the answer is clear: the Sartre of 'Drôle d'amitié' is an anti-Communist writer of almost equal perception and persuasiveness as Koestler, and the extracts have the same value as historical fiction and political analysis as *Darkness at Noon*. But it is never possible, with an author who made his views known in so many different contexts as Sartre, to forget what he said elsewhere. In 1948, in a comment on an article by Claude Lefort, the editorial staff of *Les Temps Modernes* defined their position by saying:

> Pour lui, l'U.R.S.S. est l'accusée. Pour nous, avec ses grandeurs et ses horreurs, elle est une entreprise en panne.[34] (For Lefort, the U.S.S.R. is in the position of prisoner at the bar. For us, with its greatness and its horrors, it is an enterprise which has temporarily broken down.)

Unlike Koestler, Sartre never denounced the Soviet Union and all its works. Indeed one of his most frequently quoted remarks was: 'un anti-communiste est un chien. Je ne sors pas de là'[35] (an anti-communist is a swine. I shall never change my mind on that). In July 1952, in a series of articles entitled *Les Communistes et la Paix*, he stated that 'Russia wants peace and proves it every day'[36] and claimed that however hard he looked, he could, over the previous ten years, find not a single instance of Russian aggression. At no point in his career did Sartre ever mention the repeated Russian attempts to force the Western allies out of West Berlin, and he fully endorsed the view that the Korean War of 1950–3 was caused by South Korea and the United States and not by an unprovoked invasion by the Communist North. But his literary work often contradicts the implications of his public stance, and this is as true of 'Drôle d'amitié' as of his best political play, *Les Mains Sales*. There, the plot offers as damning an indictment of Communist opportunism as the account in 'Drôle d'amitié' of how the Communist Party is prepared to use any means, including telling the German guards that French prisoners-of-war are trying to escape, in order to get rid of heretical members. Indeed, it is in this play that the most instructive commentary on 'Drôle d'amitié', and on Sartre's failure to complete *Les Chemins de la liberté*, is to be found.

Hugo, a relatively new member of the Proletarian Party in the Eastern European country of Illyria, is sent to kill Hoederer, one of the Party leaders suspected of wishing to change the Party line. He succeeds, only to discover on being released from prison for what had been interpreted as a *Crime Passionnel* – the title of the English translation – that it had all been a mistake. After he had killed Hoederer, orders had come from Moscow showing that the line he was trying to pursue had been the right one all along. Rather than accept this, Hugo has himself killed, an action interpreted by most spectators as a justified rejection of a world in which the Party line is at one and the same time sufficiently sacred to justify murder and sufficiently flexible to be changed at a moment's notice.

This was not, however, the way Sartre wanted the play to be interpreted. He said so on a number of occasions, and between 1952 and 1960 refused permission for *Les Mains Sales* to be performed because of the way in which it was being seen by everybody as an indictment of the Communist Party. The previously unpublished drafts for the continuation of 'Drôle d'amitié', which were not made public until the 1982 *Pléiade* edition, suggest that he also tried to change his mind about the implications of the events in 'Drôle d'amitié'. It appears, for example, from Sartre's unpublished drafts, that Brunet was wrong to think that it was Chalais who told the Germans that he and Vicarios were going to try to escape. In fact, it was another prisoner, Moûlu, already presented in the closing pages of *La Mort dans l'âme* as a rather nasty piece of work, who was the real traitor.

Sartre was not, as a novelist, in any way averse to telling the reader what to think, and Moûlu is a suspect character from the moment he makes his appearance. He refuses to take a shower or wash his feet, and behaves most irresponsibly towards his fellow prisoners by scattering over a field the letters from their families which he is supposed to distribute to them. It is not therefore much of a surprise when the unpublished extracts from *La Dernière Chance* show that it was he who told the Germans about the projected escape of Brunet and Vicarios. Any final version of the novel would have had to make it clear that the Brunet of 'Drôle d'amitié' was mistaken about who was really responsible for Vicarios' death, and Sartre would certainly have been able to rewrite the novel in this way if he had wanted. The last quality he lacked was technical skill. There might nevertheless have been something suspicious about the way the novel changed from being an indictment of the Communist Party to a book in which the blame was placed on one of the more traditional targets of Marxist hostility, the lower-middle-class Moûlu.

Technique, Ideas and a Sense of Ending

One of Sartre's most interesting and frequently quoted remarks about fiction occurs in a review which he published in July 1939 of the French translation of William Faulkner's *The Sound and the Fury*:

> Une technique romanesque renvoie toujours à la métaphysique du romancier. La tâche du critique est de dégager celle-ci avant d'apprécier celle-là.[37] (The technique of a novelist always implies a metaphysic. The task of the critic is to bring out the second before appreciating the first.)

Les Chemins de la liberté is an attempt to put this idea into practice, with the style and technique of presentation changing from volume to volume according to the idea or ideas that Sartre wishes to emphasise. Each of the sections in *L'Age de raison* is told from the point of view of one character, as in the interior monologues in Virginia Woolf's *The Waves* or Faulkner's *As I lay dying*. In presenting events in this way, Sartre is also respecting the rule which he laid down in his criticism of François Mauriac's *La Fin de la Nuit* when he wrote:

> Le roman est action, et le romancier n'a pas le droit d'abandonner le terrain de la bataille et de s'installer commodément sur un tertre pour juger les coups et rêver à la fortune des armes.[38] (The novel consists of action, and the novelist has no right to leave the battle field and install himself comfortably on a hillock, judging the blows given and received and dreaming of the fortunes of war.)

Mauriac's mistake, he claimed, like that of most French writers, was to try to ignore the fact that

> la théorie de la relativité s'applique intégralement à l'univers romanesque ... et dans un vrai roman, pas plus que dans le monde d'Einstein, il n'y a de place pour un observateur privilégié.[39] (the theory of relativity is wholly applicable to the world of the novel, and ... in a real novel, as in the universe of Einstein, there is no place for a privileged spectator.)

Although most of the events in *L'Age de raison* are told from
Mathieu's point of view, there are a number of incursions into the
more limited thought processes of young Boris, and even of
Marcelle. This enables the reader to see Sartre sticking to his own
rules and to be aware, through the way the story is told, of the
isolation of people one from another. This failure to communicate,
which is constant throughout *L'Age de raison*, and more convincing
than in the ending of the affair between Roquentin and Anny in *La
Nausée*, is one of the features of the novel which make it into a
portrait of what Sartre described as 'le marasme français de
l'entre-deux-guerres'[40] (the stagnation of French society in the
inter-war period). Here, Sartre is quite conscious of what he is
doing, and offers a perfect coincidence between technique of
narration and subject matter. In *Le Sursis*, Mathieu sees himself as
already transformed into a historical character by the imminent
outbreak of the Second World War.

Il y avait eu un homme tendre et timoré qui aimait Paris et qui s'y
promenait. Cet homme était mort. Aussi mort que Waldeck-
Rousseau, que Thureau-Dangin; il s'était enfoncé dans le passé
du monde, avec la Paix, sa vie avait été versée dans les archives de
la Troisième République; ses dépenses quotidiennes alimenter-
aient les statistiques concernant le niveau de vie des classes
moyennes après 1918, ses lettres serviraient de documents à
l'histoire de la bourgeoisie entre les deux guerres, ses in-
quiétudes, ses hésitations, ses hontes et ses remords seraient fort
précieux pour l'étude des moeurs françaises après la chute du
Second Empire.[41] (There had been a shy and sentimental man
who loved Paris and liked walking through its streets. This man
was dead. As dead as Waldeck-Rousseau or Thureau-Dangin; he
had sunk into the past, together with Peace; his life had been put
into the archives of the Third Republic; his daily expenses would
provide statistics concerning the standard of living of the middle
classes after 1918, his letters would be useful as documents for
the study of the French middle class between the wars, his
worries, hesitations, his fits of shame and remorse would be
invaluable for the study of French customs after the fall of the
Second Empire.)

The factual portrait of a historical period provided by the plot,
attitudes and incidental details of *L'Age de raison* is supplemented

by the way the story is told, and in the first volume of *Les Chemins de la liberté*, Sartre sticks to his rule about not letting the reader see him playing God the Father with his characters. Even the description of Daniel Sereno emerging from the confectionery shop in the rue Vercingétorix after Boris has turned down his offer of a drink, holding

> dans la main droite le glaive de feu de Saint Michel, et dans sa main gauche un paquet de bonbons pour Mme Duffet[42] (carrying in one hand the flaming sword of Saint Michael and in the other a box of sweets for Madame Duffet)

does not quite go against Sartre's proclaimed intention of doing away with the omniscient narrator. This is not how God the Novelist sees Daniel. This is how Daniel, at that moment, sees himself. Marcelle habitually addresses him as 'l'archange', as a tribute to his exquisite manners and air of saintly beatitude; and Daniel does not lack the ironic self-awareness which enables him to see how funny the contrast is between how she sees him and what he is really like. He knows perfectly well that his inner certainty of carrying out a mission of divinely inspired vengeance is quite invisible to anyone else, who will see him simply as an old queen carrying a box of sweets. His determination to avenge himself for a sexual disappointment by playing a dirty trick on an old friend is something which the reader knows about because of the plot, not because the novelist has nudged him to tell him about it.

Sartre is, here, fully in command of his material. The events mean what he wants them to mean, and this meaning comes out in the way he presents them to the reader. However preoccupied the characters in *L'Age de raison* are with their private lives, international politics are never far away. The book opens with Mathieu being accosted by a man who gives him a letter with a stamp on it from the besieged Republican garrison in Madrid, and he is haunted throughout the novel by his failure to go and fight on the Republican side. In *Le Sursis*, international politics dominate everything that happens. Everybody is going to be affected by the crisis set off by Hitler's demand to incorporate the German-speaking population of the Sudetenland mountains in Czechoslovakia into the Third Reich, and Sartre made no secret of his debt to the technique which he borrowed from the American novelist John Dos Passos to express this idea. The narrative switches, often in

mid-sentence, from one group of characters to another, always to
come back to

> la guerre, redoutée par Pierre, acceptée par Boris, désirée par
> Daniel, la guerre, la grande guerre des debout, la folle guerre
> des blancs[43] (the war, feared by Pierre, accepted by Boris, longed
> for by Daniel, the great war of the men who can walk upright,
> the mad war of the white men),

seen here by one of the most moving characters in *Le Sursis*, a man
compelled by bone marrow disease to spend the whole of his life in
a horizontal position. It is a *tour de force* of applied technique, the
ideal book to read at a time of international crisis, even one caused
in the days of the Cold War by the Russia of whom Sartre said in
1952 that however hard he sought, he could find no aggressive
intentions in its foreign policy. When Mathieu thinks about what is
happening, the multiplicity of characters and viewpoints take on a
philosophical meaning as he reflects that:

> Si on essayait de regarder la planète en face, elle s'effondrait en
> miettes, il ne restait plus que des consciences. Cent millions de
> consciences libres dont chacune voyait des murs, un bout de
> cigare rougeoyant, des visages familiers, et construisait sa des-
> tinée sous sa propre responsabilité. Et pourtant, si on était une
> de ces consciences, on s'apercevait à d'imperceptibles effleure-
> ments, à d'insensibles changements, qu'on était solidaire d'un
> gigantesque et invisible polypier. La guerre: chacun est libre et
> pourtant les jeux sont faits. Elle est là, c'est la totalité de toutes
> mes pensées, de toutes les paroles d'Hitler, de tous les actes de
> Gomez: mais personne n'est là pour faire le total. Elle n'existe
> que pour Dieu. Mais Dieu n'existe pas. Et pourtant la guerre
> existe.[44] (If you tried to look directly at the planet, it disinte-
> grated into tiny fragments, with nothing left but individual
> minds. A hundred million minds, all free, each aware of a wall, a
> glowing cigar butt, a familiar face, and each constructing its own
> destiny for which it alone is responsible. And yet if one were one
> of these minds, one realised, by imperceptible contacts and
> undetectable changes, that one was a cell in an immense but
> invisible coral growth. War: everyone is free and yet the die is
> already cast. The war is there, everywhere, it makes up the whole
> of my thoughts, the whole of Hitler's words, the whole of

Gomez's acts; but nobody is there to add it all up. The war exists for God. But God does not exist. And yet the war exists.)

Only if God existed could there be complete knowledge of any event, especially as complex and complicated a one as a world war. Later on in his work, Sartre was much preoccupied in his political thinking by the concept which he and other Marxist thinkers call 'totalisation'. What the etymology of this word suggests that it means is the adding up of everything so that it makes one, immense, but nevertheless coherent sum. But since no human mind could ever understand such a sum, the concept of totalisation is meaningless outside a religious context, and the insistence which Marxists place upon it is yet another indication of how right the critics of this philosophy are to say that it is an alternative form of religious belief. The attraction it exercised over Sartre would also seem to stem, in this respect, from the fact that he was one of those men who could see the advantages of believing in God without ever managing to do it.

Sartre's idea that the novelist can only know what the individual characters in his novels know is not one that stands up to even the most superficial analysis. What he really means is that the novelist should not tug too obviously at the reader's sleeve in order to tell him what to think. From this point of view, Sartre is often just as open to criticism as the François Mauriac whom he accuses of intervening in the narrative to make sure that the reader does not get the wrong idea. In *Le Sursis*, France and the United Kingdom have no sooner decided to give way to Hitler than the cowardly bourgeois Jacques Delarue brings out the best champagne. As the Czech diplomat Mastny reads out the details of how his country is going to be dismembered, this account of what the text of *Le Sursis* makes a point of calling 'un assassinat historique'[45] alternates with a description of how Ivich is virtually raped by her boy friend. There is, perhaps understandably, no attempt at historical objectivity. *Le Sursis* was not published until 1945, when hindsight had made political judgements of the Munich agreement relatively easy.

But although Sartre was quite happy in 1945 to condemn the way that the French and British governments had behaved in the period before the Second World War, he had much more difficulty in expressing a consistent view of the Soviet Union. George Orwell did this, in allegory in *Animal Farm* and by implication in *Nineteen-Eighty-Four*, and it is disappointing for English admirers of Sartre to discover that he does not seem to have expressed an opinion on Orwell's work. For in 1936, Orwell had done what Mathieu Delarue realised that he ought to have done and gone off to fight for the Spanish republicans. He thus had the best record of any twentieth-century writer for political commitment in what he did as well as in what he wrote, and it would therefore have been even more interesting to find out what Sartre thought about him. Yet just as the way in which a novelist tells his stories can, as Sartre observed, be itself full of significance, so too can his silence about another writer. Sartre did not talk about Orwell because he could not bring himself to look closely at the work of a man who had behaved as he sometimes suspected that he ought to have done: commit himself actively to the left in the 1930s, and come right out and condemn the Soviet Union unreservedly as a tyranny and betrayal in the 1940s and 1950s. Sartre's inability to bring his most ambitious undertaking as a novelist to a satisfactory conclusion can be just as eloquent about the feelings he had and the problems he faced.

It is in this respect that the unfinished tetralogy of *Les Chemins de la liberté* stands as a monument to the death of the illusion to which André Malraux gave poetic form when he wrote, describing the death of the Communist militant Kyo in *La Condition humaine* (*Man's Fate*):

Il aurait combattu pour ce qui, de son temps, aurait été chargé du sens le plus fort et du plus grand espoir; il mourait parmi ceux avec qui il aurait voulu vivre; il mourait, comme chacun de ces hommes couchés, pour avoir donné un sens à sa vie. Qu'eût valu une vie pour laquelle il n'eût pas accepté de mourir? Il est facile de mourir quand on ne meurt pas seul. Mort saturée de ce chevrotement fraternel, assemblée de vaincus où des multitudes reconnaîtraient leurs martyrs, légende sanglante dont se font les légendes dorées! Comment, déjà regardé par la mort, ne pas entendre ce murmure de sacrifice humain qui lui criait que le coeur des hommes est un refuge à morts qui vaut bien l'esprit?[46] (He would have fought for what in his time was filled with the most potent meaning and the greatest hope; he was dying by the side of those with whom he would have wanted to live; he was dying, like all those lying outstretched around him, because he had tried to give meaning to his life. What would a life for which he would not have accepted to die been worth? It is easy to die when you do not die alone. Death interwoven with the fraternal murmurs of the dying, congregation of the conquered in which the multitudes of the future would recognise their martyrs, bloodstained legend of which the stuff of golden legends is composed! How, already face to face with death, could he not hear this murmur of human sacrifice, crying out to him that the virile heart of men is as great a refuge for the dead as is the human mind?)

After 1950, Sartre did not try to write any more novels, and his comment on the end of this illusion takes the form of a silent literary death knell.

His work as a playwright continued, producing a highly entertaining vehicle for Pierre Brasseur to exert his talents for deliberate overacting in *Kean*, and giving rise in 1959 to his most fascinating and complex play, *Les Séquestrés d'Altona*. In it, he argued that France's role in Algeria was no different, morally or politically, from Germany's attempt to conquer Russia in the Second World War, and suggested that France could become as prosperous by accepting defeat in North Africa as Germany had become by losing the Second World War. In 1965, he adopted Euripides' *The Trojan Women* in such a way as to make it an obvious attack on what he always described as the war waged by the United States against the people of Vietnam. The play was brilliantly performed at the *Théâtre National Populaire* and well received by the public, but it did little to bridge the increasing gap between Sartre the creative writer and Sartre the left-wing polemicist.

In 1971, this gap became unbridgeable. On the one hand, there was the publication of the first two volumes of *L'Idiot de la famille* (*The Fool of the Family*), the study of Flaubert on which he had been working for over ten years. It contained over 2 million words, but stopped short before offering a full analysis of *Madame Bovary*, the novel which Flaubert had published in 1857, when he still had fourteen years to live and almost all his other major works still to write. On the other hand, in complete contrast to a work which not even Flaubert specialists fully understand, there was Sartre's increasing involvement, through speeches, interviews, public appearances and statements to the press, in various left-wing causes such as the protection of Maoist newspapers against attempts at press censorship, or the protests against the treatment of political activists in West German prisons. Herbert Marcuse's insistence that

Sartre was, whether he liked it or not, 'the world's conscience'[47] applied – if at all – more and more to Sartre the polemicist and less and less to the Sartre the creative writer.

It is always tempting to apply to his own performance anything that an author says about how books ought to be written. In Sartre's case, the application to his own performance as a novelist of his remark about a novelist's technique of narration 'reflecting a metaphysic' produces some odd results. It is an acceptable coincidence that Brunet should be taken prisoner at the village of Padoux at the very moment when Mathieu is becoming a hero of the last cartridge at exactly the same place. But when Brunet and Maurice Tailleur then both turn up at the same prisoner-of-war camp as Mathieu, you feel you are reading a version of Anthony Powell's *A Dance to the Music of Time* in which the long arm of coincidence is no longer being used as a comic device. It is, instead, the expression of a mysterious providence totally absent from Sartre's other work, and unconvincing for other reasons apart from that.

Sartre could not finish *Les Chemins de la liberté* because he could not believe, in his heart of hearts, that the kind of political progress he hoped for was possible, and in this respect his remark about the technique of a novelist expressing a metaphysic applies to him in a way that he never intended.[48] His pathological dislike of the French middle class prevented him from seeing what was really happening in the France of his time. As Raymond Aron observed, he was not sufficiently interested in seeing what was going on around him in the 1960s and 1970s to realise that everything was changing. He did not therefore notice that the French economy was, under a mixed economy of the type which orthodox Marxism always said was impossible, enabling everybody to improve their standard of living.

In the unpublished extracts of *La Dernière Chance*, Mathieu tells himself that he will never again think of what he is, only about what he does.[49] It is a remark which is especially welcome to all the readers of *L'Etre et le néant* who feel that the argument goes badly wrong in the closing section, *Avoir, Faire et Etre* (Having, Doing and Being). For it is here that Sartre begins to argue that all human beings share the same fundamental desire to make what he calls the *Pour-Soi* (the For-Itself, or human consciousness) coincide with the *En-Soi* (the In-Itself, the world of natural objects).

What Sartre means by this is that everybody has the same basic ambition: to be as totally themselves as a stone is a stone – or, as Daniel Sereno puts it, an oak tree is an oak tree – while at the same time remaining absolutely conscious of what they are. This, Sartre argues, is impossible. The price we pay for being aware of ourselves is the knowledge that we could always be different. If we were absolutely what we are, then we would not, in Sartre's view, even know it. We should be totally opaque, with as little ability to see within ourselves as a piece of coal. Human beings, according to the views set out in the closing pages of *L'Etre et le néant*, are totally aware of themselves, but totally incapable of fulfilling their basic desire, which is really to be themselves. They are thus doomed to perpetual frustration.

This argument may or may not be true. Since it is impossible to see what kind of empirical evidence would prove it either right or wrong, it is tempting to say that it is neither true nor false but simply meaningless.[50] While it is true that few human beings are completely happy – something which Sartre's theories require – not many of them would agree to see themselves as unhappy for the reasons set out in *L'Etre et le néant*. In this respect, Sartre is once again rather like a Christian or a Freudian. The Christian maintains that people are unhappy because of original sin, and dismisses as an illusion any statement that a person is unhappy because she or he is not rich, clever or attractive enough, not very good at games, had a persecuted childhood, or has just been turned down for a job. The Freudian has a similarly dismissive view of the reasons which people put forward to explain why they are unhappy. Instead, he claims to find the root cause for all frustrations in an unresolved Oedipus complex.

Sartre is like the Christian or the Freudian in that the closing pages in *L'Etre et le néant* claim that all human frustration and unhappiness have the same fundamental cause. He differs in that he sees this as neither original sin, nor an unresolved Oedipus complex, but the inability to bring together the *En Soi* and the *Pour Soi*. In so far as the Sartre of *L'Etre et le néant* holds out no hope of the contradictions in the human condition ever being resolved, his version of existentialism is more pessimistic than either Christianity or Freudianism. While Christianity has the concept of salvation, and Freudianism offers the practice of psychoanalysis, Sartre maintains that human beings are inspired by a desire which is not only unattainable but self-contradictory. We cannot become like a stone because we have self-consciousness, which is the one quality that the stone lacks.

The oddness of these ideas provides yet another reason for regretting the unfinished nature of *Les Chemins de la liberté*. Mathieu Delarue develops into such a good critic of the theory of perpetual frustration which dominates the last pages of *L'Etre et le néant* that it is very disappointing not to be able to see him showing, in practice, just why so many of the gloomier ideas of his creator are wrong. The first sign that Mathieu is growing up comes when he reads the letter in which Daniel explains how he has finally found an escape from the constant and meaningless flow of thoughts in his head. This is because he has 'discovered God'. Although it would have been very interesting to see Daniel combining his new religious faith with his solicitude for Marcelle and continued tendency to chat up handsome young gardeners, it is impossible not to sympathise with Mathieu when he throws Daniel's letter out of the window of the train taking him off to join the army in September 1938.[51] By doing so, he dismisses the major illusion which dominates the closing passages of *L'Etre et le néant*, and which has been part of his own undoing until then: the belief that human beings are more interested in being than in doing.

For the first thing which strikes anybody who tries to look at the behaviour of his fellow human beings with the lack of preconceived ideas said to characterise the phenomenological attitude is that the one quality we all have in common is a taste for doing things. Any combination of the *En-soi* with the *Pour-soi* would lead to a state of inactivity which would be insufferably dull, just as anyone putting into practice Pascal's idea of avoiding unhappiness by staying quietly in a room would be as boring to himself as to other people. Mathieu's decision to give up trying to be, and concentrate instead on doing, is a most salutary reaction against the argument that dominates the closing pages of *L'Etre et le néant*. If Sartre had proceeded to show Mathieu acting according to this insight, he would have done more than put another nail in the overdue coffin of metaphysics by offering a welcome rejection of the argument put forward in the closing pages of *L'Etre et le néant*. He would also have put his finger on the main illusion which made Mathieu so inadequate a character in *L'Age de raison*. The reason why Mathieu is so incapable, in the first volume of the series, of dealing with ordinary life, is precisely the desire to be free rather than to use his freedom. Now, when it is almost too late – there can be no other translation of *La Dernière Chance* except *The Last Chance* – he has come to his senses.

This does not mean that Mathieu regrets his failure to use his freedom to make Marcelle happier by marrying her and keeping the child. Nothing could be further from his and Sartre's value system than the idea which Choderlos de Laclos, the author of *Les Liaisons dangereuses*, told his wife that he was going to illustrate in his next novel: that true happiness can be found only in the bosom of the family. Mathieu's idea of action is a much more macho one. It consists of taking part in exciting and possibly violent political activity. If he does have the passionate affair with his brother's wife, Odette, which Simone de Beauvoir mentions in her autobiography, this is because of the tradition whereby the true reward that women offer heroes is sexual satisfaction, not because he is interested in the idea of a wife and children.

When Brunet meets up again with Mathieu in the German prisoner-of-war camp, it is at the very moment when Mathieu has just finished arranging for the traitor Moûlu to be executed.[52] The need to ensure that traitors be punished became a central preoccupation of the French left as early as 1793, when the law was passed enabling counter-revolutionaries to be sent straight to the guillotine without a lot of legal fuss and bother as to whether or not they were guilty. There was still an obvious anxiety to ensure that nobody who had betrayed the cause escaped due punishment as late as 1960. A careful reading of Jean Genet's play *Les Nègres* (*The Blacks*) brings out the real purpose of the elaborate ceremonies whereby the Blacks are shown as trying to attain greater awareness of the blackness by playing at being black: it is to distract the attention of the audience from the execution off-stage of a traitor to the black cause.

This scene suggests yet another reason why Sartre did not finish *Les Chemins de la liberté*. By 1950, he had become so interested in politics, and especially the violent and exciting politics of the left, that he would have found any exploration of ordinary human relationships a bit dull. From 1945 onwards, when the popularity of existentialism made it easy and necessary for him to explain precisely what it was, he insisted on the fact that it was a philosophy for a time of crisis. Once the crisis began to fade, the kind of books in which murder, torture, betrayal and other extreme experiences were shown as making up the stuff of human existence became less easy to write and less fashionable. The second and third volumes of *Les Chemins de la liberté* dwelt very fully on the tumult and the violence of politics in mid-twentieth-century Europe. Sartre clearly enjoyed writing about such things, and *Le Sursis* and *La Mort dans l'âme* proved as popular as *L'Age de raison* and all his other works. His failure to bring the narrative forward into post-war France suggests that he found the arrival of more peaceful times rather boring.

It is, however, equally possible to argue that Sartre did not complete *Les Chemins de la liberté* – and, indeed, gave up conventional forms of literary expression altogether – because he was far more interested in exploiting the resources of the modern media. He was, of course, prevented from using the television and radio. Even nowadays, it is not customary in France to allow dissident intellectuals to use the most powerful instruments of modern communication to express their ideas. The series of programmes on the history of France which Sartre prepared in the 1970s were never put on television, which was a great pity and a sign of considerable weakness on the part of the French political system. An inability to stand criticism, even if it does seem manifestly wrong, is the surest sign that any political party gives of its unfitness to govern. Whereas the BBC put the adaptation of *Les Chemins de la liberté* on television, the French restricted it to the apparently safer medium of radio. But as Michael Scriven argued in the special number which *Les Temps Modernes* published in 1990 to mark the tenth anniversary of Sartre's death, the frequency with which he allowed himself to be interviewed by the press, together with his readiness to have a film made of his life, suggests that he was conscious of how anyone wishing to have a genuine influence on the modern world had to use modern rather than traditional methods of expressing himself. Sartre's abandonment of fiction, in this context, is a recognition of what Marshall McLuhan argued in the 1960s was the beginning of the death of the book.

The reader who comes to the novels of Jean-Paul Sartre expecting the traditional pleasures of fiction is bound to be slightly disappointed. Like Aldous Huxley, the English writer whom he most resembles, Sartre is much more interested in ideas than in people. Except for the relationship between Boris and Ivich, whose slightly incestuous feelings for each other were acknowledged by Sartre himself as having been fed by some of his private obsessions, the only important emotional links in *Les Chemins de la liberté* are between men. Even then, the only one where any kind of emotion comes into play is in the strange friendship between Brunet and Vicarios, and this ends fairly quickly when Vicarios is killed. It is not that Sartre cannot think up relationships. In *La Nausée*, the affair between Roquentin and Anny has considerable promise, as does the marriage between Gomez and Sarah in *Les Chemins de la liberté*. He is sensuous, self-indulgent and ruthless, she the epitome of self-denial and abnegation, a vegetarian pacifist married to a carnivorous warrior. But the relationship is not then developed, and the reader for whom the novel reaches its height in books such as *Middlemarch* or *Anna Karenina* cannot avoid a sense of disappointment at the way Sartre invites him to be interested in a character or a relationship only to drop them just as they are becoming interesting.

It would, for example, have been fascinating to see Marcelle and Daniel bringing up Mathieu's child, and equally compulsive reading to learn how Ivich finally copes with her in-laws, or Boris with the problems of growing up. *Le Sursis* and *La Mort dans l'âme* are full of characters about whom one would like to learn more, especially the man referred to simply by his first name of Georges. He knows himself to be ugly and unattractive, and is sad not for his own but for his child's sake that he has to leave for the war. He realises that his daughter, now a baby, will inherit his ugliness and lack of physical charm, and that when he comes back she will be ashamed of him in front of her pretty and elegant friends.[53] Sartre's early philosophy is one in which all difficulties, in the last resort, at least in theory, can be solved by making correct use of the freedom of the will. It is pleasing to see that he is capable of at least imagining how things are in reality, as well as of recognising how some people's lives are very much more dominated than others by their physical make up.

Like Aldous Huxley's essays and novels, the plays, prefaces, interviews, critical studies, autobiographical fragments, reviews, philosophical essays, short stories and novels which made Sartre the best known French writer of the mid-twentieth century are best seen, as I suggested in Chapter 1 of this study, as forming part of one book, Sartre's own intellectual autobiography. In the various volumes which make up this autobiography, Sartre found out what he thought by writing down his ideas, and seeing how they worked out on paper. French culture has always been intensely interested in ideas, and he found a public constantly eager to find out what he thought next. The growing internationalisation of intellectual and literary life in the twentieth century meant that this public rapidly came to include every civilised country. In 1964, even the Soviet Union allowed *Les Mots* to be translated and put openly on sale.

There may, however, have been political reasons for this unexpected relaxation of what was then a policy of strict censorship. *Les Mots* called into question the whole existence of what was known as 'bourgeois literature', and it was perhaps because Sartre seemed to be arguing that literature was always less important than politics that this autobiographical fragment proved so popular in a totalitarian state. When Sartre said 'En face d'un enfant qui meurt, *La Nausée* ne fait pas le poids'[54] (by the side of a dying child, *La Nausée* weighs nothing) he was expressing a guilt feeling characterising the middle class in the whole of the developed world. The Soviet authorities must have been very happy to be able to make their citizens realise how unhappy one of the most successful authors in the capitalist West really was.

At first sight, *Les Mots* seems as fictional as any of Sartre's novels. According to Simone de Beauvoir, Sartre's mother claimed that 'Poulu n'a rien compris à son enfance',[55] and it is certainly tempting to argue that the story of a man becoming a writer because his grandfather once talked to him seriously is more improbable than most novels. Sartre's description of his unhappy childhood – 'Je déteste mon enfance et tout ce qui en survit'[56] (I hate my childhood and everything still remaining of it) – is as good as anything in Dickens or Daudet, and has the unexpected quality of being one of the best arguments in favour of a normal, well-balanced childhood ever written. But the way in which Sartre's career developed also bears out, in a way that he cannot have intended, the basic accuracy of his account of how and why he became a writer. Only a man brought up to think that literature could offer some kind of spiritual salvation would try so many ways of writing, only to find each of them ultimately unsatisfactory.

For *Les Chemins de la liberté* was not the only book that Sartre failed to complete. He never finished either *Les Communistes et la paix*, or *Le Fantôme de Staline*, or the book on Flaubert, or one of the most intriguing of his essays in art history, the study of Tintoretto entitled *Le Prisonnier de Venise*. *L'Etre et le néant* promised an *Ethics* which he never bothered to publish in his lifetime, leaving the *Cahiers pour une morale* to appear as a result of the efforts of his literary executors in 1983. The existentialist biography of Dostoievski, also promised in *L'Etre et le néant*, never seems to have been even begun, and there is no trace of his having tried to fulfil the promise in *Les Mots* of describing the 'acids' which he said ate away his conviction that literature offered the kind of religious salvation which had attracted such praise from his grandfather.

Sartre did not always leave his public with its tongue hanging out asking for more. His *Baudelaire* is as perfectly finished a work of art as *Huis Clos* or *Les Séquestrés d'Altona*, *L'Age de raison* a beautifully constructed novel, the 1957 essay 'Le colonialisme est un système' a perfect illustration of the Leninist theory of imperialism. But the extraordinary versatility which enabled Sartre to write so much, so differently and so well had its darker side. The impression which it leaves is not only that of a literary craftsman who can turn his hand to anything. It is also that of a man casting desperately around, looking to literature for something which it cannot give.

It is also doubtful if anyone who had not had something like the childhood experience described in *Les Mots* would have made the extraordinary statement that

Si la littérature n'est pas tout, elle ne vaut pas une heure de peine.[57] (If literature is not everything, it is not worth spending an hour on it.)

It is true that Sartre did then go on to offer an explanation of what he meant which reads very much like a watering down of the original statement. Literature, he goes on to say, 'sèche sur pied si vous la réduisez à l'innocence, à des chansons' (dies on its feet if you reduce it to innocence or to songs) and his argument becomes slightly more understandable when he writes that:

Si chaque phrase écrite ne résonne pas à tous les niveaux de l'homme et de la société, elle ne signifie rien. La littérature d'une époque, c'est l'époque digérée par sa littérature. (If every sentence does not echo at every level of man's experience, it means nothing. The literature of a historical period is that period digested by its literature.)

It is certainly possible to see what he means by this, and his hostility to literature as entertainment recurs in the idea he expressed when he said in the interview with Jacqueline Piatier in 1964 in *Le Monde* that *La Nausée* weighed very light in the scales when placed by the side of a child dying of hunger. This is very similar in tone and meaning to the remark which Tolstoy made about a good pair of boots being more valuable than the complete works of Shakespeare. Nobody who has spent his life reading or writing books, or indeed following any of the undemanding professions which the world of late-twentieth-century capitalism offers to verbally adroit members of the middle class, has not at some time felt the utter worthlessness of it all compared to the problems of the undeveloped and even of the developed world. St Paul's reassurance in I Corinthians 12 about there being 'many gifts but the same spirit' does not always offer adequate consolation especially when one recalls the statement in Ecclesiastes XII that 'Of the making of many books there is no end, and much study is a weariness of the flesh'.

But not even these comparisons make it possible to say precisely what Sartre meant when he said that if literature is not everything, it would not be worth a moment's trouble. Is this trouble the author's? the reader's? the publisher's? the critic's? What about people who write political literature? What about people who never read a book in their life? What about somebody who simply wants to read a book because he likes a good story? Are they to be damned completely, just as Sir Toby Belch thought that Malvolio was going to deny cakes and ale to everybody because he himself was virtuous? As is often the case when one reads the remarks about politics and literature made by politically committed writers, one comes away with the feeling that they have done neither their country, nor literature, nor themselves, any particular service.

Sartre's remark reflects such an odd attitude that it can be explained only by the very peculiar kind of experience described in *Les Mots*. Only a man brought up as curiously as Sartre claims to have been could have developed so extreme a set of attitudes towards writing. It is, as I suggested earlier, almost as though he had been one of those children exposed too early in life to the complex, violent and intense emotions inseparable from the sexual experience of adults. Such children never quite succeed in coming to terms with their own sexuality, and there is a similar oddity about Sartre's attitude towards an activity which other writers, in no way inferior to him in talent, interest and achievement, have been able to contemplate with much greater equanimity.

Les Mots also suggests, albeit indirectly, that the attitude towards literature which Sartre absorbed in his childhood did not fit him very well for a career as a novelist. The concept of literature as metaphysical salvation does not sit easily by the side of an activity such as story telling. Neither is it very compatible with analysing society or studying human relationships. In so far as Sartre tells some good stories, creates a number of entertaining characters or depicts an interesting collection of intriguing situations, he shows how good a writer he could have been if he had settled for the apparently more modest and certainly more understandable definition of the aims of fiction put forward by Jane Austen:

> Only a novel ... or, in short, some work in which the most thorough knowledge of human nature, the happiest delineation of its varieties, the liveliest effusion of wit and humour are conveyed to the world in the best chosen language.

Had Sartre ever read *Northanger Abbey*, he would have dismissed the anonymous young lady's remarks as symptomatic of such bourgeois illusions as the existence of human nature or the need for the author to entertain. The view of literature which he developed in reaction against his grandfather's influence, and which 'Qu'est-ce que la littérature?' made famous throughout the world, runs parallel to the view of philosophy set out in Marx's eighth thesis on Feuerbach: 'Philosophers in the past have only interpreted the world. Our task is to change it'.

In so far as French middle-class society was more strongly established in 1980, at the time of Sartre's death, than it had been when the publication of *La Nausée* in 1938 marked the beginning of his literary career, he may have been tempted to look back on his life as a failure. He would have been wrong to do so. The closing pages of *Les Mots* contain a kind of anticipatory epitaph.

Nulla dies sine linea.
C'est mon habitude, et puis c'est mon métier. Longtemps j'ai pris ma plume pour une épée. Maintenant, je connais notre impuissance. N'importe: je fais, je ferai des livres; il en faut; cela sert tout de même. La culture ne sauve rien ni personne, elle ne justifie pas. Mais c'est un produit de l'homme: il s'y projette, s'y reconnait: seul, ce miroir critique lui renvoie son image.[58] (*Write a line every day.* It's my habit and it's my job as well. For a long time, I took my pen for a sword. Now, I know how powerless we are. It doesn't matter. I am writing books, and I shall write more books. They are necessary. Culture saves nothing and nobody. It offers no justification. But it is a human product. Man projects himself and recognises himself in it. This critical mirror is the only place where he can see his face.)

If anyone wants to know what attitudes, feelings and ideas were current in the middle of the twentieth century, there are few better places to start than the novels of Jean-Paul Sartre. Such a reader may also find out quite a lot about himself.

Notes

Chapter 2 *La Nausée*

1. Sartre, *Oeuvres Romanesques*, Pléiade (Paris: Gallimard, 1982) p. 1699.
   The existence of the Pléiade edition has naturally made the study of
   Sartre very much easier, and I am deeply indebted to the work done
   by Michel Contat and Michel Rybalka. In the rest of the notes, this
   edition is simply referred to as *Pléiade*.

2. 'L'Existentialisme est un humanisme' (Nagel, 1951) p. 94. According
   to Francis Jeanson's *Sartre par lui-même*, p. 46, Sartre later regarded
   this lecture as a mistake, and it certainly presents his ideas in a
   disconcertingly understandable form. This was not, however, the view
   of C. E. M. Joad, who said that he had never met 'a more pretentious
   farrago of metaphysical abracadabra', and added, in the *New Statesman
   and Nation* for 8 August 1948, that 'if Monsieur Sartre has conceived
   the unutterable, he should not attempt to utter it'. The lecture was
   given at the Club Maintenant in October 1945, in one of Paris's livelier
   evenings. Fifteen people fainted and thirty chairs were broken.
   Professor Joad was not the only English writer to give public expression to the reservations felt by some of his compatriots. In 1950, the
   humorist Paul Jennings published an article entitled 'Report on
   Resistentialism' which attributed to the 'bespectacled, two-eyed Pierre-
   Marie Ventre' the 'sombre, post-atomic philosophy of pagan, despair-
   ing nobility' which 'advocates complete withdrawal from Things' on
   the grounds that things themselves are always against us – like slices of
   toast which fall marmalade side down more frequently on to expensive carpets than on to cheap ones (See *Oddly Enough*, London:
   Reinhardt & Evans, 1950, p. 150).

3. The article originally appeared in *Les Temps Modernes* in March 1951,
   and is reprinted in *Situations* IV (Gallimard, 1964) p. 88. Sartre's
   attitude to homosexuality in this article is quite different from his
   treatment of it through the character of Daniel. He admires Gide for
   having tried to base a new set of moral principles on the need to
   recognise the existence of justifiable sexual difference, and in his essay
   on Baudelaire makes a very favourable comparison between Gide's
   ability to 'eat away' at the austere moral rules which had characterised
   his Protestant upbringing and Baudelaire's inability or refusal to work
   out a set of moral values for himself. However, in his 'Une Nouvelle

littérature en France', a lecture he gave in the USA in 1945, Sartre wrote that Gide had now lost almost all his influence over young French people and claimed that 'sa philosophie, qui convenait à l'époque heureuse d'avant l'autre guerre, ne peut être d'aucun secours en nos temps de misère'. (His philosophy, which suited the happy times before the First World War, can be no use to-day in our time of suffering.) There are also some unflattering remarks about Gide in 'Qu'est-ce que la littérature?' reprinted in *Situations* II (Gallimard, 1948).

4. Interview in *Le Monde*, with Jacqueline Piatier, 18 April 1964.
5. Thus in the autumn of 1936, he wrote of a production of *Julius Caesar* that Shakespeare's characters had the same reasons for anger, disappointment and frustrated ambition as the French people of the 1930s and continued:

> Les jeunes surtout s'y reconnaissent, bien que la plupart des personnages soient des hommes mûrs: si la jeunesse est l'âge de la générosité et des erreurs, quelles fautes plus généreuses et plus irréparables peut-on trouver que celles de Brutus, – et si c'est l'âge des amitiés, quelle amitié sera plus tragique et plus belle que celle de Brutus et de Cassius? (The young, above all, recognise themselves in it, although most of the characters are men in their prime. If youth is the age of generosity and mistakes, what more generous and more irredeemable faults can you find than those of Brutus – and if it is the age of friendship, what finer and more tragic friendship can there be than the one between Brutus and Cassius?)

6. Simone de Beauvoir, *La Force de l'âge* (Gallimard, 1960) p. 47.
7. 'Réflexions sur la question juive' (Gallimard, 1946) p. 82.
8. *Pléiade*, p. 209. Roquentin describes the jazz tune of 'Some of these Days' as having been written by a Jew and performed by a Negress. In fact, the singer best known for performing the song, Sophie Tucker, was Jewish, while as the notes to *Pléiade* p. 1747 point out, the name of the composer, Shelton Brooks, might have suggested to Sartre that he was Jewish, like other well-known composers such as Irving Berlin and George Gershwin, when in fact he was a gentile. Sartre's choice to associate Roquentin's aesthetic solution with the two groups whom he saw as most excluded and persecuted by capitalist society looks forward to his later political development. In 1938, it would still have been regarded by respectable members of the French middle class as provocative to express admiration for American jazz, especially when this admiration is linked with praise for Jews and Negroes.
9. *Les Mots* (Gallimard, 1964) p. 14.
10. *Pléiade*, p. 110.
11. *Correspondance*, Conard edition, Vol II, p. 345 (1852).
12. 'Le Livre, instrument spirituel' (1895). *Pléiade*, Oeuvres Complètes, p. 378.
13. *Horizon*, March 1946. 'Novelist-Philosophers'.
14. Letter dated 20 February 1871. Quoted in *The Life and Letters of Thomas Henry Huxley* (Macmillan, 1900) Vol I, p. 162.

15. See *Those Barren Leaves* (1925). Quoted from the Chatto & Windus standard edition (1962) p. 162. For the 'second law of thermodynamics', see Huxley's *Island* (Penguin edition, 1964) p. 243.
16. *Pléiade*, p. 158.
17. *Philosophical Investigations* (Blackwell, 1953) pp. 47 and 51.
18. See *TLS*, 23 March 1949. The *Pléiade* edition makes no reference to these criticisms but does translate part of the review in the *TLS* for 3 December 1938, when *La Nausée* was still untranslated, and which described Sartre as 'halfway between Céline and Kafka' and an 'accomplished and original writer'.
19. *Pléiade*, p. 62.
20. *Pléiade*, p. 52.
21. *Pléiade*, p. 117.
22. *Pléiade*, p. 118.
23. *Théatre* (Gallimard, 1947) p. 102.
24. *L'Imaginaire* (Gallimard, 1940) p. 245.
25. See the passage in Renan's *Souvenirs d'Enfance et de Jeunesse* (1883) in which he explains how the intellectual training he had received in order to become a priest had given him complete faith in the rationality of Christian doctrine and the reliability of the Bible, and how this faith entered into conflict with the discoveries which he made about the unreliability of the Biblical texts. Renan's argument is that it is better, in such a case, for the intellectually honest man to make a clean break with the Church rather than trying to reach a compromise. As the notes to the *Pléiade* edition of the novels point out, however, Sartre disliked Renan intensely, seeing him as a typical nineteenth-century humanist.
26. *L'Etre et le néant*, p. 404.
27. *L'Etre et le néant*, p. 409.
28. *L'Etre et le néant*, p. 404.
29. *Situations* I (Gallimard, 1947) p. 83.
30. See *Lettres au Castor* (Gallimard, 1983) pp. 177, 432, 477. Jeanson, *Sartre par lui-même* (Seuil, 1956) p. 187.
31. *Les Mots*, p. 143.
32. *Les Mots*, p. 185.
33. *Lettres au Castor* (Gallimard, 1983) pp. 131 and 224.
34. *Pléiade*, p. 209.
35. *Situations* III (Gallimard, 1949). From an article entitled 'La République du silence', originally published in *Les Lettres françaises* in 1944.
36. *Pléiade*, p. 443.
37. 'Baudelaire', *Les Essais* (Gallimard, 1949) p. 28.
38. *Ibid.*, p. 34.
39. Quoted in *The Age of Enlightenment*, edited by Isaiah Berlin (New York: Mentor Books, 1956) p. 163.
40. Iris Murdoch's remark is quoted on the jacket of the Penguin translation of *Nausea* (1965). For a full discussion of *L'Etranger*, see my study of Camus in the Macmillan Modern Novelists series (1989). Iris Murdoch discussed Sartre more fully when interviewed by Bryan Magee in the mid-1970s. She agreed with Magee that *La Nausée* was 'a

magnificent novel', but added that 'For better or worse, art goes deeper than philosophy'. Cf. *Men of Ideas* (OUP, 1977) p. 243.

41. *Of Human Bondage* (1915) ending of ch. XVIII.
42. *Les Mots* (Gallimard, 1964) p. 210.
43. Ibid., p. 210.
44. *Pléiade*, p. 56.
45. *Gulliver's Travels, A Voyage to Brobdignag*, Part II, ch. 6.
46. *Pléiade*, pp. 110 and 1773.
47. *Pléiade*, p. 52. In February 1971, Sartre took part in an unsuccessful attempt by a group of left-wing militants to occupy the Sacré Coeur. The protest had been organised to mark the centenary of its construction by reminding people of the fact that the church was a monument to the reactionary spirit of the French middle classes.
48. *Lettres au Castor*, p. 271.
49. *Situations* X (Gallimard, 1976) 'Les Maos en France' (1972) p. 39. In 1968, the French police had dealt with the student protest movement with their customary brutal and indiscriminate vigour.
50. *Pléiade*, pp. 1702–5.
51. So, too, is Mathieu Delarue, a more obvious self-portrait of Sartre, who was under 5 feet 5 inches tall. In 1974, Sartre explained to Michel Contat and Michel Rybalka why he did not want to make his two heroes small men: at the time, the convention in fiction was that heroes had to be tall in order to win the respect of readers. (*Pléiade*, p. 1949).
52. On page 1780 of the *Pléiade* edition, Jacques Derrida is quoted as saying, in 1978, that Sartre was now the target of all the 'anti-humanists' in the French literary world, and that this accusation was justified in so far as his philosophy was fundamentally humanistic and presented itself as such. However, added Derrida, it should not be forgotten that Sartre had published in *La Nausée* one of the most devastating and successful of all attacks ever penned against humanism and humanists, and ought therefore to be forgiven. The notes to the *Pléiade* edition are of the highest possible scholarly standard, and provide by far the best basis for the study of Sartre's work. The edition of Sartre's *Oeuvres de Jeunesse* which Michel Rybalka and Michel Contat published in 1990 is equally scholarly and fascinating. However, just as Sartre's own works cast a conscious as well as an unconscious light on the history of his times, so the notes to the *Pléiade* edition of his *Oeuvres Romanesques* are an invaluable and sometimes involuntary guide to French intellectual fashion, both in the immediate post-war period and in the 1980s. Thus on p. 1929, Christian Grisoli's review of *L'Age de raison* in *Paru* in December 1945, contains the phrase 'chacun sait, depuis Hegel et la dialectique du maître et de l'esclave, que personne n'est libre si tout le monde n'est pas libre' (everyone knows, since Hegel and the Master-Slave dialectic, that nobody is free if everybody is not free). This may or may not be true, but it was certainly not something which everybody knew to be the case at the time, when the reputation of Hegel was at its lowest ebb in English-speaking philosophical circles, and he was seen principally as one of

the fathers of modern totalitarianism. There is also the claim in Henri Hell's review of *L'Age de raison* in *Fontaine* for January 1946 that Sartre's hero is 'celui même de notre temps' (p. 1932), a statement which runs parallel to Sartre's own ambition, expressed in a letter written on 23 April 1940 (p. 1907), to write a novel which would make people feel that they are living in 'l'âge du fondamental'. This echo of the claim in Malraux's 1939 novel about the Spanish civil war, *L'Espoir*, is instructive about intellectual fashion, but no more a guarantee of the value of Sartre's or Malraux's books than Voltaire's contention – after he had read Shakespeare and Sophocles – that Racine's *Athalie* was still 'le chef d'oeuvre de l'esprit humain'. It is symptomatic of French culture to imagine that what is written in Paris has a universal value to which the productions of London, New York or Moscow aspire in vain.

Here, Contat and Rybalka are merely quoting, and it may be that comparably ambitious claims were being made at the time in English-speaking countries about T. S. Eliot or Graham Greene. The editors of Sartre's work also reveal how deeply they were imbued with the intellectual atmosphere of the 1970s and 1980s in France when they accompany the reproduction of these claims with the statement on p. 1668 that *La Nausée* is 'un des piliers de notre modernité' (one of the pillars of our modernity), and hint what this might mean by saying on pp. 1892–3 that in *Les Chemins de la liberté* 'le *référent* du roman est moins la réalité que la littérature romanesque elle-même'. What this means is that the detailed plotting and characterisation of *L'Age de raison* are not an attempt to describe reality. They are, instead, a deliberate take-off of the traditional novel, just as for some critics – my example, not theirs – *Hamlet* is a take-off of the traditional Jacobean revenge play. Whether this statement about *L'Age de raison* is true or not – and there is no evidence that Sartre intended his novel to be read that way, and no reader unacquainted with modern French literary theory can ever understand Contat and Rybalka's suggestion – it is an interesting reflection of how influential Roland Barthes's view still was in 1982 that literature, through its various codes, talks of nothing but itself; and that the only acceptable subject matter of literature is literature.

Contat and Rybalka also offer other explanations of why Sartre did not finish *Les Chemins de la liberté*, suggesting on *Pléiade* p. 1880 that since Simone de Beauvoir's 1955 novel *Les Mandarins* carried on the story about how French intellectuals behaved after the Second World War, and which Sartre had left hanging in mid air, he did not need to finish his tetralogy. They also accept Sartre's explanation that he realised, with the outbreak of the Second World War, that 'historicity' had so taken over and absorbed both him and everybody else that it was no longer possible to write books in which people had time to devote to their private lives. In his view, which Contat and Rybalka seem to endorse on page 1865, the liberal humanist society in which authors write about people's private lives disappeared with the Second World War. Again, this is not a self-evident truth outside certain literary circles in Paris, any more than a more anecdotal claim which Michel Contat made in an article in *Le Monde* on 3 January 1987 is supported by all the evidence available. In his review of Alain Buisine's *Laideurs de Sartre* (Presses Universitaires de France) Michel Contat wrote that he felt that he had met more or less all Sartre's critics, at least those who had really read him, and discovered that: 'Aucun n'est beau. On bien, ce sont des femmes, des étrangers, des gens un peu aux confins, toujours un peu exclus, un peu infirmes, à qui il manque quelque chose – d'identité, par exemple?' (None of them is good-looking. Or else, they are women, outsiders [?foreigners], people who are a bit on the edges, cut off from society, slightly ill and odd, who are lacking in something – a sense of identity perhaps?)

When I wrote to point out to Michel Contat that I am the most ordinary-looking person imaginable; that I have a wife, children and grandchildren; that I play golf and have played cricket; enjoy working with the Civil Service; rarely miss an episode of *Coronation Street*; am a member of the Conservative Party; live in a semi-detached house in a cul-de-sac called The Nook; dress like a bank manager and delight in lunching with like-minded men in the Senior Common Room, I received no reply. This, of course, is par for the course when English teachers of French write to their colleagues in France; even when they do so in French.

In Bryan Magee's *Men of Ideas*, Sartre is discussed only incidentally, and compared very unfavourably with Heidegger (p. 70).

53. *Pléiade*, pp. 69–70.
54. *Pléiade*, p. 176. Anny has clearly made the same discovery about emotions which Sartre sets out in his 'Esquisse d'une théorie des émotions'. Either she or Sartre nevertheless confuses Good Friday with Pentecost, or Whit Sunday.
55. *Situations* III (Gallimard 1949) p. 184. It is instructive to place this compliment by the side of Jim Hacker's reply to his daughter Lucy's comment that it should be 'quite easy' to change a particular piece of legislation: 'Just get yourself adopted as a candidate, serve with distinction on the back benches, be appointed as Minister and repeal the act'. *Yes Minister* (BBC publications, 1981) p. 140.
56. *Pléiade*, p. 1848.
57. *Pléiade*, p. 1952.
58. I have unfortunately not been able to track down the story in which Leslie Charteris's hero the Saint pens his little ditty, but do remember it from a childhood which resembled that of Sartre in one important respect: I read a lot of bad books. He himself remarked in *Les Mots* (p. 61), that even now he preferred reading the violent detective novels of the *Série Noire* to Wittgenstein.
59. Established in 1945, and an almost obligatory first step for a career in France as a professional politician. Jacques Chirac, Michel Rocard and Laurent Fabius are all graduates. For a discussion of the role and function of *Les Grands Corps de l'Etat*, see *Faux Amis and Key Words. A Guide to French Society by Lookalikes and Confusables*, by Philip Thody and

Howard Evans (Athlone Press, 1985). While it is true that it is much easier to succeed in the competitive entrance examination entry into l'ENA if you have made a sensible choice of parents and been born to a senior civil servant in the Paris area, there is some distance between the way in which French and British society recruit their elites and the imaginings which underline Roquentin's (and Sartre's) vision.

60. See Brand Blanshard, *Retreat from Truth* (OUP, 1958) p. 153.
61. By Joseph Grubb in 'Sartre's Recapturing of Lost Time', *Modern Language Notes* (November 1958) pp. 515–22.
62. *Les Mots* (Gallimard, 1964) p. 10.
63. See p. 146 of *Situations* X, 'Politique et Autobiographie'. It is also very tempting to see the three-volume study of Flaubert, like the two biographical fragments of Tintoretto in *Situations* IV and IX, as novels, and Sartre himself said as much in an interview with the *New Left Review* on 26 February 1970. Cf. *Situations* IX (Gallimard, 1972) p. 123.
64. *Pléiade*, p. 210.
65. *Pléiade*, p. 117.
66. *Pléiade*, p. 21.
67. 'L'Existentialisme est un Humanisme', pp. 35–6.
68. In *Pléiade* p. 1772, Contat and Rybalka say that Sartre did mention Talleyrand to them as a possible if distant model for Rollebon.
69. *Situations* II, p. 143.
70. Cf. Présentation des *Temps Modernes* (1945). *Situations* II (Gallimard, 1947) p. 13.
71. *Murder in the Cathedral* (Faber and Faber, 1935) p. 56.
72. *Pléiade*, pp. 49–50.
73. *Pléiade*, p. 133.
74. (Gallimard, 1943) p. 11.
75. *Pléiade*, p. 114.
76. *Pléiade*, p. 36.
77. *Situations* V (Gallimard 1964) p. 183. For a comparably uncritical presentation of the case for violence in late-twentieth-century Europe, see *Situations* X, 'Les Maos en France', p. 45: 'Pour les maos . . . partout où la violence révolutionnaire prend naissance dans les masses, elle est immédiatement et profondément morale, car les travailleurs, jusque-là objets de l'autoritarisme capitaliste, deviennent, fût-ce pour un moment, les sujets de leur histoire' (For the Maoistes, wherever revolutionary violence stems from the masses, it is immediately and profoundly moral, for the workers, until then the victims of capitalist authoritarianism, become, if only for a moment, the subject and driving force of their own history).
78. *Pléiade*, p. 113.
79. *Pléiade*, p. 83.

Chapter 3   Le Mur

1. See 'The Story Teller' in Saki's *Beasts and Super Beasts*.
2. See *Lettres à Sartre, 1930–1939* (Gallimard, 1990) p. 211.
3. See *Dialogue with Death*, translated by Trevor and Phyllis Blewitt (Penguin edition, 1942) p. 55. For the discussion of Heidegger, see *L'Etre et le néant*, pp. 615–42.
4. See *L'Etre et le néant*, pp. 431–508.
5. 'L'Existentialisme est un humanisme', p. 94.
6. *Sartre par lui-même* (Seuil, 1956) p. 83.
7. In 'Ecrire pour son époque' (1946). Text available in Contat and Rybalka, *Les Ecrits de Sartre* (Gallimard 1970). This is an invaluable account of Sartre's life and work, to which I owe much of the information reproduced in this study.
8. *Pléiade*, p. 360. It is instructive to see one of the received truths of modern conservative thinking put forward in such obviously ironic form.
9. *Situations* IV (Gallimard, 1964) p. 160.
10. See the magazine *Lire*, No. 75 (April 1990) p. 38. Part of the reminiscences of the corporal, Jean Pierre, with whom Sartre was in the army in 1939–40.
11. *Pléiade*, p. 368.
12. See *The Code of the Woosters* (1938) p. 215 of the Standard Autograph edition (1962). It will be recalled that Roderick Spode had to make his followers wear black shorts because by the time he formed his association, there were no shirts left. He and his adherents wear black shorts.
    'Footer bags, you mean?'
    'Yes.'
    'How perfectly foul.'
    'Yes.'
    'Bare knees?'
    'Bare knees.'
    'Golly!'
13. He discusses this in *Situations* VIII (Gallimard, 1972) p. 240, part of a series of interviews and articles showing his strong support for the most radical proposals brought forward by the students.
14. *Les Existentialistes et la politique, Idées* (Gallimard, 1966) p. 186.
15. *Pléiade*, p. 1849.
16. *Situations* III (Gallimard, 1949) p. 237.
17. *Situations* VII, p. 135.
18. *Pléiade*, p. 375.
19. *Pléiade*, p. 383.
20. 'Réflexion sur la question juive' (Gallimard, 1954 edition) p. 65. The text was written in 1944. Extracts appeared in *Les Temps Modernes* in December 1945 and the essay itself was first published in book form in 1946.
21. In *Le Petit Marseillais*, 9 February 1941.
22. *Punch*, 7 December 1949.

23. See Simone de Beauvoir, *La Force de l'âge* (Gallimard 1960) p. 139. The idea of using Dowson's poem first came to them when they visited London in 1933, and saw Kay Francis (best known for the passion she aroused in the breast of King Kong) in the recently released film, *Cynara*. The poem itself does not tell the story of a philosophically accepted and calculated series of infidelities, but the state of mind of a man who cannot rid himself of the memory of a particular woman, however hard he tries.

24. 'L'Existentialisme est un humanisme', p. 86.

25. *L'Etre et le néant*, pp. 89–93. Stekel is quoted on p. 93.

26. Annie Cohen-Solal, *Sartre, a Life* (Heinemann, 1985) passim. See also Ronald Hayman, *Writing Against: A Biography of Sartre* (Weidenfeld & Nicolson, 1986) p. 204: 'throughout his life, Sartre had remarkably few friendships with men of his own age'.

27. *Pléiade*, p. 283.

28. Hayman, *Writing Against*, p. 137, quoting a remark that Sartre made to Simone de Beauvoir in one of the interviews she had with him between August and September 1974. Thus on p. 385 of *La Cérémonie des adieux* (Gallimard, 1981) she quotes him as saying: 'Les rapports sexuels avec les femmes, c'était obligé parce que les rapports classiques impliquaient ces rapports-là à un moment donné. Mais je n'y attachais pas une telle importance. Et, à proprement parler, ça ne m'intéressait pas autant que les caresses. Autrement dit, j'étais un masturbateur de femmes plutôt qu'un coïteur.' (Sexual relationships with women were something you had to have because they were required at a certain moment in a relationship. But I didn't give them much importance. And in fact, that side of it didn't interest me as much as the caresses. In other words, I was a masturbator of (?by) women rather than a copulator.)

  There is some abiguity in the 'de', which could mean either that he masturbated women or that he achieved orgasm in a masturbation session in which they played a part.

29. *L'Etre et le néant*, p. 93. Sartre quotes from *La femme frigide*: 'Chaque fois que j'ai pu pousser mes investigations assez loin, j'ai constaté que le noeud de la psychose était conscient.' Stekel's book was published in a French translation by Jean Dalsace under the Gallimard imprint in 1937. Stekel (1868–1940) thought that Freud gave far too much importance to the unconscious, and developed an active method of treatment to replace what he considered to be the excessively passive Freudian technique of free analysis. 'Day after day', he said, 'I attack the patient's system by storm, showing that he can get well betwixt night and morning, if only he will discard his fictive aims' (J.A.C. Brown, *Freud and the Post-Freudians*, Pelican, 1961, p. 42). Being treated by him must have been rather like a spell in the US Marines or at one of the older English Public Schools. In the 1930s, Sartre was able to stand sufficiently apart from his theory of liberty to be able to look at it with an element of ironic detachment. Thus on 8 November 1939, when he was serving with the French army during the phoney war, he wrote to tell Simone de Beauvoir how he had outlined his

theory of liberty to a certain Paul, explaining to him how suited the
post-war period would be to the establishment of 'une dictature de la
liberté' in which he could roast Paul's feet in front of a hot fire until
the unhappy man agreed to declare himself free. Jean-Jacques Rousseau, who rarely made jokes, talks in *Le Contrat social* about forcing
people to be free if they refuse to obey the General Will.

Sartre, like Rousseau, is in the camp of those whom Isaiah Berlin, in
his 1946 *Two Concepts of Liberty*, describes as wishing to change society
in a positive direction in order to make people free. The other
tradition, more frequently associated with liberal capitalist democracy
than with the thinkers who stem from Rousseau and Marx, takes the
view that the best way to make people free is to remove as much
external pressure and discipline as possible.

A number of critics of Oreste in *Les Mouches* have complained that
he does not, after freeing the inhabitants of Argos, do anything
further to help them to realise their freedom. Such critics are inclined
to be politically on the left, and thus to endorse the positive concept of
liberty. Others are quite happy for Oreste to go off and leave the
inhabitants of Argos to work things out for themselves. They tend to
be politically on the right, in so far as to be on the right in the second
half of the twentieth century is to wish to limit the powers of
intervention of the state.

30. *Thérèse Desqueyroux* (1927) Livre de poche, pp. 47–8.
31. Anouilh, *La Valse des toréadors* (1949) *Pièces grinçantes* (Table Ronde, 1961) pp. 171–2.
32. *Pléiade*, p. 306.
33. See Simone de Beauvoir, *La Force des choses* (Gallimard) p. 104.
34. *Pléiade*, p. 1296.
35. *Pléiade*, p. 302.
36. For Barthes, see *Essais Critiques* IV (Seuil, 1984) pp. 167–74. For the other details, see *Pléiade*, pp. 1309, 37, 1427. On my first visit to France, in 1949, I was given sardines au beurre as an hors d'oeuvre. When I complimented my hostess on their excellence, she replied: 'Oui, monsieur, ce sont des sardines de Munich'. Her husband explained that his wife meant 'sardines she had bought in September 1938, at the time of the Munich crisis'. When I admired the foresight of someone able to lay on enough sardines to provide for her family and guests for over ten years of privations, her husband added, lest I should be suspicious of what I was eating: 'Vous savez, cher monsieur, la sardine a cette particularité de se bonifier en boîte' (improves in the tin).
37. *Les Mots*, p. 185.
38. *Les Séquestrés d'Altona* (Gallimard, 1959) p. 146.
39. *Lettres au Castor, 1926–1939* (Gallimard, 1983) p. 237.
40. Ibid., p. 211.
41. The theory of 'la psychanalyse existentielle' is set out on pp. 643–62 of *L'Etre et le néant*. Michael Scriven has studied Sartre's ideas and practice in more detail in his very interesting *Sartre's Existential Biographies* (Macmillan, 1984). R. D. Laing's and D. G. Cooper's *Reason*

and Violence: a decade of Sartre's philosophy, 1950–1960, was published by
the Tavistock Press in 1964, with a preface in which Sartre wrote that
he agreed with them in seeing mental illness as 'l'issue que le libre
organisme, dans son unité totale, invente pour pouvoir vivre une
situation invivable' (the way out that a free organism invents, in its
total unity, so as to be able to live out an unlivable position). It is not
clear what aspect of Pierre's experience has been unlivable, and there
is a hint on p. 241 that he was already giving signs of mental stress
before marrying Eve. The idea of madness as a 'way out that we
invent' recurs in *Les Séquestrés d'Altona*, though in a more critical
manner. Franz would like to escape into madness from the memory of
the tortures he inflicted on the Russian partisans, but cannot do so.
Sartre also sees genius as 'a way out that one invents', writing on p. 536
of *Saint Genet comédien et martyr* that his aim in analysing Genet has
been to show that genius is not a gift but 'l'issue qu'on invente dans les
cas désespérés' (a way out that you invent in desperate cases).

Sartre's essay on Genet is not reliable in the details it gives of Genet's
early life. A carelessly written sentence on p. 13 implies that Genet was
7 years old when he was sent as a foster child to a peasant family in the
Morvan area, to the south east of Paris. The researches of Dichy and
Fouché in their *Jean Genet. Essai de chronologie 1910–1944*, Bibliothè-
que de Littérature française contemporaine, Vol. 7 (Paris 1988) have
shown that he was only 7 months. Sartre also seriously misrepresented
Genet's foster family by describing it as one of fairly brutish peasants.
Charles Regnier was a skilled artisan. He and his wife adored children
and did everything they could to make Genet happy. Dichy and
Fouché also failed to find any evidence for Sartre's claim that Genet
was punished for stealing by being subjected, at about the age of 8, to a
village ceremony in which he was publicly labelled a thief. Neither was
Genet sent away from his foster family in disgrace. He left at the age
of 14, which was the norm for the practice of fostering out orphans at
the time, and was offered a chance of an apprenticeship in a printing
works. For a fuller discussion, see Philip Thody, 'The Decline and Fall
of a Literary Myth', *Salisbury Review* (June 1989).

42. *Pléiade*, p. 1841.
43. *Pléiade*, p. 271.
44. See *Les Existentialistes et la politique* (Gallimard, 1966) p. 185.
45. *Sartre, a Life*, p. 108.
46. *Writing Against*, p. 38.
47. *L'Etre et le néant*, pp. 471–2.
48. Editions de la Pensée Moderne (Paris, 1953). It appeared in the
    section entitled realistic eroticism.
49. One of the most entertaining illustrations of this is in Paul Bailey's *An
    English Madam* (Jonathan Cape, 1982). There was also an interview on
    BBC television with a prostitute about to leave for the seaside resort
    where the Conservative Party was going to hold its conference. She
    always, she said, took a wider and more exotic collection of corrective
    equipment than when following the flag at the Labour Party confer-
    ences.

50. 'Qu'est-ce que la littérature?' p. 196.
51. *Situations* II, p. 196.
52. Ibid., pp. 111, 113.
53. Ibid., p. 16; 'Présentation des *Temps Modernes*'.
54. *Pléiade*, p. 37.
55. Cf. especially pp. 176–80 in his 'Autoportrait à soixante-dix ans' in *Situations* X (Gallimard, 1976).
56. *Pléiade*, p. 465.

Chapter 4   *Les Chemins de la liberté*

1. Thus on p. 63 of her *Mémoires d'une jeune fille rangée* (Gallimard, 1958) Simone de Beauvoir writes: 'L'image que j'ai de moi-même à l'âge de raison est celle d'une petite fille rangée, heureuse, et passablement arrogante' (the image I have of myself at the age of eight (see p. 62) is that of a well-behaved, happy and fairly arrogant little girl). It is nevertheless clear that the expression can be applied to older people, since Simone de Beauvoir describes Sartre on p. 218 of *La Force de l'âge* as being reluctant to pass 'de l'âge de raison à l'âge d'homme'.
2. *Situations* III, p. 172.
3. 'Questions de méthode', in *La Critique de la raison dialectique* (Gallimard, 1960) p. 29. Theoretically, of course, and in a Marxist context, Sartre is right. The production of wealth is still based on a system whereby those who own the means of production, distribution and exchange get a lot more money than those who merely work. What is more open to question is whether this can be avoided without destroying both the economy which produces wealth and the political system which allows people their intellectual and political liberty. The experience of the two states who have based their political system on Marxism, China and the Soviet Union, suggests that it cannot.
4. *Pléiade*, p. 1891.
5. *Pléiade*, p. 409.
6. *Le Figaro littéraire*, 7 May 1949.
7. *Pléiade*, p. 438.
8. Sartre himself categorically denied that he had ever wanted a son, and did not accept that the relationship which he sought to establish with the young men in his circle had anything paternal about it (*Situations* IX, p. 212). G. K. Chesterton once said that the aim of literary criticism was to tell the author something that would make him jump out of his boots. An analysis of *Les Mains Sales* and *Les Séquestrés d'Altona* which explained the relationship between Hugo and Hoederer, and between Franz and his father, in terms of a father-son relationship would presumably have just this effect.
9. *Pléiade*, p. 118.
10. *Pléiade*, p. 493.
11. *Pléiade*, p. 723.
12. *Pléiade*, p. 729.
13. *Pléiade*, p. 443.

14. *Pléiade*, p. 850. Sartre's use of the word 'pédéraste' as a synonym for homosexual suggests that the word has wider connotations in French than in English, where it tends to mean a man attracted to young boys. As the episode with Bobby in *L'Age de raison* suggests (*Pléiade*, pp. 533–40; 685–70), Daniel is not averse to the occasional adventure in the rough trade.

15. In his *Métamorphose de la littérature* (Gallimard, 1952).

16. *Pléiade*, p. 724.

17. *Pléiade*, p. 1218.

18. Cf. *Pléiade*, pp. 1789–90, where the extracts from Simone de Beauvoir's mémoires, as well as reports from independent witnesses, show her to have been a pain in the neck.

19. *Pléiade*, p. 1075.

20. *Pléiade*, p. 1266.

21. In *Paru* (December, 1948) with Christian Grisoli.

22. For a full account of how Sartre intended *Les Chemins de la liberté* to end, see *Pléiade*, p. 1864 and p. 2015, an account based on Simone de Beauvoir's mémoires.

23. *L'Etre et le néant*, p. 474. Sartre's account of Alleg's courage is in 'Une Victoire', reprinted in *Situations* V.

24. Cf. p. 443 of *Situations* IV in which he talks about 'l'unique objet possible de la littérature' now being the expression of an author's feelings in the context of his own time and as a means of enabling his readers to understand what their own social position is.

25. 'Merleau-Ponty vivant', *Situations* IV (Gallimard, 1964) p. 190.

26. In addition to the long account in the section of 'La Critique de la raison dialectique' entitled 'Du groupe à l'histoire', there is shorter summary on pp. 265–7 of *Situations* VIII.

27. *Pléiade*, p. 1491. On p. 44 of *Les Existentialistes et la politique*, M.-A. Burnier points out that the *Temps Modernes* team regarded the Attlee government of 1945–50 as providing 'a modern form of British imperialism'.

28. See *Pléiade*, p. 2115.

29. See his *Causes and Lessons of the Second World War*, Marx, Engels, Lenin, Stalin Institute (Toronto 1990). For a full discussion of the way the Communist Party of Great Britain reacted, see *The Communist Party and the War*, edited by John Attfield and Stephen Williams (Lawrence & Wishart, 1984). There was no unanimity on the line to take, and many comrades did regard the Nazi-Soviet Pact as a betrayal. So, too, did many French Communists, but party discipline in France was stricter.

30. *Pléiade*. p. 1534.

31. *Pléiade*, p. 1512.

32. *Pléiade*, p. 1517.

33. *The Invisible Writing* (Hamish Hamilton, 1954) p. 15. Later in his autobiography (pp. 402–4) Koestler discusses the difference between the relatively small interest aroused by the book in England, where it was published in 1940 but had sold fewer than 4000 copies by the end of the war, and the storm that accompanied its publication in France

under the title *Le Zéro et l'infini*. It immediately became a bestseller, partly because the Communist Party bought up whole stocks of it so as to reduce the number of people who could read it, and partly because it happened to be what Koestler described as 'the first ethical indictment of Stalinism to be published in post-war France'. Its publication coincided, in Koestler's view, with the attempt of the French Communist Party to take over the state by a reign of terror, and he points out that fear of reprisals was so great that the French translator declined to have his name appear on the cover. In 1946, Sartre's friend and political ally, Maurice Merleau-Ponty, published an article in *Les Temps Modernes* entitled 'Humanisme et Terreur', which reappeared in book form in the Gallimard collection *Les Essais* in the following year. In it, he argued that Gletkin, the Party functionary who finally persuades Rubashov to confess, was right. The whole question, argued Merleau-Ponty, was not whether Communism respected the rules of liberal democracy, which it obviously did not, but whether or not the violence it practised was revolutionary, and therefore capable of creating genuinely human relationships among human beings. There is a long and enthusiastic account of Merleau-Ponty's arguments in Simone de Beauvoir's *La Force des choses*, pp. 120–2. This book also contains a number of remarks which suggest that Simone de Beauvoir did not like Koestler.

34. *Les Temps Modernes* (February 1948) p. 1516.
35. *Situations* IV (1964) Merleau-Ponty, p. 249. Earlier in the same article, Sartre wrote (p. 227): 'quels que soient ses crimes, l'U.R.S.S. a sur les démocraties bourgeoises ce redoutable privilège: l'objectif révolutionaire' (whatever its crimes, the USSR has one extraordinary superiority over bourgeois democracies: it wants to bring about the revolution).
36. *Les Temps Modernes* (July 1952) p. 18.
37. *Situations* I, p. 71.
38. Ibid., p. 41.
39. Ibid., pp. 56–7.
40. *Pléiade*, p. 1912. Part of the 'Prière d'insérer' (publisher's blurb aimed at telling critics what to say and readers what to think) distributed with *L'Age de raison* in 1945.
41. *Pléiade*, pp. 1046–7.
42. *Pléiade*, pp. 559.
43. *Pléiade*, p. 794.
44. *Pléiade*, p. 1025.
45. *Pléiade*, p. 1120.
46. *La Condition humaine* (1933) Part VI, p. 289 in the 1968 University of London Press edition by Cecil Jenkins. The action is taking place in 1927, when Tchang Kai Chek, having overthrown the old, warlord government of China by allying himself with the Communists, turns against them and massacres all those he can find. The rest, led by Mao Tse-tung, head north in the Long March, and finally bring China under Communist control in 1948.
47. Quoted in *Pléiade*, p. xcviii.

48. Sartre's own explanation for his failure to complete *Les Chemins de la liberté* links up with his view that the Second World War completely changed his attitude towards himself. Once he became aware of his own 'historicity', it was no longer possible for him to describe so obvious an alter ego from his pre-war self as Mathieu Delarue. Moreover, Simone de Beauvoir's *Les Mandarins*, an account of the behaviour of French intellectuals during the Occupation and the immediate post-war period, continued the story of Mathieu and his friends in such a way as effectively to cut the ground away from under Sartre's feet. (*Pléiade*, p. 1880).
49. *Pléiade*, p. 1617.
50. In 'Resistentialism', Paul Jennings writes: 'The third great concept of Ventre is *le néant* (the No-Thing). Man is ultimately, as I have said, a No-Thing, a metaphysical monster doomed to battle, with increasing non-success, against real Things.'
51. *Pléiade*, p. 1099.
52. *Pléiade*, p. 1643.
53. *Pléiade*, p. 840.
54. *Pléiade*, p. lxxxiv, extract from an interview with Jacqueline Piatier, *Le Monde*, 18 April 1964.
55. See Simone de Beauvoir, *Tout Compte Fait* (Gallimard, 1972) p. 107. On p. 104, Simone de Beauvoir reports Sartre's mother as saying 'j'ai été deux fois mariée et mère, et je suis toujours vierge' (twice married, and a mother, and still a virgin); a remark which suggests that she had been as unlucky in her choice of men as Sartre's heroines.
56. *Les Mots*, p. 137.
57. *Situations* IX (Gallimard, 1972) p. 15.
58. *Les Mots*, p. 211.

Select Bibliography

All Sartre's fiction is available in paperback, either in the Gallimard *Livre de Poche* or the Folio edition.

The same is true of his plays, with *Les Mouches*, *Huis Clos*, *La Putain repectueuse* and *Morts sans sépulture* still being best read in the 1947 Gallimard edition of his *Théâtre*.

His two major philosophical works, *L'Etre et le néant* (1943) and *La Critique de la raison dialectique* (1960) are in the standard Gallimard edition, as are the three volumes of *L'Idiot de la famille* (1971–4).

There are also ten volumes of his *Situations*, the long, 1952 study *Saint Genet, comédien et martyr*, and the short, 1946 essay on Baudelaire, as well as a number of other books mentioned in the 'Main Events in the Life and Times of Jean-Paul Sartre' at the beginning of this study.

Suggestions for Further Reading

Sartre has been much studied. The best account of his life is Ronald Hayman's *Writing Against. A Biography of Sartre* (Weidenfeld & Nicolson, 1986). The two best studies of his ideas are Joseph P. Fell III, *Emotion in the Thought of Sartre* (Columbia University Press, 1965) and George Howard Bauer, *Sartre and the Artist* (University of Chicago Press, 1969). The account of his life likely to make most appeal to readers in sympathy with Sartre's political ideas is by John Gerassi, son of one of the models for the character of Gomez in *Les Chemins de la liberté*. It is called *Jean-Paul Sartre, Hated Conscience of his Century*, and will be in two volumes. The first volume, *Protestant or Protestor*, was published by the University of Chicago Press in 1989.

Other works likely to be useful to the student are mentioned in the notes. The study of *La Nausée* by Paul Reed in Grant and Cutler's *Critical Guides to French Texts* is particularly recommended, as is Denis Boak's study of *Les Mots* in the same series. English-speaking critics writing on Sartre tend to take a more detached stance than their French colleagues. As suggested in the notes, Francis Jeanson's 1956 study, *Sartre par lui-même* still provides the best account of how Sartre's admirers would like him to be seen.

Index

Ainger, Arthur Campbell 18
Alleg, Henri 8, 130
Anouilh, Jean 88, 137
Appleby, Sir Humphrey 49
Arnold, Matthew 16–17
Aron, Raymond 3, 149
Askey, Arthur 15
Auden, W. H. 9
Austen, Jane 158
Ayer, A. J. 22–3, 34

Bad faith (= *mauvaise foi*) 63–4,
   86–7, 90, 129
Bains, Hardial 137
Balzac 60, 88
Barrès, Maurice 82
Barthes, Roland 45, 51, 91, 164
Baudelaire, Charles 6, 33, 51, 52,
   92, 97–8, 126
Beauvoir, Simone de 2, 3, 5, 17,
   66, 68, 73, 79, 84, 89, 94, 97,
   105, 117, 128, 130, 152, 164,
   168, 171, 173, 174
Beckett, Samuel 37, 99, 104, 108
Beethoven 27–8
Belloc, Hillaire 49, 69
Blanshard, Brand 50
Boisdeffre, Pierre de 124
Bonfire of the Vanities, The 118
Bradbury, Malcolm 115
Brasseur, Pierre 7, 148
Breton, André 99
BBC 15, 109, 153, 165
Burnier, Michel-Antoine 78, 100

Camus, Albert 5, 7, 8, 15, 29, 30,
   31, 36, 37, 45, 69, 71, 99, 105,
   108, 124
Carp, Augustus 27
Catcher in the Rye 118
Cause du Peuple, La 11
Céline, Louis-Ferdinand 51
Chesterton, G. K. 24, 171
CIA 6
Cohen-Solal, Annie 87, 100
coitus interruptus 89–90, 115, 127
Conan Doyle 74
Commune, La 42, 46, 58
Contat, Michel 164–5, 167
Cooper, Andrew 95, 169–70

Darwin, Charles 15, 16, 19, 23
dénatalité française, la 4, 89
Derrida, Jacques 45, 163
Descartes 76, 86
Diderot 56, 58
Dos Passos, John 17, 30, 144
Dostoievski 36, 56
Dowson, Ernest 84, 168
Dreyfus, case 82, 137

Ecole Nationale d'Administration 49,
   166
Eliot, George 85
Eliot, T. S. 37, 58–9, 164
Evans, Howard 166
Existentialism 14–15, 33
   compared to Christianity,
      Freudianism and Marxism
      37, 150–1

Fanon, Franz 10, 64
Faulkner, William 30, 142
Flaubert, Gustave 11, 22, 25, 58,
    98, 148, 155, 166
Franco 67–8, 74
Freud 52, 86, 97, 168
Fromm, Eric 90

Galsworthy, John 113, 122
Gaulle, Charles de 9, 45, 54, 72,
    128, 135
Genet, Jean 52, 97, 104–5, 152,
    170
Gibbons, Stella 43
Gide, André 15, 46, 51, 119, 127,
    160–1
Gould, Stephen Jay 17, 18
Greene, Graham 34, 37, 164
Gray, Thomas *Elegy in a Country
    Churchyard* 110
Guillemin, Henri 7
Guillemin, Louise (Sartre's
    grandmother) 1, 52
Gunn, Thom 93

Hamlet 41, 71–2
Hamlet 164
Hayman, Ronald 8, 87, 101
Hegel 129, 163–4
Heidegger 69–71, 165
Hitler 3, 4, 5, 32, 42, 67, 68, 72,
    112, 135, 137, 145, 146
humanism (Boo word in modern
    French) 45–6, 99, 163–4
Hume, David 35, 71
Hurricane (keeps humanism a
    Hurrah word in modern
    English) 45
Husserl 17
Hutton, Joseph 15
Huxley, Aldous 23–4, 36, 94, 136,
    153
Huxley, T. H. 23

index, all Sartre's work on 6

Jeanson, Francis 8, 31, 71, 60, 175
Jennings, Paul 160, 174
Joad, C. E. M. 160

Jolivet, Simone 126
Joplin, Scott 21

Kafka 101, 108
Kant 115
Kierkegaard 14, 32, 108
Kipling 130–1
Knox, John 65
Koestler, Arthur 67–9, 138–40,
    172–3

Laclos 152
Laing, R. D. 95, 169–70
Laval, Pierre 82
Larkin, Philip 92
Lawrence, D. H. 83–4
Libération 8, 11
Lodge, David 115

MacArthur, General Douglas 7
Mae West 18
Mallarmé 22
Malraux, André 36, 71, 124, 147–
    8, 164
Mancy, Joseph (Sartre's
    stepfather) 2, 5, 48–9, 75,
    100, 101
Marcuse, Herbert 148–9
Marxism 7, 8, 9, 37, 38, 59, 113,
    133, 146, 149, 158, 171
Maugham, W. Somerset 38, 96
Maupassant 58
Mauriac, François 30, 51, 87, 92,
    115, 142, 146
Maurras, Charles 82
Merleau-Ponty, Maurice 122, 173
Michelangelo 24
Mikado, The 91
Mirbeau, Octave 43
Mitterrand, François 10
Mosley, Sir Oswald 78
Mozart 24
Munich crisis and agreement 3,
    17, 72, 110, 118–19, 146, 163
    sardines 92, 169
Murdoch, Iris 36, 85
Mussolini 67, 72

Napoleon I 57, 110
Napoleon III 7
New Woman 63
Nietzsche 16
Nizan, Paul 2, 4, 126, 135–7
Nobel Prize 10, 13

Orwell, George 91–2, 110, 146–7

Pascal 32, 34, 108, 124, 125, 151
Perrin, Marius 4
Pétain, Philippe 5, 45, 46, 75, 82
Peter, Laurence 92
phenomenology 62–3, 151
Plato 30
Pléiade edition of Sartre's fiction
    12, 78, 99, 129, 136, 141, 160,
    162, 163
Pooter, Charles 26
Powell, Anthony 149
Proust 50–1, 127

Racine 51
Renan, Emert 28, 162
Russell, Bertrand 10
Rybalka, Michel 99, 100, 102,
    164–5, 167
Rousset, David 6, 81

Saint-Exupéry, Antoine de 51,
    124
Saki 67
Salisbury Review 170
Sartre, Jean-Baptiste (Sartre's
    father) 1, 21, 51, 116
SARTRE, Jean-Paul-Charles-
    Aymard
  admiration for Shakespeare 17,
    161
  advises *coitus interruptus* 89
  attitude to: Afghanistan, invasion
    of by USSR 12; *Algérie
    Française* 5, 8, 9, 130–1, 148;
    Baader, Andreas 11; Berlin,
    Soviet threats to 9, 140;
    contingency 13, 14–22;
    French Communist Party 7, 8,
    112–13; homosexuality 120–
    1, 126–8, 160–1; Israel 6, 10,

11, 80; Korean war 7, 140;
    student rebellion of 1968 10,
    43, 79, 167; USSR 6, 8, 10,
    140–1, 145, 173; Vietnam,
    American policy in 10, 12,
    148; women 86–7, 102, 105,
    127–8
  childhood 1–2, 54, 92–3: impact
    on concept of literature 11,
    53–4, 114, 155–7
  concept of: committed
    literature 39, 74–5, 136–7,
    156–7; existential psycho-
    analysis 52–3, 97–8, 104, 169;
    freedom 6, 62–3, 85–6, 90–1,
    123–4, 130–2, 168–9, *see also*
    bad faith; love 95–6
  cult of violence 11, 65, 128, 166:
    possible reason for abandoning
    the novel 152–3
  defines existentialism 14–15,
    56–7, 71, 79, 152–3
  discrepancies in work 106–8,
    148–9
  dislike of nature 31
  dissatisfied with own literary
    talents 92, 114, 158
  fails to complete books 155
  few men friends 87, 168
  good appetite 30–1
  indifference to science 17, 79
  intellectual snob 44
  interest in: madness 93–5, 106,
    170; non-literary techniques of
    communication (possible
    reason for abandoning the
    novel) 153
  loses at chess 76
  many women friends 87
  military service 3, 4, 67, 129,
    132, 134 (regrets not having
    taken a commission 132)
  obsessional images 28–31, 77,
    94
  offers unconscious portrait of his
    time 28, 38, 44–5, 73–5, 89–
    90, 100–2, 111–12, 149, 163–5
  one mention of Christ 19
  preoccupation with: defining

literature 53–5, 114, 131, 155, 156–7; father-son relationship 116–17, 171
Protestant characteristics in work 64–6, 83
relationship with audience and readership 43, 46
sight in only one eye 2, 134
successful sex life 84: if odd 87, 168
successful as teacher 77, 101
unhappy adolescence 2, 20, 101
whole work an intellectual autobiography 51, 114–15, 154, 157, 166
SARTRE, J-P, works mentioned and discussed
L'Affaire Henri Martin 8
L'Age de raison 4, 6, 33, 87, 89, 109, 114–24, 126, 142–4, 164
Baudelaire 6, 126, 156
Bariona 4
'Chambre, La' 62, 93–6
Chemins de la liberté, Les 4, 36, 73, 85, 102, 103, 107, 109–153, 164
Communistes et la Paix, Les 7
Critique de la raison dialectique, La 9, 133, 171
Derrière Chance, La 110–11, 141, 149, 151
Diable et le Bon Dieu, Le 7, 87
'Drôle d'amitié' 110, 114, 132–4, 134–5, 141
'Enfance d'un chef' 48, 67, 73, 75–83
'Erostrate' 93–105
'Esquisse d'une théorie des émotions' 76, 80, 81, 86, 102
L'Etre et le néant 4, 9, 28–9, 62, 69, 70, 74, 85, 102, 106, 130, 149, 151, 155
'L'Existentialisme est un Humanisme' 6, 14, 56, 85, 160
Huis Clos 5, 72, 86, 94, 102, 120, 130–1, 156
Intimacy (*Le Mur* in translation) 67, 83, 84

'Intimité' 67, 83–92
L'Imaginaire 27
L'Imagination 27
Kean 148
Lettres au Castor et à quelques autres 17
Mains Sales, Les 67, 73–4, 133, 140–2, 171
'Materialisme et Révolution' 48, 112
Mort dans l'âme, La 6, 100, 114, 119, 126–9, 141, 155
Mots, Les 10, 20, 31, 39, 51–3, 92–3, 101, 116, 154–5, 156, 157, 158
Mouches, Les 5, 27, 132, 167, 169
Mur, Le (collection) 4, 48, 63–108
'Mur, Le' (short story) 3
Nausée, La 3, 13–66, 74, 87, 103, 105, 106, 107, 122, 143, 155, 158, 163
Nekrassov 8, 73, 86
'Orphée Noir' (preface) 80
Putain respectueuse, La 6, 87
'Qu'est-ce que la littérature?' 6, 39–40, 53–4, 57, 73, 81, 106, 114
'Questions de Méthode' 8, 57
'Réflexions sur la question juive' 33, 75, 78–82
Saint Genet, comédien et martyr 7
Séquestrés d'Altona, Les 9, 86, 93, 94, 95, 102, 117, 148, 156, 171
Sursis, Le 4, 6, 17, 85, 110, 114, 118, 126–7, 137, 143, 144, 146, 154
Schweitzer, Albert 1, 9, 64
Schweitzer, Anne-Marie (Sartre's mother) 1, 2, 5, 51, 155, 174
Schweitzer, Charles (Sartre's grandfather) 1, 52–3, 54, 95
Scriven, Michael 153, 169
Shaw, G. B. 18
Spitfire 45
Stekel 85–6, 87, 168
Stendhal 85, 125
Swift 41

Talleyrand, Maurice de 57, 166
Templar, Simon 49
Temps Modernes, Les 6, 106–7, 110,
    132, 135, 136, 153
Tennyson 15–16, 110
Thibaudet, Albert 53
Thody, Philip, self-portrait 111,
    165
Tintoretto 155, 166
Troyat, Henri 38
Tucker, Sophie 20, 161

Ulysses (Joyce) 116

Varin, René 103–4

Védrine, Louise 42
Vichy régime 45, 75, 82
Vietnam 74
Voltaire 34, 35, 58, 164

Wilde 70
Wittgenstein 25, 165
Wodehouse, P. G. 77–8, 167
Wordsworth 92, 137

Zola 51, 88, 110
Zonima, Lena (= Madame Z) 10